AMERICAN COSTUME
★★1840-1920★★

AMERICAN COSTUME
★★ 1840-1920 ★★

written and illustrated by

ESTELLE ANSLEY WORRELL

Stackpole Books

The frontispiece depicts outdoor clothing of the 1870s and 1880s. Clockwise from the left are Figures 144, 131, 144, 185, 183.

AMERICAN COSTUME: 1840 TO 1920
Copyright © 1979 by Estelle Ansley Worrell

Published by
STACKPOLE BOOKS
Cameron and Kelker Streets
P.O. Box 1831
Harrisburg, Pa. 17105

Published simultaneously in Don Mills, Ontario, Canada
by Thomas Nelson & Sons, Ltd.

Printed in the U.S.A.

Library of Congress Cataloging in Publication Data

Worrell, Estelle Ansley, 1929-
　American costume, 1840 to 1920.

　Includes index.
　1. Costume—United States—History—19th century.
2. Costume—United States—History—20th century.
I. Title.
GT610.W67　　391′.00973　　78-25854
ISBN 0-8117-0106-9

Contents

Preface　7

Acknowledgments　9

Chapter　1　Creative Costumes　11

Chapter　2　1840s: Rustic Simplicity and Fantastic Growth　15

Chapter　3　1850s: American Styles Develop as Trouble Brews　27

Chapter　4　State and Local Militias: A Diversity of Styles　43

Chapter　5　The Civil War and Mass Production　51

Chapter　6　1860s: The War Ends and the Western Era Begins　61

Chapter　7　1870s: The Economic Revolution and the Styles It Influenced　81

Chapter　8　1880s: Troubled and Extravagant Times and the New Folklore　99

Chapter　9　1890s: New Sports, New Jobs, and New Problems　119

Chapter　10　1900s: A Modern Sophistication, the Arts, and Ecology　139

Chapter　11　1910s: World War I and the Modern Woman　155

Chapter　12　Design and Construction　173

Index　201

Preface

Clothes are the mirror of history. Clothes make history and history makes clothes. To look only at the expensive European-inspired fashions of the sophisticated and well-to-do would be like studying the history of automobiles by looking only at the Rolls-Royce.

In order to understand women's fashions of today one must understand something of past attitudes toward women and of women's attitudes toward themselves and their world. You can't really understand men's fashions of today without realizing that much of what a gentleman of today considers proper was once considered crude or ungentlemanly.

Just about anywhere in the world today you can find people who know about gingham dresses and sunbonnets, shirtwaist blouses and sports skirts, buckskin and hunting shirts and country-western clothing. Fashion magazines in Europe and England pictured "American style hunting clothes" as early as 1850 while fashion "experts" in America still considered them coarse, or low-class. People in other parts of the world recognized the American style and understood American folk clothing while fashionable Americans were slavishly copying European styles.

Our costume, as well as our music, was recognized and appreciated abroad long before it was at home. We have made important contributions in both fields. We supplied the world with cotton and we led the world in shoe design and manufacture. We gave the world comfortable, practi-

cal, beautiful sportswear and casual clothes. We fostered the idea of separates. We led in liberating women—physically by their clothes as well as legally and politically. We gave the working person clothes that were designed to assist him in his work, to make it safer, more comfortable, and attractive. Our children's clothes allowed little ones to run, jump, and play in safety and comfort while at the same time freeing their mothers from the drudgery of laundering and ironing. Most importantly, we gave the world the idea of ready-to-wear stylish clothing which enabled individuals to express their own taste and lifestyle without reference to their social or economic class.

My story tells of the building of America, the people who built it, and how they looked when they acted out their own individual or group roles. I tell that story even when it's shameful because I show what slaves and Indians wore as well as child laborers, minority groups, and angry protesters trying to bring about changes. I also show the drama of women making clothes out of old curtains and bonnets out of wheat straw and of their untiring efforts to outfit their fighting men in homespun, handwoven, vegetable-dyed, and homemade uniforms. I tell how desperate soldiers wore oilcloth piano covers for rain ponchos or fought in "Sunday" clothes because they had no uniforms.

The story of our clothing is fun, too, as we see the Keystone cops, our delightful biking and automobile clothes, the cowboy's hair pants, and some of the outlandish things women have resorted to in the name of fashion. Did you know that the Pullman car brought about the idea of pajamas for men? Who wants to walk through a sleeping car in a nightshirt or underwear? Why did men wear suspenders until after 1910? That's when the belt loop became a regular part of men's trousers. How early aviators came to wear jodhpurs and why early cowboys refused to wear denim are other interesting parts of our history.

Americans have called their clothes by the most colorful names. Did you ever hear of any of the following items: a fish, batwing chaps, shotgun breeches, the crash suit, a jellybag, or hard-knock shoes? Our ancestors have also worn: the brownie suit, railroad trousers, sack coats, pommels, and slickers.

Each stage of our westward migration produced folk heroes and styles of folk clothing which will forever be associated with it, such as the mountain men, the gold miner, or the cowboy. Our military history has produced some folk clothing of its own, such as that worn by the World War I aviator and the sailor, and has directly influenced the clothing of all ages of Americans including women, boys, and even little girls. The working people and the military have had as much influence on America's costume as has European fashion.

Inventions such as the bicycle, automobile, electric light, and the motion picture have contributed directly to American costume history. Our own arts have influenced our clothing, too, through the old minstrel shows, theatre, the dance, and the movies.

It is significant of our interest in costume that our Confederate soldiers were called "butternut soldiers" because of the vegetable dye used for their homemade uniforms and that "coppers," one of our slang terms for policemen, came about because of their early uniform buttons. Our very first professional sports team took their name from their clothes—the Cincinnati Red Stockings.

The story of American costume is the story of events, wars, inventions; social, religious, cultural, and political movements; and economic situations throughout our history. It is the story of the folks of all ages and walks of life who wore those clothes.

Acknowledgments

A very special thanks to those institutions which shared their collections and opened their files to me and to their staffs who were so generous with their time: The Library of Congress, The National Archives, The Smithsonian Institution, and the National Gallery of Art in Washington; The Whitney Museum of American Art, The Museum of the City of New York, The Print Division of The New York Public Library, The New York Historical Society and the Metropolitan Museum of Art, in New York; The Confederate Museum and the Valentine Museum in Richmond; The Museum of Fine Arts, Boston; the Brooklyn Museum; and the City Art Museum of St. Louis.

Each art collection shared adds to our total knowledge of how Americans have dressed throughout history. I express my gratitude to those individuals who have assembled extensive and important collections of American art and shared them so generously: Edgar William and Bernice Chrysler Garbisch, New York; Mrs. John Nicholas Brown, Providence, R.I.; Mrs. Catharine McCook Knox, Washington; Clarence P. Hornung; and Alexander McCook Craighead.

For over three decades Nashville Academy Theatre (formerly Nashville Children's Theatre) has provided so many of us with an environment that stimulates and encourages creativity. I am grateful to the Board of Directors and to Director Tom Kartak for presenting me with design challenges and for allowing me to explore, take chances, and to grow.

I would like also to thank the following museums and historical societies: Addison Gallery of American Art, Andover, Mass.; Detroit Institute of Arts; Philadelphia Museum of Art; Syracuse Museum of Art; Yale University Art Gallery; Abby Aldrich Rockefeller Folk Art Collection, Williamsburg; Tennessee Fine Arts Center, Nashville; Walters Art Gallery, Baltimore; Fogg Art Museum, Harvard University; The William Rockhill Nelson Gallery of Art, Kansas City; and the Remington Art Memorial; Kansas State Historical Society, Topeka; Georgia Department of Archives and History, Atlanta; Western Reserve Historical Society, Cleveland; New York Historical Society; the Chicago Historical Society; Arizona Pioneer's Historical Society; the Society of California Pioneers; and the State Historical Society of Colorado.

Thanks to: Sears, Roebuck Company; Osh Kosh B'Gosh Co.; American Telephone and Telegraph Company; U.S. Bureau of Public Roads; Bureau of Aeronautics; The Navy Department.

I am indebted to Mr. Bill Colsher of the Nashville Public Library, and Mr. William Baker of the Tennessee State Museum who assisted me in research, and to Jo Anne Chrisman, who shared old family photographs with me.

And finally, I am grateful to members of my family who have assisted and encouraged me in so many ways: my husband Norman; daughters, Anne, Elizabeth, and Clare; my son Sterling, and my brother Sterling Ansley, Jr.

Chapter 1

Creative Costumes

A costume can express a person's fundamental values because we all care what people think about us. We are careful that our clothes give the "right" impression and are concerned that we not wear something that will give anyone an erroneous impression of us.

Our attitudes toward clothes are so ingrained in us that the head of the F.B.I. cautioned that we might invite harm to ourselves by the way in which we dress. When we dress to go somewhere we might actually be determining our destiny by the clothes we select from our closet. Politicians hire consultants to tell them how to dress to attract the votes they seek. Lawyers tell clients how or how-not-to dress in order to sway juries. School principals expel students for their dress or hair styles, restaurants and clubs refuse admission to people because of their clothes, and parents get emotional over what their children wear. Preachers preach about the way people dress. Newspapers always describe what well-known personalities are wearing when they receive awards, are arrested, get married, or divorced and so on. They describe what both the prosecution and the defense wear to court each day of the trial and they sometimes describe the clothes of the jurors. Anytime a group engages in some kind of public protest you can count on the media to describe what the individuals were wearing at the time.

We leave our homes where they are when we go someplace, we even park our cars eventually, but our clothes always go with us. For this reason they are considered a part of our character. Clothes are so personal that sometimes when we are asked to describe a person we describe their clothes instead.

Americans are considered the most visual-minded people in the world today, possibly because of our free enterprise system and our use of advertising and television. All indications are that we will become even more visually oriented in the future. It is estimated that between eighty and ninety percent of all impressions are received through our eyes. In view of all this it seems that theatre today is not living in the present if it does not consider the impact of well-designed costumes on today's audiences.

Costume design means organizing ideas, feelings and information. It means thinking in terms of the entire play or production and then moving toward the central characters whose feelings are most apparent and most important.

The role of the costume should be to establish a time, a location, or a state of being. A primitive or advanced state must not be confused with time and place. The American frontier, for instance, was not a specific place or time in history; it was a stage of development at the edge of a settled area which was constantly moving. You might, as a result, be called upon to design frontier costumes for any period in American history.

A costume can establish the economic condition of the character wearing it. It also can make a statement about the climate, the season, the weather, or the geographic location. Attitudes toward religion, politics, and regional or geographic traditions can be illustrated through clothing.

Most important of all, a costume should say something about the specific individual who is to wear it. A well designed costume can make a statement about the character even before the actor wearing it says a word of dialogue. Some facts about how one lives are quickly determined. If a person did not hang up his clothes the night before, or if he wipes his hands on them or drips food on them, you would know at first glance, wouldn't you? More subtle are those things that a person reveals because he *wants* to make a certain impression concerning his wealth, status, or taste. Still more subtle, but nonetheless a part of a person, are those qualities, faults, and attitudes that he shows about himself without even being aware of it. The designer should consider both the deliberate and the subconscious statement each character can make through costume.

Eliza Doolittle in *My Fair Lady* is transformed outwardly as she changes inside. Even she realizes, in the play, that the professor cannot simply send her back to her old life because the Eliza of that former life does not exist anymore. She is an educated, graceful, beautiful, and soft-spoken woman now and everything about her appearance illustrates this but she realizes it before Professor Higgins does. Eliza is easy to design for because her transformation is extreme. Most changes you will be called upon to illustrate will be far more gradual—although just as important.

One of the most dramatic things that a designer can do in theatre is to indicate visually a subtle change either in a character's attitudes or the attitudes of others toward that character. In the *Rainmaker* Lizzie takes great pains to conceal her hunger for romance yet under the surface of her personality there are indications which reveal it to those who are open to it. As she experiences the joy of being loved her costume should include a symbol of that joy. (If she has a complete change of costume then her new dress and hairstyle can be just a bit more soft and feminine. If your budget does not allow complete changes, you can still change her hair slightly or alter the manner in which she fastens or arranges her clothes to indicate her fulfillment.) Just the addition of a simple accessory can often be sufficient but when an experience, revelation, or a change of some sort in attitudes takes place within a character you should, in some way, indicate it visually. *Your audience expects some outward proof of a character's inward feelings.* Don't just depend on the actors to *tell* them—show them!

The script usually determines the period and sometimes the exact date and setting of a play. The playwright indicates age, social and economic status, and those attitudes of each character as they concern the plot. A costume designer is left to draw conclusions concerning some aspects of a character's attitudes. A designer's challenge is to illustrate those conclusions and the intended attitudes as indicated in the script in a way that the audience can understand and enjoy.

By reading a script you can determine what is *physically* expected of a costume in certain scenes. For instance, a script might indicate a need for a pocket somewhere, or a garment that can be pulled off instantly, or require that a piece of clothing be sturdy enough to be pulled by someone. An actor may have to change costumes on stage as part of the play or he may have to change off stage in only a minute or two. Even before you begin your design you may have a short list of physical requirements already determined by the script as well as by each character's attitudes.

The lifestyle of a character is the expression of what and who he is and once you determine some things about that lifestyle you will have the essence of your design.

One example from my own exprience concerned designing costumes for three young boys in the same period and of the same age but of very different attitudes and lifestyles. They were Tom Sawyer, Huck Finn, and Sid from the musical *The Adventures of Tom Sawyer*.

Aunt Polly loved Tom and Sid and would have seen to it that they were clean and properly dressed when each day began. It was what they did to their clothes that was the basis for my designs. Sid stayed dressed, he did not remove his shoes or jacket, and he remained clean and neat all day like the obedient boy he was. Tom could hardly wait to remove his jacket, roll up his shirt sleeves, open his collar, stuff his pockets full, and remove his shoes and stockings. He was soon dirty and rumpled but it was just dirt from that day's play—"fresh dirt" you might say. Now Huck was a child of the river who probably slept in his clothes. They were more than likely castoffs to begin with and he thought of them as just something to hang on his body to cover him. He hated shoes and if only one suspender would hold up his breeches then two would be too many.

Once the proper historic period and the geographic location had been determined, each boy's individual lifestyle had to be analyzed.

Wealth and status. A successful businessman deliberately plans his outfit to tell others that he is successful, tasteful, and well coordinated. He must look as successful as he is. The successful man's wife dresses so that her husband's success shows through her by perhaps first acquiring the little mink stole and later the mink coat as he climbs up the ladder of success. There are numerous books on the subject of dressing to look successful and even powerful.

As far as fashion is concerned, there are two kinds of socialites. There is the woman or man of wealth who only wears what is new and expensive. As soon as those "beneath" acquire it the socialite tosses a fashion aside and buys the next newest style. This person constantly must prove his/her wealth and status by untiring efforts to stay "out front." The other, more conservative type socialite never wears the very latest fashion, always waiting until a style is in its second phase, when others in the circle of friends are wearing it. This way the socialite never competes with or outshines the established leaders but only obediently follows where they lead. Designing for the very rich social-leader character is often where an amateur designer fails. You must learn to determine whether leading is a matter of life and death to the socialite or if slavishly following is the way of life. In this book I have shown the transitional styles as well as those that were fashionable at the beginning, middle, and end of each decade. When new, the dress of Figure 106, for instance, would be worn by a very fashionable woman because it was predicting the new styles to come.

The dresses of the '70s and '80s demonstrate how the bustle started high, moved down onto the legs, then went back up to the waist, and finally disappeared. In order to show that a character in your play is very rich and fashionable you might make her bustle style newer than those of the other ladies. You will have to keep her in her proper relationship to the others.

Remember that it is better to understate "rich" rather than to overdo it lest the lady end up looking cheap instead of expensive. We have all seen plays in which the designer apparently thought "rich" meant more jewelry, more make-up, and more decoration on the clothes.

Poverty and hard times. Designing for your poor characters at first seems simple but much can be expressed through old worn clothes. A character, for instance, can be very poor but just that fact in itself will not necessarily solve your design challenge. Determine something about his lifestyle and his attitudes. A garment, especially on a young poor person, might not fit properly indicating that it was a hand-me-down from an older person or a charity gift. The person's basic outlook can be shown through the costume perhaps by patches and by buttons that don't all match. The clothing might be clean and neat in order to state that this person or another caring person still has pride in his looks. He is poor, yes, but has taken the trouble to cover the holes and replace the buttons and enjoy the dignity of being clean.

On the other hand, if the poor, misfitting garments are dirty, rumpled, unpatched and uncared-for, it might indicate that the character no longer has the will to fight back. A really downtrodden character might no longer care about the impression he makes. Even among the lowest of people you will find a variety of attitudes toward life, other people, and one's self. Don't just put the character in rags without considering the fact that he still might have a great deal of pride and hope.

Suffering or discomfort of various kinds and degrees can be expressed through costume. One of the most effective ways to accomplish this is to think of a scene as an artist's painting. You have no sound effects, dialogue, or body movement to depend on so you will have to use some visual evidence of the character's misery.

One example might be a young soldier who is damp, cold, and miserable. He will evoke strong feelings from the audience if he *looks* damp, cold, and miserable and if they are made to feel that he is not just any soldier but that particular soldier at that very moment experiencing that particular misery. Just having him wear a coat, rehearse shivering and saying "Brrrr, I'm cold," is not going to involve the audience. You must, through your design,

make them *feel the cold.* For example, the soldier of Figure 71 which was inspired by an old Civil War photograph can be the basis for such a design. The addition of a non-military scarf might be worn in one of various ways in a visual attempt to keep warm. He might wrap it around his neck as shown or wrap it around the head and then around the neck as did the little boy of Figure 19. He might wear it either over his cap or under it to warm his head and ears. Worn underneath the collar, the scarf would hold it up to protect his neck. The coat might be tattered and muddy and the young man might clutch a quilt around his shoulders or wear an oilcloth piano cover poncho (Figure 128). In an extreme situation he might have resorted to a pathetic attempt to close an old coat which had no buttons left on it by lapping it over in front and tying a rope around his waist. The more desperate his attempts to keep warm, the colder he will seem.

After you have successfully expressed his misery visually, the addition of the body movement, dialogue, and sound effects will involve the audience still more. The creative use of costume can capture and express the mood of a scene and impart it to today's visually minded audiences as effectively as the dialogue.

A character's roots. For Injun Joe, the villain of *Tom Sawyer,* I designed a costume to illustrate his heredity. He was referred to in the script as a "half-breed" so I built part of his clothes like the white man's and part like the Indian's. The costume was similar to that of Figure 133 which is also representative of two cultures. My Injun Joe not only wore the white man's trousers but his black riding boots as well. I decided his shirt should be a fiery orange-red (to represent anger) and made dirty from constant wear. He wore the feathered hairstyle of Figure 98 as well as a black vest over his belted shirt. There are many opportunities to use a character's ancestry or nationality as a source for your designs. If not the entire costume, sometimes just one small element can express a hint of a character's background if that background is important to the play.

Body language must be considered in costume design. In studying body language it is interesting to find how often clothing plays a part in human expression. One example is the romantic "preening" ritual. Visualize a young man at a party and a girl across the room talking to a friend: he adjusts his coat, straightens his tie, and clears his throat as he looks across the room at the girl. She in turn, realizing he is coming her way, arranges her clothes, moistens her lips, fluffs her hair, and checks her neckline. If a mirror is nearby she will take a quick look to see if her clothes and make-up are right. She may quickly ask her friend if her clothes look right. This whole scene is so visual that it can be played without dialogue; the actions of the characters and their relationship to their clothing and to each other are apparent.

An intimate love scene can be indicated by the simple,

deliberate removal of a hair-ribbon or a coat. *How much is removed is not as important as the manner in which it is taken off.* A skillfully designed costume and the creative use of it can have more impact than an awkward scene played in an embarrassing attempt at realism.

A swinging skirt on a young girl can convey a message as do the tight pants of a modern rock singer or an unbuttoned shirt. One famous example in *How To Succeed in Business Without Really Trying* was the office party scene. Every girl in the office showed up wearing the same dress but the men only noticed one particular girl's dress because she was conveying messages to them by the way she walked and moved. Her attitudes toward men came through loud and clear by the way she wore the dress and the way it fit.

Every girl knows that the way she feels in a dress can determine how she looks in it. A dress that she doesn't feel is right for her can spoil her evening even though others insist that she looks great in it. She will move differently in a dress that makes her *feel* beautiful.

Hairstyles accompanying the costume drawings are authentic to the period and to the type of costume so that you can design hair with the proper historical silhouette.

Hair design for theatre must be more than just historically correct, for it like the clothes, should tell something about the character.

For centuries the question of hair has provoked emotion and even violence. Even in ancient Rome the elders worried and fumed over the young men's habit of wearing their hair too long.

There actually is no correlation between lawlessness, academic capacity, or morals and hair length yet juries, judges, school principals, parents, and personnel directors consistently show an irrational fear of the influence hair has on young people. Psychologists admit that there is no evidence to substantiate this fear.

Historically and anthropologically, long hair has been a symbol of aggressive power and sexual activity—ever since Samson! Throughout history young men with long hair have been labelled lawless, immoral, anti-government, unclean, primitive, irresponsible, aggressive, and uncontrollable. Older generations invariably view long hair as a threat from the younger generation to the status quo.

In theatre the hair style can go beyond the fashionable silhouette and express something of the individual. Longer hair on an older person might express some rebelliousness or change in attitudes. Traditionally in theatre the "letting down" of the hair has demonstrated submission on the part of women. After you establish the proper historical hairstyle for the play you must then treat it in relation to the symbols connected with it in order to make your statement.

Basically, throughout history, long hair on a man has symbolized rebellion and independence while short hair symbolized conformity, morality, and submission. With women it has been traditionally the opposite, long hair symbolizing submission to authority and to men while short hair has been interpreted as rebellion and independence. There are some periods in history when this is not the rule, however, so you must first study the correct period and then inject the emotional symbolism into your designs. Beards and mustaches have at times provoked strong feelings, too.

One third of the total time spent looking at a person is spent looking at the face. We glance up and down the entire figure one or more times but concentrate on the face. Perhaps this is why the hairstyle is so important to us.

A critic with a knowledge of costume design and of what a good costume should do, can, by comments and advice, encourage theatre groups of all levels to take costume seriously.

A word of advice to any aspiring critic: ask yourself, Did the costume confirm or contradict the attitudes of the character? Did it tell anything about the character's lifestyle? When all critics begin to expect more of costume design in our visually oriented society, the result will be that we will receive more enjoyment not only from costume but from theatre as a whole.

One of the best ways to learn about something is by example so I offer the following quotation from Clara Hieronymus, drama and art critic for the *Tennessean* newspaper concerning character is *Blithe Spirit*:

> It would help enormously if Madame Arcati, the medium who inadvertently "materialized" Ruth and Elvira, were more eccentric in dress and manner. . . . We are told that Arcati (every comedienne must want to play this wacky role) has ridden her bicycle 7 miles to hold the seance at the Condomines' house; her entrance has been "stageset" before she arrives.
>
> But her appearance doesn't jibe with our expectations. Might there have been bicycle clips on her pants legs, and her robe hitched up? As it is, [she] looks very much like any present day woman dressed for a cocktail party, and on her return visit she wears a sedate black suit. It isn't enough, we need more to meet the eye.

The following drawings and discussions give a broad view of American costume from the smartest fashions to the clothes of those who suffered hard times. Just as art and music reflect the tempo, tensions, aims, attitudes, hopes, failures, and successes of the times, so do clothes. The view includes military, work, and play clothes as well as the apparel of those people who were just beginning a new life in a new place. Each decade of costume represents a cross section of America.

Costume is never revolutionary but is always evolutionary. Everything in costume is related to what has gone before and what will follow.

CHAPTER 2

1840s

Rustic Simplicity and Fantastic Growth

At the beginning of the 19th century the United States exported 5,000,000 dollars worth of cotton a year and by 1840 it was 63,000,000—America was sending cotton all over the world. Wheat and corn production increased dramatically during these years, too. The North was in the midst of an industrial revolution, the South remained primarily an agricultural society. More than five times as many people lived on farms in both sections of the country as lived in towns and cities.

Immigrants were arriving by the tens of thousands while the vast areas of the West were beginning to be opened for settlement. Systems of transportation were growing at a fantastic rate. Between 1845 and 1848 the United States would have a war with Mexico, the annexation of Texas, and the settlement with Great Britain of the Oregon boundary.

The sewing machine would revolutionize clothes making, while the newly invented plate photography would be greatly improved to record for history the clothing Americans were wearing. There was another revolution beginning at this time as Amelia Bloomer and Elizabeth Cody Stanton shocked the nation by wearing short dresses over trousers.

American Costume

Seen in the industrial cities of the North, on southern plantations, on river-boats or trains, and in small towns throughout the nation, the frock coat was widely popular. At this period it was usually single-breasted with flared skirts as shown here. In hot weather or in the southern climate white linen coats were favored with wide-brimmed straw hats. Tan, green, brown, blue, and gray were favorite colors, as were tweeds in winter.

The tailcoats of the early 19th century were still worn by some men at this time, too.

Vests or waistcoats were either embroidered or made of brocade and often colorful. Watch fobs were worn in the vests. This gentleman's shirt collar has the points turned down over a large cravat of black. Cravats were frequently red at this time too.

Trousers were often checked or plaid. Sometimes they matched the coat, sometimes not. The trousers worn by this man are the older, shorter pantaloons favored in the South and rural areas. Gentlemen in the city favored the longer, sometimes strapped trousers of Figure 2.

Curly hair and long bushy sideburns were popular. His black slipper-shoes lace through three holes over large tongues.

Figure 1

Figure 2

A coat of new design appeared at the beginning of this decade and was destined to influence men's coats right up to the present time. It was the box coat. It had no waistline seam as coats had always had, but was made in a straight line from the shoulders to the hem. The shawl collar was sometimes of satin; in winter it might be velvet or fur.

Another coat of almost identical line was the Moscow coat of wool with a fur collar. It was often fur-lined or even fur all over. It had tabs going across the front to join the buttons as on the smoking jacket of Figure 83 and the cowboy's coat of Figure 125. Buttons were often cloth-covered.

Trousers, strapped under the foot, might be striped, checked, or plain. The hat was a cut-down hat or a high straw. Much like a top hat, it had a rounded crown. Black boots were preferred in cold weather, worn under the trousers. Slippers were worn in mild weather in the city.

Fancy waistcoats underneath the coats usually had shawl collars and might be either double- or single-breasted. Curly hair was immensely popular and sideburns came down on the cheeks making cheek-whiskers.

In the cities the volunteer fireman was a popular hero. Fire companies competed with each other with their dashing uniforms and polished equipment.

Coats were made on the same lines as the fashionable coats but were decorated with a great deal of braid and buttons. Some were cutaway at the front skirt corners as in Figure 23, and some were single-breasted. The variety of styles of braid trim illustrate a great deal of creativity and competition among the fire companies. Black leather belts were favored, but some coats were beltless. This fireman wears a horn suspended from his belt. The horn and the bell on the fire engine were the 1840s equivalent of our present-day sirens.

His trousers have a matching braid stripe down the side and a strap under the foot.

Hats with a wide protective brim in back had been worn in France for many years by men whose work kept them out in the rain. It was a natural style for Americans to adapt for fire fighting. Decorative metal plates stood up in front, often with the name of the fire company embossed on it.

Some fire companies wore shirt-smocks very similar to the one worn by the soldier in Figure 37. They wore long trousers and fireman's hats. A shirt of almost identical design was pictured decades later in an 1897 mail-order catalog labelled "Fireman's Shirt" so it must have been commonly used as such during the second half of the century.

Figure 3

By 1850 more than five times as many people lived on farms as in towns and cities. Although popular fiction has led many to believe that all southern farmers were plantation owners, only about 300,000 out of 6,000,000 owned slaves in 1850. Of those only about 37,000 owned twenty or more slaves. Most farmers, both northern and southern, were small independent farmers.

For generations English and many European farmers had worn smocks. When they came to America they brought the tradition with them and wore them throughout the seventeenth and eighteenth centuries and—paintings indicate—right up to the Civil War.

The decorative stitching on these smocks eventually became known as "smocking." Blue and gray were favorite colors of many European farmers, green or natural of the English, and black of the German. These smocks were also worn belted in the manner of Figure 5, becoming a hunting shirt.

This farmer wears dark pantaloons and shirt with the thigh-length smock. He wears a feather in his flared top hat of former years. In summer in the fields these smocks were often worn without trousers.

Figure 4

American Costume

The farmer's smock met the Indian's deerskin tunic in America and became the hunting shirt. There are many references in American history to "hunting smocks." Early hunting shirts were often decorated in the Indian manner with quiltwork or beads as this one is on the sleeves.

This man, who might be a trapper, hunter, explorer, or western settler, wears his shirt belted, but some were unbelted like the smock of Figure 4. Shirts of all styles still opened only at the neck. In warm weather a linen shirt was decorated with fringed linen; a deerskin shirt worn in winter was also fringed. In Figure 5 the shirt's long fringes are tied in knots at the dropped shoulder line. This man wears a white shirt underneath. These shirts were sometimes high-necked like the Indian one in Figure 38.

Soldiers at the battle of the Alamo during the war with Mexico wore outfits such as this.

Leather Indian leggings are drawn up over the trousers. A strap on each side is attached to the trousers' waist. A garter is tied under each knee to hold them in place. He wears Indian moccasins. A strap holds a canteen and other equipment.

The fur hat, introduced by early French trappers, can be turned down over the ears. American trappers were fond of feather decoration on their hats. They preferred Sharp's buffalo rifle.

In 1843 the Oregon Trail was marked off and by 1845 more than three thousand people had settled in Oregon.

Figure 5

Gold miners, Mormon pioneers, riverboat men, farmers, young boys, and slaves wore many variations of the loose pantaloons, drop-shouldered shirt, and suspenders. Many paintings and photographs show that only one suspender was worn. Suspenders at this time were two separate straps, not joined as they are today. There might be many reasons why a man or boy might wear only one—he might have lost one, only had one cast-off one to start with, have broken one, didn't want to bother with two, or perhaps just improvised one out of some material in an emergency. The reasons were as unique as the individuals who wore them.

This man's pantaloons are rolled up showing his heavy lace-up work shoes. Many men are pictured barefoot or with boots. Shoes for slaves were made right on the plantation by a slave trained as a cobbler.

His hat is a wide-brimmed straw seen most often in rural areas, around rivers, and in the South.

Mormon pioneer men were pictured dressed like this man as described in Figure 17.

Figure 6

Between 1844 and 1854 3,000,000 immigrants from Europe flooded into eastern seaports and moved across America to settle. Of these, 1,300,000 came from Ireland (see Figure 90) and a million from Germany.

Many of these immigrants were farmers, musicians, railroad workers, miners, artists, teachers, scientists, engineers, lumbermen, brewers, steel workers, printers, and musical instrument makers. These immigrants brought us the idea of the town band and the glee club. It was said that fifty percent of all miners were foreign-born. The most important pre-Civil War activity in the West was mining.

The full drop-shouldered shirt and suspenders were worn by men of all classes. This man wears his union suit under his shirt and a vest over it. His trousers or pantaloons are tucked into canvas-lined boots which are turned down showing the canvas and the boot straps.

His cap is the one issued to the U.S. Army in 1841. This cap originated in Prussia in 1813 during the Napoleonic War. It was introduced by both European immigrants and former army men and was widely worn until the early 20th century (see Figure 161).

See Figure 17 for description of Mormon pioneers.

Figure 7

During the war with Mexico, United States soldiers wore the close-fitting short jackets adopted during the early part of the century. They were designed after those worn during the French Revolution and the Napoleonic War. For the cap history see Figure 7.

The cavalry wore dark blue jackets with light blue trousers; the infantry light blue jackets to match the trousers. Both groups had yellow stripes on the trousers for corporals, sergeants, and higher officers. The cavalry jacket had yellow piping on the curved, side-back seams (like those on the back bodice of Figure 188). Yellow was also used on the cap band, collar, and cuff trim.

An eagle was embossed on the plate of the white shoulder strap and "U.S.A." on the belt buckle. (These white straps were not worn after the 1840s except by military schools and a few state militias.) Brass buttons were used. Cavalry troops wore black boots.

Some of these jackets had very small coat tails in back, as in Figure 57.

The first regiment of mounted troops to serve against the Plains Indians was raised in 1833. This regiment of dragoons allowed each man $3.50 a month for clothes and $6.00 a month salary. By 1840 it was raised to $8.00!

In 1847 Colonel Sterling Price (later a major general of the Confederate army) attacked the Pueblo Indians of Taos with volunteers from Missouri and a group of mountain men. Mountain men also fought at the battle of the Alamo (see Figure 5).

Figure 8

American Costume

Of all the southeastern Indians the Cherokees made the greatest contribution to history. Sequoyah, a mixed blood Cherokee of Tennessee, developed a writing system during the 1820s. Within the following years the tribe had learned the system and even published a bilingual newspaper during the '30s. They translated the Old Testament into Cherokee. By 1840 these people along with the Creeks, Choctaws, Chickasaws, and Seminoles were pushed from their eastern capital to Indian Territory in the West.

These Cherokees had adapted to the life of their white neighbors, wearing the clothes, building homes and towns, and promoting traditional education through their written language.

This Indian wears a wraparound garment similar to a kimono over his white dress shirt, waistcoat, and cravat. It had the drop shoulder of shirts of the period. These dressing-gown style coats were of brightly colored exotic prints and stripes. A solid color cummerbund was worn.

Fitted Indian leggings or trousers and moccasins covered the legs and feet.

This Indian wears a metal medallion around his neck. A flower-striped fabric is wrapped around his head to form a turban.

Figure 9

Southeastern Indian women wore short sarongs and lots of feathers in the 16th and 17th centuries but later adopted cloth dresses similar to those of white women. They eventually were much like that of Figure 166 in both one-piece and blouse and skirt styles.

This woman wears an older style dress of deerskin or cloth with decorations of pierced metal and shell ornaments around the wide neck and collar. It is gathered in at the hips. The sleeves are gathered onto a dropped shoulder.

Indian leggings cover the lower leg and the top of her moccasins. Tan or red were favorite colors for these leggings which were gartered beneath the knee.

Southeastern Indian women were recorded as having worn their shiny black hair long either parted in the middle or with bangs.

By 1849 most members of the Seminole tribe had been captured by the army and sent to Oklahoma.

Figure 10

20

Southern Plains Indians were originally woodland Indians who were pushed out of their tribal lands as America grew westward. They based their plains culture on the horse and the buffalo. As they changed, so did their clothing which became more and more decorative and dashing.

The image most people have of the American Indian is that of the Plains Indian on horseback with the long fringe and feathers of his clothing moving dramatically in the wind. Fringe has a marvelous way of reflecting and intensifying almost every little motion of the body. Its use developed out of aesthetic expression as well as for its practical purpose of diverting water away from seams.

Long tufts of hair, both human and animal, are tied into the shoulder yokes, around the neckline, down the length of the sleeves and around the uneven hem of this man's deerskin tunic. Quillwork or bead medallions are attached at the chest with strips of leather; other strips are attached around the middle.

His close-fitting leggings are held up by a belt like those of Figure 95. They are decorated with quillwork and hair tufts of black and red.

His long wavy hair is almost covered with feathers and strips of leather.

Figure 11

Women of the southern plains, woodland, Great Lakes areas, and the Northeast all wore blankets much like this. Occasionally they are shown wearing undecorated tunics similar to that of the man in Figure 11 and tied at the waist with a belt.

Eighteenth and early nineteenth century blankets were plain, often blue or tan, but toward the end of the century they were woven in striped and plaid designs. These bright, fancy blankets were probably received in trade from the whites.

This woman carries her baby inside a blanket on her back. When the blanket was pulled up to form a head covering, sometimes the baby peered out to one side of the mother's head. In some paintings of Indian villages one must look carefully to see the little face in the darkness of the mother's hood.

Her leggings, attached with leather garters just below her knees, are red, her plain moccasins, tan. Her long hair is parted in the middle.

Figure 12

21

Women's sleeves of the 1840s were often fitted at the upper arm, flaring above the elbow. Tucked bodices, diagonal lines, and dropped shoulder lines were the fashion.

This dress, probably a party dress, is off the shoulder with a tucked swag around the neckline that is sewn into the front seam. The point in front and curved side-front seams were boned for stiffness.

For really formal occasions the sleeve ruffles might be several layers of lace or fabric. Sometimes there was more than one skirt flounce, too.

Dresses were made of silk, cotton plaid, checks, or calico. They varied in length, many of them being a few inches off the floor like this one.

Hair was always parted in the middle at this time and pulled across the forehead and sometimes the cheeks. This young lady's is pulled behind her ears into bunches of slender sausage curls. A ribbon headband crosses her forehead and is fastened with a small brooch. She wears a bracelet with stones to match her neckline brooch.

Her shoes are flat-heeled slippers.

Figure 13

Figure 14

Howe's lock-stitch sewing machine made sewing easier and faster by 1843. For the first time, machine-stitching was as strong as hand stitching. Things could be made by machine in less time, so it was inevitable that the world of clothing would never be the same.

Shirring became so prevalent on clothes that dresses like this one had bodices and sleeves almost entirely shirred.

Here, fabric is shirred at the shoulders, then released to spread out and conform to the bust before being caught into the front seam at the waist and point. The neckline is filled in with a sheer cloth and trimmed with a grosgrain ribbon bow at the throat.

Sleeves were caught in row upon row of shirring. Sometimes a row of shirring alternated with a solid band. Cuffs were drawn up by numerous rows of stitching to fit the wrists. Sheer fabrics were often used for sleeves, gray being a favorite color on the pastel-colored dresses.

Skirt flounces were trimmed with lace or bands of shirring. They varied in number and size.

This lady's hair style is similar to that of Figure 13 except that it covers the tops of her ears.

22

Both Amelia Bloomer and Elizabeth Cody Stanton faced ridicule and scorn when they shocked the country by wearing short dresses with men's trousers. The matching full trousers were gathered in at the ankle by a drawstring. The demand by women for equality would continue right up to the present.

The shockingly short skirt came to a little below the knee. More conservative women wore long skirts like that of Figure 42, made of one to three flounces. This one appears as though the lower, third flounce has simply been removed.

This crusading lady wears a fashionable bodice jacket with dropped shoulders which form caps over the flared, three-quarter-length sleeves. Underneath she wears a full, flared-sleeve blouse with a small collar. Both jacket and skirt are trimmed with dark braid. In warm weather partial sleeves with drawstrings or elastic at the elbow gave the appearance of a complete blouse underneath while being much cooler than a blouse.

Bonnets were trimmed at the sides with satin ribbons or flowers. Figures 104 and 110 show similar bonnets from the side.

High-buttoned, low-heeled shoes and gloves complete her history-making outfit which gave us a new item of apparel and a new word—bloomers!

Figure 15

Older or more conservative women still wore crisp white caps with lappets hanging down in either back or front. This one is folded back into a cuff and decorated with satin ribbon rosettes on each side.

Although she clings to earlier styles for her cap, this lady wears a dress of fashionable lines with the diagonal bodice tucks from shoulder to the center front waist point. The shoulder line is dropped down onto the arm.

Her wide neckline and fitted long sleeves are trimmed with starched white collar and little cuffs. Although her dark dress with the prim white trim and her cap tell us she is very prim and proper, her dress also tells us she can afford the latest style.

Her hair is parted in the middle and twisted into a bun in back. Her slippers are flat-heeled and she carries an embroidered handkerchief.

Figure 16

American Costume

In 1847 the Mormon pioneers set out on their journey to the valley of the Great Salt Lake. By 1856 two thousand people had made the trip, pushing and pulling hand carts. Later, ox carts were used, and by 1860 three thousand Latter-Day Saints had made the trip.

In a painting owned by the Church of Jesus Christ of Latter-Day Saints most of the men in a large party of pioneers are dressed like those of Figures 6 and 7.

Mormon women of all ages were dressed like this young woman in the painting already mentioned. The jacket, sometimes called a "poke" jacket, has the prevailing dropped-shoulder line and flared sleeves. She wears no blouse underneath but has a bandanna around her neck. The bandanna, the jacket, and the skirt were often of different colors making a colorful costume. Usually the skirts were dark colors with the jackets lighter.

Although the bonnets of Figures 15, 43, and 46 are shown in the painting, most of the women wear the charming, wide-brimmed, straw hat tied on with a scarf or ribbon. It has a rather romantic look.

Figure 17

Little girls' dresses had tucked bodices and wide or off-the-shoulder necklines like their mothers'.

On the left, the dress bodice has an interesting tucked panel gathered into a curved shape just above the waistline. A yoke is sewn in at the shoulders, becoming part of the sleeves. The neck and sleeves are trimmed with lace with a pink satin bow on each shoulder of the blue dress. A matching pink ribbon is tied around her waist and she carries a reticule purse.

On the right, a little girl wears a mauve-colored dress with a tucked bodice. The off-the-shoulder neckline has a bertha collar trimmed with black lace and a rosette. The small, fitted sleeves are trimmed with black lace also.

Her apron, with its pointed waistband, is a sheer black fabric with lace on the edges. She wears amber beads and has a handkerchief in her apron pocket.

Both children wear lace-trimmed pantalets. Both have middle-parted hair with sausage curls or back bun like their mothers.

Blue high-topped laced-up shoes are worn by the girl on the left, flat black slippers by the one on the right.

Figure 18

Dressed for play, a little girl wears a full, gathered smock over her long-sleeved dark green wool dress. Her wool stockings are red, her high-topped shoes black.

Her interesting bonnet is a kind of stocking cap bunched in back and tied together (in the manner of ancient homemade stocking caps). It is also gathered at the neck and tied under the chin.

A young boy wears brown pantaloons buttoned onto a gray sweater, worn over a shirt. He also wears high-topped black shoes; his stockings are tan. His mittens are gray, as are the girl's.

His cap is also of interest. It is the popular cap of Figures 7 and 8 worn over a red, tan, and white striped wool scarf with tasselled ends. The scarf goes over the head and ears, crosses under the chin, and then wraps around the neck before it ties in front—a very warm and snug headdress!

Figure 19

Very little boys' clothes during the 19th century were more like their mothers' than their fathers'. The little boy on the left wears an off-the-shoulder dress of black wool or taffeta. It has black velvet panels which flare out over the very full, elbow-length sleeves. A sheer white ruffle trims the neckline.

The gathered skirt opens in front to show the white pantaloons which have a little split at the hem. His slippers are black.

His visored cap is much like those of Figures 7 and 8 but is a very dressy interpretation with gold braid and two silk tassels on one side.

Young boys wore peasant or European worker-style smocks over long trousers. They were usually tan, gray, or blue. This one, on the boy on the right, is pleated onto a square yoke and belted with a wide belt. The yoke, neckline, and sleeves are trimmed with white sheer lace. The smock skirt opens in front to show the trousers.

He wears low-cut black slippers. His hair is parted on the side and curled.

Figure 20

25

American Costume

Figure 21

Not all little boys wore skirts although even their trousered suits reflected women's styles.

On the left a little boy wears a blouse with sleeves which become full at the lower arm. The neckline has a wide white collar. His cream-colored pantaloon-style trousers button onto his dark blouse. Pleats at the waist give fullness to them in further imitation of women's full clothes.

His wide-brimmed, shallow hat of either silk "beaver" or fine straw is trimmed with two silk tassels on a cord. (Felt and silk were brushed to give the appearance of beaver fur.)

On the right an older boy wears trousers pleated onto a waistband like a full skirt. They taper to a slim ankle. The full blouse (or top) has collar and cuffs of a darker color. The wide neck reveals a shirt underneath with a cravat. He carries a rounded top hat like that of the man in Figure 2.

The little boy wears black patent-leather slippers with bows, the older boy, lace-up high tops with pointed toes called "high-lows."

CHAPTER 3

1850s

American Styles Develop as Trouble Brews

During the 1850s America began the change from a rural society to an industrial one. Permanent settlements were made in North Dakota while Iowa, Michigan, Minnesota, Wisconsin, and Oregon joined the Union. It was said that gold created the states of California and Nevada early in the decade. Kansas was opened to settlement in 1854.

The steam locomotive brought about the idea of casual sport clothes. The great steamboat era was beginning. It was possible to travel all the way to Montana by steamboat in this decade. Another form of travel, bike riding, was a new sport and along with the train and boat would inspire new sports clothing.

Lincoln and Douglas shared the stage for their famous debates (1858) and John Brown struck at Harper's Ferry in 1859. The war between North and South was soon to grow out of the emotion-filled disagreements.

Our folk clothing such as buckskins, sunbonnets, denims, cowboy clothes, double-breasted shirts, bloomers, the shirtwaist and tailored suit, and slave clothes was already being recognized abroad as typical American styles. The sewing machine was becoming a part of the American home, and the American factory too, as the first attempts were made to mass produce clothing. It was in the '50s that a sewing machine was first used for shoemaking.

Women's fashion magazines and men's sack coats were new and both remain popular right up to today.

By 1858 Iowa, Michigan, Minnesota, and Wisconsin had joined the Union and with Indiana, Illinois, and Ohio made up the new region of the "Middle Border" states.

One outfit commonly seen in the new region as well as in eastern cities was this redingote or frock coat of tan, green or white. In 1858 Abraham Lincoln wore an almost identical outfit in his debate with Stephen A. Douglas. His was a medium gray, Douglas's either brown or black. Lincoln wore a small tie.

The double-breasted coat has a fitted bodice and flared skirt with a split in back. The lapels are curved almost like a shawl collar with a split.

Fawn-colored trousers were down on the boots, even touching the floor in back, sometimes with a strap under the foot.

This man wears a black satin vest with a collar and a black cravat on his high shirt collar. White cravats were also seen. Only the points of the collar turn down.

His top hat, slightly flared, may be black, gray, or sometimes beige or yellow. He carries the fashionable walking stick and may have a monocle in his vest pocket. His hair is curly with broad sideburns.

Figure 22

Although there were no railroads farther west than the Missouri River except for a few in California, one could go all the way up to Montana by steamboat. One outfit worn by gentlemen on those steamboats is shown here.

The frock coat with rounded-off skirt corners appeared at this time and was known as the morning coat. The shawl collar had no slits as does Figure 22. The coat was usually a dark color except in the South where white linen was worn.

Moire or brocade vests were often double-breasted as is this one. This man has his shirt collar turned down the tiniest bit all the way around instead of just the points. Red or black satin cravats were popular and the idea of the pre-tied ties and cravats which fastened in back was new. His white shirt has ruffles at the chest but tucked shirts were worn, too.

Trousers still often had the front fall with buttons instead of the front fly which was being worn in Europe. When this coat and trousers were of the same fabric it was called a "ditto suit."

His hat of leghorn straw was called a "plug" or "stovepipe" hat. The band was wide grosgrain ribbon. Top hats of either rounded or flared shapes were worn also.

Figure 23

The steam locomotive brought about the idea of casual, sporty clothes as people traveled to health springs and seaside resorts.

A shoulder pouch for personal things and valuables became a necessity for these travelers and remains so today. Binoculars were carried in the pouch, too.

The box coat, of straight lines with no darts or waistline seam, was a familiar sight at this time because of its comfort during travel. This design is, with few changes, still worn today. Green, blue, and gray were popular colors in a variety of fabrics, including velvet. Many of these box coats were trimmed with dark braid accenting the lapels and cuffs. Most often worn instead of the suit jacket, this coat, in a longer length, could also be worn as an overcoat.

Trousers at this time were often decorated with braid as these are. Light, solid colors as well as checks, plaids, and stripes were fashionable.

Although boots would remain immensely popular with all classes, the laced-up shoe was worn also.

This man wears the tall black silk hat with gray ribbon band. The derby or bowler hat was worn, too.

Figure 24

The raglan sleeve topcoat, named for Lord Henry Raglan, made its appearance in the 1850s and remained in fashion for over a hundred years! Raglan is said to have lost (or at least lost the use of) an arm in the Crimean War and designed this comfortable, easy coat which eliminated the traditional armhole. Gray, lined with checks or plaid, was fashionable.

Practicality was becoming more important as men traveled about in our "nation on wheels." The starched, detachable collar and cuffs were now worn. A man could change his collar and cuffs while on the go, without having to change his shirt!

This gentleman wears a tucked shirt with his pre-tied bow tie and detachable collar.

The high, rounded hat of Figure 2 was now pushed in, forming a bowl-like depression on top, and was referred to as a bowler. These hats were often of fine straw.

Sideburns and curls were worn. The walking stick and the monocle were popular accessories. This man holds a monocle in his hand. The pince-nez was worn by men as well as women.

Figure 25

American Costume

Not only was traveling by train or steamboat a popular pastime but riding the newly invented bicycles and hiking were the fashion. America was destined to become the world leader in sportswear before the end of the century.

These sports outfits were usually of corduroy, tweed, or checked wool with linen in summer. They were often edged with either matching or contrasting braid. This coat has cutaway front corners for ease in pedaling, stepping up into trains or gangplanks, or bending. Plenty of pockets with buttons or buttoned flaps provide secure places for small accessories. A shoulder strap and pouch were added for carrying large items necessary to one's particular sport. The pouch might be brown, black, or sometimes white.

Trousers were protected, or gotten out of the way, by buff-colored gaiters with buttons on the sides. Black lace-up shoes were worn.

A visored, fitted cap sometimes had flaps inside which could be pulled down to protect the ears.

A gentleman wore a white shirt with turned-down collar points and a bow tie.

Figure 26

Smoking cigarettes was a fashionable habit so smoking jackets and dressing gowns were proper at-home attire. They can be made in any length.

Velvet and quilted taffeta were favorite fabrics with bright-colored or black braid trim. Fancy silk braid or cord frogs and beautiful buttons were used as well as decorative quilting and embroidery. This dressing gown has slits in the flared sleeves but many gowns had plain cuffed sleeves. A heavy silk cord with tassels served as a belt. These lounging costumes had several pockets to hold a cigarette case or other accessories.

Turkish or "house" caps of black velvet with multicolored embroidery were worn. They were edged with silk cord and decorated with large tassels either on top or side.

Underneath a shirt and tie were worn as well as trousers. In cold weather a waistcoat would be worn too.

Mustaches were fashionable as were curly sideburns.

Figure 27

Until 1860 our nation's farm products were worth more than the products of our factories. Although the independent small farmer was still in the majority, it would all be changed in a few more years.

High-waisted pantaloons with matching button strap suspenders were worn by farmers, rivermen, young boys, slaves, and other men who worked outdoors. These strapped pantaloons were the beginning of our American invention, the overalls, although not until the 1890s would they take their present form. In some paintings they are blue, possibly denim.

Shirts still had full sleeves and drop shoulders. This man wears a shirt with several tucks running from the shoulder to the waist on each side. Shirts at this time had a waistline seam in front with a slightly gathered skirt added on to it. He wears the collar open although some paintings show that men wore them buttoned or with tied cravats or bandannas (see Figure 66).

His hat is the wide-brimmed straw hat worn by rural people for centuries. His shoes are heavy brown lace-ups but Wellington boots were often worn.

Figure 28

After the detachable collar came to be the fashion, work shirts like the one on this working man appeared everywhere. The long trousers, the vest, and the boots of Figure 7 and the pantaloons of Figure 28 were worn with striped, checked, calico, or colored shirts.

This man wears a blue-and-white striped shirt which still has the dropped-shoulder line although the collar is gone. Only a narrow neckband of white is used at this time.

His work apron is leather, held on by leather strips. These protective aprons were necessary for steel workers, blacksmiths, wagon makers, and anyone who worked with hot or very rough materials—the hotter the metal, the thicker the leather. Slaves are pictured wearing similar clothes at this time.

One folk painting in the Chrysler Museum shows steel workers wearing black stovepipe hats at work! The blue trousers are rolled up showing the black boots.

The blue trousers were possibly denim. Denim came to America from France where it was woven in de Nimes. It came unbleached and one had to dye it.

Figure 29

The most important pre-Civil War activity in the West was mining. Back in 1808 Lewis and Clark had opened the way and the trappers soon followed. After the explorers and trappers came the prospectors. These early westerners carried few, if any, extra clothes with them. When their clothes wore out they had to make do with leather or canvas clothes.

In these early mining days a town meant a group of rude tent-houses thrown up in haste. They were once described as "board and canvas cities." Canvas, being the only cloth available, was used for work clothes. Tent canvas was an early form of denim, being unbleached rather than indigo blue-dyed.

This westerner wears a shirt of the period like those of Figures 28 and 29. It could be a deerskin shirt. A bandanna is tied around his neck. Suspenders were commonly worn although this man wears none.

His trousers are protected by snugly fitting Indian leggings pulled up onto his thighs. He would have set out in shoes but eventually made or traded for Indian mocassins when they wore out.

His wide-brimmed hat, turned up in front, was used for everything from a wash basin to a drinking cup. It protected him from cold or sun and was great for carrying ore samples.

He has a pouch and gun holster on his belt and carries a Sharp's buffalo rifle.

Figure 30

Up until the Civil War the only farming done west of the Missouri was in some parts of Colorado, Nevada, California, and the Great Salt Lake Valley. Oregon joined the Union in 1859, and between California and Oregon was a vast, unpopulated, virtually unknown area. North Dakota did not have a permanent settlement until 1851.

The period between 1851 and 1860 was the peak of French, Swedish, and Irish immigration. These immigrants, many of whom went west to find gold, probably brought the idea of the double-breasted shirt to America. It was more or less the European peasant smock tucked into the trousers. (Visualize this shirt outside the trousers and belted like that of Figure 37 to see the European look.)

This man wears a red kerchief under the collar. He wears a dark belt although belt loops were not used yet. His boots are black riding boots but Wellingtons and the canvas-lined ones of Figures 7 and 34 were worn too.

The hat shown here was described in Figure 30 although the cap of Figure 7 was worn just as often with this shirt.

These shirts in blue, black, gray, red, green, and even yellow were seen in many professions all over America. They were commonplace in the mining towns as immigrants went west to seek their fortunes. They remained popular throughout the century.

Figure 31

By mid-century Americans' buckskin hunting clothes were actually pictured in many European fashion plates and labelled ''sporting or hunting clothes in America.'' Thus our folk clothing was recognized as such for decades in Europe before our own fashion ''experts'' at home looked upon them as anything more than lower class, rough, or crude!

The 18th century hunting smocks had by this time evolved into this classic American frontiersman shirt. Made on the lines of fashionable shirts with its collar, drop-shoulder line, and opening to the chest, it has a fringed capelet of deerskin.

This man wears a shoulder strap with pouch and a belt. An 1840s Colt ''pepperbox'' pistol is tucked in his belt; it was part of the costume of the early West, part of the code. The reloading gate, left open, would prevent the pistol from slipping down into his trousers or through his belt.

His deerskin Indian leggings pulled over his trousers protect them and his legs. They are held in place by leather garters tied at the sides; one holds his knife.

This man of the forest wears no shirt underneath his buckskins but gentlemen hunters wore white shirts and ties with theirs.

His wide-brimmed hat has developed a character of its own from years of service. His rifle is a Sharp's buffalo rifle of the 1850s.

In 1849 the newly organized Department of the Interior sent its first Indian agent into western territory to negotiate with the Indians.

Figure 32

Figure 33

During the gold rush years many Mexicans poured into the mining towns. When they found no gold they became railroad workers, laborers, and cowhands.

The earliest cowhands in Texas wore Mexican chaparejoes (chaps) for riding horseback but the war with Mexico soured them on anything Mexican. As a result, they adapted Indian leggings for their work clothes as described in Figures 126 and 127. The Californians were not as involved in the war and never gave up their heritage of Mexican things.

The leather overalls were worn over the trousers to protect them when riding a horse. They buttoned all the way down each side. The French cavalry in Louisiana in 1804 and the Danish and Norwegian cavalries in 1813 wore them.

This Mexican miner or railroad worker left his leather overalls unbuttoned below the knee so that they flapped when he walked. He wears a fancy bolero and shirt under his poncho or serape. The flat-topped hat, with its ribbon ties, is Mexican. The total effect is rather dramatic.

One old painting in California shows a famous bandit dressed in this manner who terrorized the gold rush towns.

American Costume

More people settled in California during the 1850s than had settled in New Hampshire in its entire history. It was only natural that during such fast growth there would be lawlessness. Americans have always had an inclination to set up governments and write constitutions so some Colorado and California communities did just that when they felt the eastern law establishment did not give them proper protection!

Vigilante uniforms were surprisingly like those that would be used in the Civil War a few years later. Paintings show coats of either black or a very dark blue, with a stand-up collar and coming to just above the knee. The single-breasted front has metal buttons and a metal plate on the black belt.

This man wears the Wellington boot favored by the military for over a hundred years. Sometimes the flaps were turned down.

His cap is the shako worn by the Prussians (in 1813), Austrians, British, and then the Americans in the war with Mexico. The top of this shako has become harder than the soft top of Figures 7 and 8. While military hats changed to the soft kepis of the Civil War, it was the civilian police who retained the stiff cap like the policeman of Figure 93. (The French gendarmes of today still wear the stiff cap.)

Instead of on a shoulder strap, the pouch is fastened to the belt in the center back. His rifle was probably a Spencer.

Figure 34

Figure 35

The U.S. Army had over one million square miles over which they were supposed to protect the westward travelers—and a little over ten thousand men to do the job. The army offered military escorts to wagon trains going west by providing two regiments of dragoons, eight of infantry, and one of mounted riflemen. In emergencies they called in extra regiments of artillery. During the first half of the decade an estimated forty-one skirmishes with Indians occurred.

Uniforms for these military escorts had already taken much the same form they would retain during the Civil War. The coat bodice was double-breasted with the two rows of buttons being closer toward the waist. The lapels lined with yellow were most attractive when turned back as shown here. The coat had a high stand-up collar. This soldier is an officer so he wears officers' epaulettes. The skirt of the dark blue coat is somewhat flared with a split in back.

The trousers, dark blue also, have a yellow stripe down the side.

He wears the black shako cap, like that favored during the war with Mexico (Figure 8), and black boots, probably Wellingtons (Figure 34), which protect the knees while riding a horse.

In 1856 and 1857 seventy-five camels were imported into Texas to be used by the army. Although they imported Turkish, Greek, and Armenian drivers with the camels, the army was in charge. A caravan journeyed from San Antonio to California in 1857.

When the Civil War began, the camels were sold to private citizens, other countries, and to a circus but some were turned loose or escaped to roam the American desert. For over fifty years there were reported sightings and, of course, there were a lot of legends concerning them.

The most interesting part of the Camel Corps uniform is the black and yellow cap. It is an example of the evolution of styles. The shako cap of Figures 34 and 35 is leaning forward. The hat is shorter in front than in back exposing the sewn-in top. It is still relatively stiff but will grow softer with the top even more squashed down toward the front as in Figures 69, 71 and 77. The pre-Civil War caps show other interesting stages as the kepi grew out of the shako.

This soldier wears a single-breasted, dark blue coat with a slightly flared skirt, split in back. The cuffs, collar trim, and stripes are yellow.

His trousers are light blue, his Wellington boots, black. The epaulettes are for officers only.

By the way, camels were not new to America. Colonial Virginia is said to have experimented with them in the 18th century.

The first U.S. dragoons were shown in dark blue double-breasted coats (see Figure 35) with a black belt. The trousers were light blue like these. For dress, officers wore red sashes under the black belt and a red pompom on the black hat. This Camel Express uniform was typical of U.S. uniforms back east.

Figure 36

Kansas was opened to settlement in 1854 and within two years was involved in clashes over the question of slavery. Border ruffians destroyed the Free State center in Lawrence, Kansas. These "ruffians" are pictured dressed in buckskins of several styles, coats like Figure 84 with gun belts on the outside, and an assortment of shirts, trousers and battered hats.

A unit of artillery is called a battery. This man of the Kansas Free State Battery wears a shirt much like a European worker's smock. It is gray with a white or yellow binding around the double-breasted front panel. It is shown with the top button unfastened. The same braid edges the cuffs and the side pocket flap as well as his sleeve stripes. A white shirt worn underneath shows at the neckline. These smocks were sometimes tucked inside the trousers.

His trousers are inside his plain black boots. His hat is a black, wide-brimmed, high-crowned hat with the crown pushed in, giving it a flat look.

Figure 37

Indians caused less hardship and death to the white settlers on the Oregon Trail than did thirst, malnutrition, accidents, and sickness.

The Overland Trail ran through the hunting grounds of the Northern Plains Indians. These Indians turned to a new life based on hunting on horseback and eventually became the stereotype of the American Indian. As far as costume was concerned everything became more intensified. Their fringe became longer and their headdress became more spectacular as shown in Figure 95.

This mountain Indian, who might have been Blackfoot, Cheyenne, or Mandan, hunted in the forest and farmed by rivers before going to the new lifestyle. He adopted the blanket from the white culture. He wears a bright red blanket over his fringed tunic and leggings.

His deerskin tunic has yellow trim and fringe down the sleeves and long fringe across the shoulder. There are red patches of quillwork across the shoulder. There is a large, colorful, round bead decoration on the front.

He wears a necklace of bear claws and beads and another one consisting of a leather strip holding a medallion.

His headdress is made of red-brown tufts of hair (human and animal) and several feathers which fan out in a fountain of color and movement.

Figure 38

This woodland Indian woman is representative of the women of several of the tribes who moved south.

Her tunic is long-waisted with a girdle of quill or beadwork around the hips. The sides of the tunic are an openworked design of small leather strips revealing part of the torso. The same openwork goes from the neck to the elbow of the sleeve. The sides of the skirt are left open and decorated with the same long, graceful fringe as that on the skirt and sleeve edges.

Her shining black hair is long in uneven locks. Two strings of beads, shells, or teeth are worn around her neck.

Her baby is laced onto a wooden papoose board with a little canopy over his head. The babies' arms and hands were laced inside the deerskin blanket in cold weather but might be left free on warm days.

Figure 39

Englishman Charles Frederick Worth rose to be the great dressmaker of the century, influencing fashions around the world, even small-town America.

In America lace could be purchased in special dress-length pieces of various sizes and shapes. Directions accompanied these pieces with suggestions for several possible designs and combinations.

This formal dress also could be made in a high-necked, long-sleeved version according to the directions which accompanied the lace pieces. Satin and lace combinations were very fashionable as illustrated here. This blue satin dress has a white lace overskirt, flounce, sleeves, and neckline flounce. The neckline and skirt flounces have a strip of narrow black lace at the top. Other favorite color combinations were black lace over yellow or pink, and white over red or pea-green. Plaid and checked taffetas were favorites too.

This woman's hair is parted in the middle and pulled back into a large bun decorated with flowers. She wears a locket and bracelet and carries a folding fan.

Ribbon sashes like those on Figure 42 were often used on formal dresses as were the two- and three-flounce skirts. Some skirts had as many as a dozen small ruffles so any number can be used and still be authentic.

Very formal gowns sometimes had detachable trains similar to Figures 137 and 168 with much lace, ribbon, and flower decoration.

Figure 40

Figure 41

This dress with matching jacket was one of the great dressmaker Worth's ideas which eventually led to the skirt, jacket, and shirtwaist combination—the tailored suit! Even remote areas in America would eventually feel the influence of this man who designed for the Empress Eugenie after going to live in Paris.

This early form of the suit has shoulder wings or rolls and peplum skirt making it reminiscent of the early 17th century doublet suits which, by the way, were much criticized by men at the time. These jackets were also worn beltless, giving a princess line like the coat of Figure 103. Both these coats are longer in back than in front, predicting the bustles of the future. Short bolero-length versions with curved fronts similar to the bodice of Figure 102 were worn too. Sleeves were tapered with front and back seams.

Skirts were sometimes longer in back too, giving a train effect. Skirts were rounded at the hips because hoops had several wires all the way up to the waist. They later were cone-shaped as the wires were only at the hem.

Both coat and skirt are decorated with dark braid designs.

This lady's hat is a flat derby-like shape with ribbon poufs and feathers, worn tilted onto the forehead.

Her hair is pulled back with little ringlets hanging down in back.

Aniline dyes were invented, making wild colors like fuchsia, magenta, and violet familiar.

This dress, which was popular with all age groups, was obviously inspired by Amelia Bloomer's dress of a few years before (Figure 15). Three-flounce skirts were as commonly seen as this two-flounce one. The full sleeves were split in front revealing the white sleeves of the soft blouse underneath. Sometimes the sleeves and crisp white collars were a part of the bodice, sometimes they belonged to a separate blouse and sometimes, in warm weather, they were just simple detachable pieces. Whether attached or not, the white collar was everpresent.

The skirt and bodice were often separate because of the immense weight of the full skirt with the stiffly boned point of the bodice coming out over the fullness to flatten it.

Braid trims the skirt flounces, split sleeves, and bodice. It covers the curved bodice side-front and dropped-shoulder armhole seams too. Wide grosgrain ribbon sashes, caught up in poufs, decorate the skirt. Sometimes flowers were added to them.

The hairpin was invented to help hold the heavy hair styles which were knotted in back.

Figure 42

Figure 43

Family portraits of this period often show the mother, the grandmother, and their slave woman who is holding a child, all wearing much the same dress in different fabrics. Portraits in all areas of the nation show dresses similar to this one on women of all ages and attitudes from conservative to very fashionable.

Coarse cottons and woolens, satins, taffetas, ginghams, calicos, and expensive patterned silks might be used.

The V-shaped, tucked bodice sometimes came to a point at the waist, sometimes was straight and belted like this one. White collars might be small and plain as on Figure 47 or sheer and embroidered as on this and Figure 42. One portrait in the Metropolitan Museum shows an elderly lady wearing the neck ruff or "betsy" of the 1830s.

Sleeves were fitted at the shoulder with no gathers at all, then flared and full at the wrist and gathered onto a cuff. Sometimes shoulder caps were added.

Skirts might be plain, flounced, or tiered like others of the decade.

Paisley and lace shawls were the rage of all age groups. Paisley ones were usually fringed like the one shown here.

Bonnets like that of Figure 15 or any of the ones shown for this decade were worn, depending on the cost of the dress and the occasion. This simple, sheer bonnet is decorated with embroidered ruffles.

The lady holds a watch which hangs from the long cord or chain around her neck. The monocle and pince-nez were commonly worn in this manner also.

Figure 44

Seen on all ages of women in all regions of America, like Figure 43, this dress was often worn in rural areas. It was made in bright colors such as green, blue, red, pink, or yellow as well as in calico and plaid or checked gingham. It might also appear in somber black, brown, or gray.

Conservative in line, it retains the wide neckline and curved bodice seams of the '30s and '40s. Clean white collar and cuffs, probably detachable, are worn. (For theatre design, these collars and cuffs can be made both plain and fancy for an inexpensive costume change.)

This woman wears a plain gathered white apron but the skirt was often pulled up and draped to protect it while working, as in Figure 109.

Her hat is the same wide-brimmed straw as that of Figure 28, long associated with rural life.

Worn in the fashionable back bun, her hair is pulled behind her ears instead of across them.

The high flat-heeled shoes of the '40s are worn adding to her conservative appearance.

Between 1850 and 1875 the sewing machine moved into both the home and the factory. Clothing factories as well as textile mills now provided employment for women, luring them outside the home.

The mills and factories forbade or discouraged the hoop; paintings and sketches of the girls always show plain instead of bouffant skirts. Certainly the hoop could be a hazard around machinery!

Much like that of Figure 15, this bodice fastens in the front. The neck is worn open. Sleeves, like skirts, are not as full as on dressier dresses. This young woman wears a blouse or possibly false sleeves, as there is no collar. The false blouse sleeves described in Figure 15 would have been practical for factory work because they could be removed during work and put back on later. Red and green were popular colors.

She wears an apron over her dress. Her dark shoes are like those of the '40s (shown in Figure 15) but laced-up instead of buttoned.

Her very charming hat is like those fashionable about 1810 and still worn for outings in the country. It is tied with a red scarf or bandanna in the back under her hair.

She carries a metal lunch pail of the period.

Figure 45

The cloth sunbonnet came to America from France and Holland and its development was much the same here as in France. By mid-century it had developed a large protective ruffle to keep the sun off the neck. It was so widely worn that it appears in paintings of New England mill girls, of farm women, of women in a crowd scene in Alabama and of Mormon women pioneers. It appears throughout the century on all ages of women, even very little girls as shown in Figure 114, on slave women along the Mississippi, on members of a wagon train, and in paintings of French rural women in their own country. The neck ruffle and the starched brim were of various sizes. In France bonnets were usually white, but American women made them in colors and calicos as well as white.

The jacket dress shown here seems to be an everyday interpretation of the fashionable one of Figure 41. Judging from the many paintings showing the absence of a hoop it would seem that the huge hoop skirts were a luxury reserved for special occasions and for very fashion-conscious ladies.

The woman on the left wears a bright-colored kerchief tucked into the neckline. It was sometimes tied in a knot on the outside as in Figure 17.

She wears a white apron tied under her jacket and carries a metal lunch pail.

These dresses were often of bright colors, sometimes with the jacket a different color than the skirt. The kerchief and bonnet often matched either the skirt or jacket but sometimes several different colors were worn all at once in this American folk costume.

Figure 46

Simple dresses of calico were seen on pioneers, slave women, and rural women throughout the country but particularly in the South and in pioneer settlements in the West. They were simple to make, inexpensive, serviceable, and comfortable. They were not boned and tight-fitting, as fashionable dresses were, nor worn over hoop skirts although petticoats were worn under them.

This woman's calico dress has small, simple white collar and cuffs with a little black ribbon bow at the neck. The bodice buttons down the front and comes to a point. It has shoulder wings at the armhole like the fashionable costume of Figure 41. Sometimes what appears to be a dress might have actually been the jacket dress of Figure 46 with the jacket tucked inside the skirt.

She wears a white apron the same length as the dress. Her shoes are soft scuff-type ones like the mules of today. These shoes were worn in summer and in the deep south. Although some photographs and sketches clearly show the scuff, some pictures show what might have been just an ordinary shoe with the back of the heel pushed in from wear. (Either type can be used for comic or dramatic expression in the theatre).

Black women wore a kerchief wrapped around the head in a turban. There is very little evidence to support the image of the slave with the kerchief tied in a large knot on top of her head. Paintings and photographs show either no knot at all or a very tiny one tied with just the tips of the kerchief. The old image more than likely grew out of the comic interpretations of the minstrel show and gradually came to be accepted as historical fact. According to the sketches of Alfred R. Waud, both white and black women along the Mississippi River also wore the sunbonnet of Figure 46, probably because of the French influence. Photographs of the period attest to his accuracy.

Figure 47

Young girls wore dresses with the diagonal tucks, dropped-shoulder line, and wide neckline of the previous decade. This dress bodice points in front over a skirt with side and back fullness. The cuffs on the short sleeves come to a point. They are trimmed with white lace as is the wide neckline. Blue was a popular color for girls.

This young girl wears long lace-trimmed pantalets under a skirt which is several inches off the floor.

The hairstyle of this girl is particularly interesting because of its modern appearance. It is parted in the middle, worn straight, and pushed behind the ear. One portrait of a woman of this period shows this same hairstyle.

Her flat-heeled slippers are black. She holds a folding fan.

Figure 48

Little boys wore short jacketed suits of velvet with pearl or metal buttons. This jacket, on the left, is quite fitted with a stand-up collar and long, slender sleeves. Burgundy was a favorite color.

High-waisted striped pantaloons of burgundy and white cotton twill button onto a cotton body or blouse. This little boy wears a tam-o-shanter with a fur ball on top. His high-buttoned shoes are made of wool or canvas. Cloth or part-cloth shoes were popular for all ages of both girls and boys.

Young boys wore European and Russian style blouses, sometimes called peasant smocks, either tucked inside the trousers, as shown on the right, or belted as shown in Figure 113. This blouse is gray-green with a white collar. It has a double-breasted panel in front like the man's shirt of Figure 37. A red cravat is tied in a large bow at the neck.

The older boy's trousers have the front panel with buttons sometimes called "railroad breeches." His black boots are particularly noteworthy. A similar pair is now in the Brooklyn Museum. They were inspired by the turned-down canvas boot of Figure 7 but the tops are purely decorative, being sewn on and of a natural colored leather. These boots are lined with red and have striped straps.

His cap is a shako described in Figure 7. (Any cap with a visor and a stiff band is technically a shako. A billed cap like Figure 252 is not one.)

Figure 49

Little girls have traditionally worn dresses in the style of a generation before. The girl on the left wears an off-the-shoulder dress with shirred bodice and double-puffed sleeves like those worn by women in the '30s and early '40s. The shoulder yoke of the salmon pink dress has a point in front. The below-the-knee skirt is very full and worn over petticoats with scalloped, embroidered pantalets.

She wears low-cut black slippers with bows and short stockings. These short stockings were probably worn in warm weather. A satin ribbon sash is a dark pink or red. Her short beads and bracelet are red.

On the right is another off-the-shoulder dress of similar, but less complicated, design, made of a yellow fabric with black dots. The bodice is gathered onto a very narrow band at the shoulders and onto a waistband at the waist. The plain sleeves are caught up into a swag effect with ribbons.

Immensely popular, the dress on the right has been shown on little girls of all classes in all parts of the country including three slave children in one lithograph in the Library of Congress. It was made of many different fabrics from calico to lace. Petticoats and lace-trimmed pantalets were worn with it.

The slippers shown with this dress have ribbons tied around the ankles. Stockings of all lengths were worn with these slippers.

Both girls wear their hair pulled straight back on top and tied with a ribbon bow. The little girl on the left has long slender "sausage" curls with ringlets at the temple, the one on the right has many shorter "corkscrew" curls which bounce as she moves.

Figure 50

Very young boys wore dresses much the same as those of little girls. On the left, the little boy's red dress has a wide neckline with interesting little triangular gussets set in where the front and back pieces meet on the shoulder. The sleeves have a seam down the center. This seam is decorated with a narrow band which continues across the neckline and down the other sleeve. It is trimmed with narrow lace and decorated with black buttons in an unusual, but most charming fashion. The sleeves have lace ruffles at the elbow.

The sewn-in waistband and the full skirt are both trimmed with white cord braid.

His lace-trimmed pantalets are full length instead of short like those of the girls in Figure 50. His blue, pointed, lace-up shoes have dark blue velvet toes and heels.

His hair is brushed toward the face in the "old fashioned" way of a generation before.

The baby in the chair also wears an off-the-shoulder dress much like that of the girl on the right in Figure 50. The bodice is trimmed with lace-edged panels down each side and lace edging around the neck and split sleeves. The full skirt has several tucks around the hem.

The baby, which could be either boy or girl, wears blue slippers with straps. Diapers were still three-cornered and tied instead of pinned.

Figure 51

42

CHAPTER 4

State and Local Militias: A Diversity of Styles

Before the Civil War and during its early months our military consisted of state militia and community or private regiments. Financial support came from state governments, wealthy citizens, and local communities in both the North and South.

President Lincoln and Jefferson Davis asked the states to help because there were no regular armies to call upon. There were many different uniforms in each state and there was no one color or design to identify any particular region or state.

Some southern regiments wore blue while some northern ones wore gray. A number preferred red or brown and at least one sported green. There were uniforms in both the South and North which were known to have cost a great deal of money while others were made by wives and volunteer seamstresses from their own neighborhood.

By 1860 the glamorous, exotic zouave uniforms were designed, sometimes at great expense to the state or community supplying them.

By seeing a sampling of the diversity of styles in American uniforms before and at the beginning of the war, the reader can gain an understanding of the origin and evolution of our Civil War uniforms. Detailed information on every regiment in each state would require an entire volume but almost all of them are represented by one or more of the following basic styles.

American Costume

Of all the items making up the uniform, the overcoat was the one which varied the least among the different groups. The coat with cape, on the left, was sometimes double-breasted as with the Seventh New York. Their cape was lined with red. Their belts and straps of white were later abandoned and more practical black was used in its place.

The Nineteenth Illinois, Eighteenth and Twenty-first Ohio, and the Seventy-eighth Pennsylvania wore the coat on the left over the uniforms of Figure 64.

In October 1859, at Harpers Ferry, Virginia, Lieutenant J.E.B. Stuart and a company of Marines wore this coat (left) with shako caps like that of Figure 8.

The Sixth Massachusetts were wearing the overcoat and cap shown on the right when they were attacked by southern sympathizers as they went through Baltimore in April 1861. An old lithograph shows them to be gray! (For southern sympathizers see Figure 66.)

Figure 52

Figure 53

The Federal Army of the Cumberland wore the uniform on the left in dark blue.

The Clinch Rifles at Augusta, Georgia, wore the long-skirted coat without the shoulder strap.

The First Michigan and the New Jersey Militia both wore uniforms of this design as did the Fifth New York German Rifles. South Carolina regiments also wore this style outfit at Fort Sumter and so did the Union forces.

The New York Fourteenth wore red trousers with a white stripe and a black coat with red patches on the collar. The shoulder patches were white and the kepi was red with a black top, band, and visor.

On the right is the pale-colored coat, probably gray, of the New York Wide Awakes. The trousers and cape lining were dark with braid trim on the cape.

The rather stiff shako cap on this man is black with a large metal plate, embossed with an eagle, standing up in front. The visor is black leather.

For the California vigilante uniform of 1856 see Figure 34.

The Army Wagon Train Escort regiments and the Camel Express Corps of the 1850s are shown in Figures 35 and 36, respectively.

Militias

The dragoons of the Fourteenth Regiment, Virginia Cavalary, wore this medium-length coat with belt and shoulder strap with large metal plates. Decorative braid on the sleeves adds to its dashing appearance.

Metal plates on the hat or cap usually indicated the regiment. Belt plates had an eagle or the initials "U.S.A." (During the Civil War the Confederate belts sometimes had "C.S.A.") The small belt clips on webbed belts usually had an eagle. Shoulder belts (or straps) often had eagle designs also.

The most dramatic part of this uniform is the Roman-style metal and leather helmet with its horsehair "mane." It must have been a magnificent sight bouncing and flying in the air as the dragoon rode his horse!

This coat was worn by the Eighth Massachusetts with the kepi. Kepis were also worn with this uniform by the Eighth Wisconsin. Their coats were dark, their trousers light.

The Heavy Infantry of Georgia wore the cocked hat of Figure 60 with this uniform. The brim was pinned up on the left.

Figure 54

This blouse or jacket is shorter than Figure 54 with sleeves gathered into a cuff. The buttons are smaller and closer together.

Alabama soldiers present at the inauguration of Jefferson Davis at Montgomery wore uniforms like this one in gray with gray caps of this design.

The Alabama Light Infantry wore a hat much like a rolled-brim sailor. It had a large plume along the left side of the brim, falling down the back a bit. The hat of Figure 66 is similar.

The Mounted Rifles of North Carolina wore this uniform with the kepi, a shoulder strap like Figure 56, and the gauntlet gloves of Figure 76.

Figure 55

45

This shorter jacket is much like that of Figure 55 but the collar is turned down and the buttons are larger and spaced further apart. The sleeves are not as full.

The Tennessee Sharpshooters wore the outfit as shown here.

The Twenty-sixth Tennessee wore kepis instead of this wide-brimmed hat.

Figure 56

The Georgia Sumter Light Guards wore this uniform, with the short jacket, shown here. The Virginia Cadets were similarly dressed.

The First Maryland had light jackets and dark trousers.

The Washington Artillery of New Orleans wore this outfit with a metal crescent-shaped gorget around the neck.

The First Ohio wore this short jacket uniform, sometimes with gaiters like those of Figure 59.

Both the Sixth Massachusetts and the Seventy-first New York had two shoulder straps crossed over the chest as in Figure 58, as well as the belt.

The Thirteenth Brooklyn wore white, crossed straps like those of Figure 58 (right) and a white belt.

Figure 57

Militias

The Boston National Lancers' (left) was one of the most European in style of all the militia uniforms. It was designed after the British Lancers whose uniform followed European lines.

The square-topped hat was reserved for Lancers. It is of Polish origin and called a schapka headdress. The cord which comes from the headdress and attaches to the coat with tassels is a cap line. Its purpose was to keep the hat from being lost when knocked off. The hat is red and black.

The short red jacket is double-breasted with the two rows of buttons in a curved design. The trousers are medium blue with a red stripe.

The Sixth Pennsylvania Lancers or Rush's Lancers were more conservatively dressed, being outfitted in regular army cavalry uniforms like that of Figure 35.

The First Virginia Cavalry were dressed in a short gray jacket. Although theirs was single-breasted, its appearance was more like that of the double-breasted jacket on the left. It had an extra curved row of buttons on each side with black braid going horizontally across the chest connecting the three rows. This gave the appearance of a gray bodice with black horizontal stripes. The collar and cuffs were yellow.

Their hat was the kepi but officers wore a large black hat with a tassel like that of Figure 68, with the long coat of Figure 53. The long coat had the same black horizontal braid on the bodice.

The U.S. Marines at Harpers Ferry, Virginia, wore the short, double-breasted jacket of dark blue with a shako cap and white, crossed, shoulder straps as shown on the right. Trousers were dark blue also. (See Figure 52 for their overcoat.)

The Volunteer Infantry of Virginia wore the short jacket shown on the right. Their long cloth cap is an early 18th century French style. It has a black visor.

The Virginia Militia wore the shako cap of Figure 8 with the outfit on the right.

Figure 58

Figure 59

Lyon's federal troops in Missouri at the beginning of the war wore the short jacket open and the trousers held by gaiters as shown here. The wide-brimmed hat was their preference.

The Marine Artillery of Rhode Island wore the jacket loose but with the plain trousers and kepi of Figure 57.

Hunting and military shirts were used instead of coats by both northern and southern troops. Here the farmer's smock or shirt of Figures 4, 6, and 7 is belted with a military belt.

The First Rhode Island wore the outfit with a cocked hat, as shown here, giving it a handsome appearance.

The Eighth Wisconsin had an almost identical uniform except that there was no yoke on the plain shirt.

For the shirt of the Kansas Free State Battery see Figure 37.

Figure 60

Figure 61

A military look is achieved with red binding on the collar and front opening of this shirt. The shoulder patches match the binding. The Rhode Island Artillery wore the shirt as shown here. It sometimes opened all the way down the front. The First Pennsylvania wore this belted shirt and the kepi also.

Militias

The Confederate Floating Battery liked the shirt tucked inside the trousers instead of belted. The kepi and gaiters were worn as shown here.

The Mississippi Rifles wore the shirt tucked in as shown but they used the cocked hat of Figure 60 instead of the kepi.

On the right, the South Carolina Palmetto State Artillery uniform adds a vest and tie to the shirt.

Figure 62

Figure 63

The Kentucky Rifle Brigade wore their traditional fringed deerskin and linen hunting shirts which had long been associated with their state. The shirt here has a military belt which holds a handgun in a holster and a knife. The kepi completes the uniform.

The South Carolina Light Infantry wore the fringed deerskin hunting shirt or smock with the wide-brimmed hat of Figure 56.

Figure 64

The native soldiers of French Algeria (the Turcos) gave the idea of the zouave uniform to the French, who dressed their own Third Zouave Regiment this way in 1854.

The first U.S. zouaves were called Ellsworth's Zouaves after Elmer Ellsworth, who started the idea in Chicago in 1860. When the war started they became the Eleventh New York or Fire Zouaves. They wore kepis although they had earlier worn wide-brim hats like that of Figure 59.

The Ninth and Fifty-fifth regiments of New York dressed like the figure on the left.

The Louisiana Tigers also were outfitted like the soldier on the left. Their breeches were blue-and-white striped and very full.

The Army of the Potomac wore red breeches and dark blue jackets. Their kepi had the cloth neck protector like that of the French foreign legion as shown on the recruit on the right.

The Eleventh Indiana, called Wallace's Zouaves, chose the uniform on the right in gray trimmed with red. They wore plain kepis.

The Twelth New York preferred the longer jacket of Figure 55 and the kepi with their zouave breeches and gaiters.

Other regiments pictured wearing zouave uniforms in newspaper engravings were the Twenty-first, Twenty-third, Twenty-fifth, and Twenty-seventh Massachusetts, and the Tenth Connecticut. The Fifty-first New York and the Ninth New Jersey are shown in them as well as the Fifty-first Pennsylvania and the Fourth Rhode Island.

In cold weather the overcoat and cape of Figure 52 (left) was worn over the zouave outfit by most regiments.

CHAPTER 5

The Civil War and Mass Production

Uniforms during the American Revolution, the War of 1812, and the War with Mexico had been handmade in France or homemade. The Civil War revolutionized the clothing industry.

It had been generally believed that in order to manufacture clothes one would have to make hundreds or even thousands of different sizes. Uniform makers discovered that certain combinations of sizes were common—for instance many men with a 36-inch waist have a 30-inch trousers length and so on. They began to keep accurate records and the science of sizing in clothing manufacturing was begun. Manufacturers discovered that they could fit a whole army with twenty basic sizes instead of hundreds.

The Confederate Congress asked southern farmers to stop planting cotton and plant badly needed food instead. With cotton production ended, the North had to modernize its wool production in order to have enough textiles for the Union's new standardized blue wool uniforms issued in 1863.

Guns were mass-produced for the first time in America at this time. One of the most important firsts as far as costume is concerned was the use of the camera. The Civil War was the first war photographed in America.

THE CONFEDERATE ARMY

The iron-clad Confederate *Merrimac* destroyed two Union ships her first day—the *Congress* and the *Cumberland*—and ran the *Minnesota* aground. The following day saw her famous engagement with the *Monitor* but neither ship was badly damaged. The Confederates' use of armored rams and gunboats caused a revolution in naval warfare.

Confederate sailors wore blue, loose-legged trousers with a front fall like that shown on the Union sailor's uniform, Figure 73.

The white blouse or middy was quite full and long as shown here. It has no braid. Some pictures show dark blue middies. The kerchief or tie is black.

This man's flat-top sailor tam is black. In cold weather a dark jacket like that of Figure 73 would be worn.

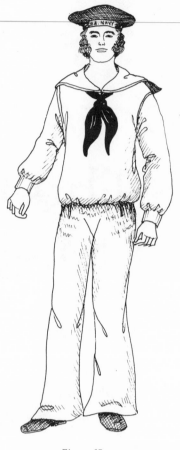

Figure 65

Figure 66

Men on the Confederate submarine *Hunley* wore red shirts and blue trousers like this man's but without the suspenders. Their hats were straw sailors like this one. Their ties were either black or red.

The U.S. *Cairo* was the first ship to be the victim of a torpedo in December 1862.

Shipbuilders working in a wartime shipyard are shown in one engraving dressed in this outfit with a vest added, making it much like that of Figure 62 (right). All the men wear this hat.

When the Sixth Massachusetts (Figures 52 and 57) was attacked by southern sympathizers in Baltimore in April 1861 a number of the rioters were dressed like this man. Some added vests and others had on well-worn coats of various styles and colors.

52

Civil War

High-ranking officers of the Confederate army wore a uniform of gray with a collar which could be worn up or turned down. The collar and lapels could be left open or buttoned double-breasted. Notice on the coat the crease in the center between the buttons. This indicates that the lapels were sometimes folded back and buttoned in the style of 18th century uniforms. The sash, belt, collar, and sleeve decorations were yellow. A clip instead of a buckle is used for the woven belt.

The famous photograph of Robert E. Lee in the Valentine Museum shows the collar open as on this officer. The painted portrait done from the photo shows the two rows of buttons in a curved design as in Figure 58, and buttoned up to the stand-up yellow collar.

This officer's wide-brimmed hat is gray. The sword case is black with gold trim. He wears a white shirt and black bow tie and sometimes adds a matching single-breasted vest. His black boots are worn under the trousers.

Figure 67

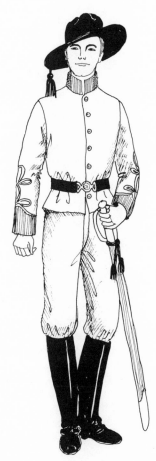

A Confederate officer wore a short jacket with braid decorations on the sleeves. The stand-up collar, cuffs, and trousers stripe were usually yellow for cavalry, red for artillery, and blue for infantry. Only officers had the braid decorations as a rule, but there was a great deal of freedom for individual expression among the rebels.

This officer, probably a colonel, wears his wide-brimmed hat tilted to one side and decorated with a large tassel on a cord. (Embellishments such as this tassel offer great potential for dramatic or comic interpretation in the theatre.)

He wears a black webbed belt with a clip. His trousers are inside his black riding boots which indicate that he is probably a cavalry officer.

Swords were quite long according to many old photographs.

Figure 68

Many rebel soldiers used Union firearms picked up on the battlefield. The Union army used Spencer rifles.

The gray Confederate uniforms were usually double-breasted with a stand-up collar. Sometimes the sleeves had cuffs of the same color as the collar. The black leather belt had an oval metal plate.

Trousers were sometimes light blue but most often gray like the coat. This infantryman wears the kepi.

Many uniforms of the southerners were made by relatives or volunteer sewing groups. Toward the end of the war the women even spun and wove the cloth from which uniforms were made. When commercial dye was not available they used a natural brown dye causing the Union soldiers to call them ''butternut soldiers.''

For bedrolls they often used quilts, bedspreads, and buggy robes. Oilcloth piano covers sometimes had to serve as waterproof blanket covers and rain ponchos (see Figure 128 for poncho).

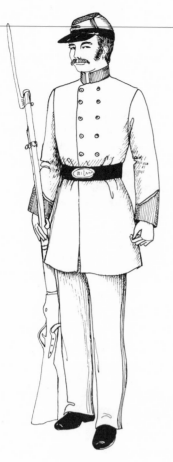

Figure 69

A shirt was worn without the jacket when the weather was hot. In many cases only the shirt was worn because the soldier had no jacket.

This man, probably in the cavalry, wears Wellington boots which were designed to give protection to the knee when the wearer was on horseback. Sometimes the knee flap was worn turned down as shown here.

Sometimes gray double-breasted shirts like that of Figure 37 were worn tucked into the trousers. Photographs often show checked trousers and suspenders and tucked shirts like that of Figure 28 with a large black tie and a top hat!

Pictures made just before or after battles show men wearing the outfit of Figure 22—top hat, tie, and vest included. The outfits are battered, dirty, and patched on the knees. They were obviously worn during the battle.

The hat most commonly seen in photos during 1861 and 1862 is a high, round-crowned gray or black hat like this one with the sides of the brim curled up.

Figure 70

Old photographs show a variety of lengths of both the gray coat and its cape. Sometimes a coat was almost to the ankles, other times up to the knees. They were more likely to be quite large and loose than too small.

When the weather was very cold and damp, woolen scarves of bright colors, plaids, or stripes would be added. Sometimes a scarf might be tied around the head, over the cap, to warm the ears.

Shoulder straps and belts were worn as shown here or in Figure 79. Sometimes the straps and belt were inside the coat.

When no coat was available, shawls and blankets were used like the gentleman's shawl of Figure 81.

Sometimes the cape is shown with buttons like that of Figure 79, other times with no buttons.

Occasionally a painting will show a red or yellow lining inside an officer's cape.

Figure 71

THE UNION ARMY

Before the Civil War the United States Navy was a small force with only sixty-nine vessels in workable order.

When the war started, Congress appropriated funds to buy up any civilian ship that could be converted to a warship—tugs, merchant steamers, and river boats.

In 1857 naval officers still wore the tailcoat of the early part of the century but by 1862 this long coat became regulation. (This remained much the same until 1947 when the frock coat was omitted.)

The Union naval officer's coat was double-breasted and usually worn with the lapels turned back as shown here. A woven belt with a metal clip was regulation. White was used for the stripes on the sleeves and white and gold for the shoulder bars. Eight stripes were for admiral, seven for commodore, six for captain, and five for commander. There was always a star above the stripes.

The cap was actually a shako but it has apparently never been referred to as such by the navy. It is referred to just as a cloth cap or navy cap. In 1862 the flare was wide but became narrower at the end of the century as shown in Figure 203. It has widened again to today's cap.

Figure 72

55

During the American Revolution there were requests for standard uniforms for the navy. They continued into the first half of the 19th century but it was not until the Civil War that any regulation uniforms were ordered. Up until that time there was little to distinguish a navy man from a merchant seaman because their dress was often the same. A certain uniformity always existed because the slop shops sold the clothes to seagoing men as described in Figure 94.

This Union tar wears dark blue slops or bell bottom trousers and a dark blue shirt. The shirt or middy was rarely worn on the outside of the trousers at this time. He has tied a black kerchief-tie under the large sailor collar.

His double-breasted, short jacket is an early form of the pea jacket which became regulation in 1886. It has steel buttons. His tam is black.

Figure 73

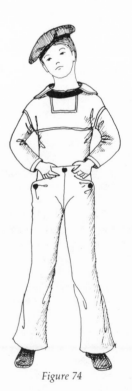

Young boys went to war, too. A boy could go to sea and serve as a powder monkey to assist the men. They were always pictured wearing small versions of the sailor uniform.

This boy wears dark blue middy and trousers. The middy has a yoke across the chest and has a drop shoulder. There is an interesting panel or yoke at the neck. This boy wears his black kerchief tied in back but they were tied in front, as in Figure 73, too. One boy's middy had brightly colored embroidered designs on the small yoke—of a heart and flowers!

His trousers or slops have a front fly and button-down pockets. Sailors' tams were usually black or dark blue.

Figure 74

Civil War

In 1863 ready-made uniforms were being worn by Union soldiers, the first time in history that clothing was factory-made. The new sewing machine had made it possible.

Clothing manufacture also meant that military uniforms could be standardized for the first time. As a result, there was less individuality in the Union outfits than in those of the Confederates.

Most photographs of high officers in the Union army show them wearing double-breasted coats like this one. The buttons were usually in groups of three rather than two as on Rebel coats (Figure 67) but some were spaced one or two at a time. Such coats might be worn as shown, or with the collar down and the lapels back. They might be folded and buttoned back at times because many photographs show an obvious crease down the center while some show them actually buttoned back. Coats were worn belted or loose. Sometimes the collar and cuffs were black or dark blue velvet. For formal wear, a sash, belt, and sword were added as in Figure 67.

Figure 75

Figure 76

Union cavalrymen wore short jackets and wide-brimmed hats. This is the uniform which became a folk symbol in the West after the war as shown in Figures 130 and 131.

The cavalry had always been considered the most glamorous part of the army. "Better to be a corporal in the cavalry than a first lieutenant in a foot company," was a commonly heard remark.

Yellow shoulder patches, collar, and trousers stripe designated cavalry on the dark blue uniform. The shoulder strap, pouch, and belt were black. This horseman wears gloves with gauntlet cuffs.

Black Wellington boots were worn to protect the knees. Some photographs show thigh-high boots. A jauntily worn hat has decorative insignia on the front. Although the gloves and boots were merely protective clothing, they, along with the large hat and jingling spurs, added dash to the uniform.

Red on the collar, cuffs, trousers stripe, and cap designated artillery, with light blue for infantry. The artillery wore the large hat and gloves of Figure 76, and some photographs show the large hats on infantrymen as well. The kepi, as shown here, was regulation for infantry.

The dark blue Union coat with brass buttons came a few inches down onto the thighs. It was usually belted with a black belt with an oval metal plate. A matching shoulder strap was worn to hold the pouch. Except for officers', Union uniforms were single-breasted.

Even when a regulation uniform was made available in 1863 it appears, from photographs, to have not included a shirt. Plaid, checked, and bright-colored shirts were worn by both officers and enlisted men. Many men just wore the union suit undershirt underneath. Suspenders or braces were commonly worn as were vests with white shirts and ties.

These Union uniforms were the basis for our present-day clothing industry because records were kept and the science of graduated sizes was developed. The army studied the records and came up with twenty basic sizes—a surprise because they expected to end up with hundreds!

Figure 77

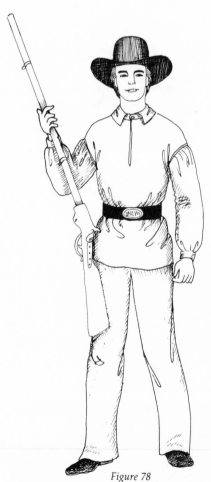

Figure 78

The Union army was outfitted with enough clothing to keep them warm in winter. Unfortunately the new woolen uniforms issued in 1863 were not designed for the heat, humidity, and stillness of southern summers and turned out to be a curse instead of a blessing. This soldier has discarded his jacket and is wearing his shirt belted.

Before 1863 officers were about the only ones who owned military coats, according to many photographs. Most men went into a fight wearing the sack coat of Figure 82. Many wore open shirt collars while others wore shirts and ties like the rebel soldier of Figure 70.

The collarless shirt of Figure 29 was often worn under wrinkled, dusty sack coats. Suspenders were usually worn under the coat.

In photographs made in the winter of '62 the federal troops usually are wearing a high-crowned black hat as shown on this soldier. Photographs made during the summer of '62 show them wearing the large straw hat of Figure 1 with a dark hat band. Only a few kepis were shown before 1863. One or two top hats invariably appear in the battlefield pictures.

Civil War

Union army overcoats were much the same as the state militia coats of several years before (Figure 52). The cape is usually buttoned as shown.

Before 1863 there was a wide variety of both color and cut. Coats were many shades of gray and blue with some regiments in brown or green. Some capes were lined with bright colors. Some state militia had been outfitted with white belts and shoulder straps but they were soon found to be impractical. All straps were black when federal uniforms were issued.

During the revolution, War of 1812, and the war with Mexico (1846) armies were composed of only a few thousand men. Clothing was (when uniforms were used) made by hand. Even socks and underwear were handmade, when worn. But in the Civil War hundreds of thousands of uniforms had to be made. Ironically enough, when it was necessary for uniforms to be mass-produced sewing machines were available.

Figure 79

The drummer boy has become a legendary figure in both art and literature since even young boys served as drummers for some companies. They were usually dressed in uniforms that were miniature copies of the men's.

This drummer boy obviously marches with a zouave company because his outfit is in the zouave style. Two such boys appear in one picture of Sherman's forces marching through Georgia.

He wears a loose blue shirt with the dropped-shoulder seam. The neckline is bound with black. His sleeves are rolled up.

The full trousers are bright red. Canvas gaiters cover his black shoes. His red cap is a tall, floppy fez with a tassel coming from the center of a small black top.

His drum is tan with a large eagle painted on the side. The metal strips are red with black tension cords. The shoulder strap is white.

One very famous painting of a drummer shows him in a blue overcoat with cape like Figure 79.

Figure 80

CHAPTER 6

1860s

The War Ends and the Western Era Begins

The census of 1860 showed there were 31,500,000 people in the United States with about half of them living west of the Appalachians. St. Paul, Minnesota, had a population of 10,000. By 1863 newspapers reported that 1,000 emmigrants were coming into New York every day.

Clothing became so scarce in the South during the war that a lady's bonnet cost up to $250.00, and new dresses were either nonexistent or exorbitantly expensive.

When the war was over young men from both the North and South went west to become railroad construction workers, cowherders, miners, and land speculators. The real beginning of the cowboy era was in 1867 when some miners-turned-cowherders decided to settle down and become ranchers. Permanent settling began as men brought their families to the west.

Frederick Worth, the English designer in Paris, influenced women's fashions the world over. In 1867 there were 300 million dollars spent on dry goods in the United States. That same year fashionable Americans were spending money on French fashions at the Paris Exhibition.

By the end of the decade men's clothing was settling in the somber plain state where it remained for 100 years, and women were being seen at beaches and swimming holes wearing bathing suits.

When the east and west railroad lines were joined in 1869, people could ride from the Atlantic to the Pacific. Travel was to have an important influence on American clothing design.

Fashionable coats of the 1850s continued to be worn during the 1860s. The frock coat was worn till the end of the century.

Shawls had been immensely popular with women for years and now the shawl was the fashion for men, too! Instead of folding the shawl into a triangle, men folded theirs into a rectangle. Many were of plaid wool and some were fringed. Men often wore the shawl when traveling.

Light colors for top hats were very fashionable. As the new sport hats came into use, the top hat was more and more associated with formal wear.

Coats were becoming more somber in color with black, brown, and gray being most common. This man wears a tucked shirt, large black tie, and vest under his coat. He wears a mustache and goatee. Trousers with the braid or stripe down the side, as in Figure 83, were the height of fashion as well as plain ones.

Figure 81

The Prince of Wales visited the United States in 1860 and created great interest in English clothes, especially sporting clothes.

This man wears a very fashionable sport suit buttoned in the latest manner. It has a shawl collar and several pockets. These coats were tweed, checked, or solid color, either stitched around the edges or bound with braid like the box coat of Figure 24.

When worn for hiking, hunting, and riding the newly invented bicycle, or for some other sport, the trousers were covered with leather or canvas gaiters fastened with metal clips or buckles as shown.

Sport hats were of felt or straw with the new low crowns. This man holds a fashionable straw hat with a ribbon band. Bushy cheek whiskers and the middle part in the hair were worn.

Figure 82

When so many uniforms had to be made during the war, manufacturers discovered that certain waist sizes usually accompanied certain trouser lengths. They began to keep records and analyze the information until eventually clothes could be manufactured that actually fit as well as homemade ones.

Enterprising merchants opened clothing stores and women were at last relieved of the job of making their husbands' or brothers' clothes.

The new clothes plus the popularity of the cigar and the cigarette brought about the new smoking jacket shown here. It is much like the box coat of Figure 24.

Collars and cuffs were often quilted, as were the facings around the pockets and coats. One museum example is pale blue with pink silk trim and a red lining! Another is tan with bright-colored embroidered flowers around collar, cuffs, pockets, and edges. It too has a red lining. The breast pocket was for "cigarette makin's."

Turkish or "house" caps were velvet, usually black, and embellished with bright embroidered flowers. A tassel always hung from the top or side. These exotic caps were similar to some of the zouave uniform caps (Figure 64).

Figure 83

After going to war and growing up, many young men could not bear to go back to the routine of farming or eastern small-town life. They went west to become prospectors, miners, land speculators, railroad construction laborers, and cowhands. By the end of the 1860s men were bringing families, and permanent settling was the rule. Soon lawyers, teachers, bankers, merchants, barkeeps, and gamblers followed.

Outfits such as this one were seen in western towns, southern docks, railroad and overland freighting stations, saloons, and just about anywhere in any section of the United States. It is much the same outfit as in Figures 22 and 81.

Gun belts with holsters were either inside the coat, as shown, or on the outside. Sometimes a Colt pistol was tucked in the high boot.

Often ties were worn, and the trousers were on the outside of the boots, about as often as inside, for town wear. The hats of Figures 7, 23, 25, 81, 82, and 87 were commonly worn, as well as the kepi.

Figure 84

American Costume

The fashionable shawl was enjoyed by men in all walks of life in all areas of our fast-growing country. After the Homestead Act of 1862, settlers went as far as the new state of Minnesota where Red River land was free. Immigrants from Ireland, Norway, and Sweden flooded into the country and many of them settled new lands. Many of the Irish stayed in the East and South.

Such simple, comfortable attire was preferred by many of these farmers and homesteaders who discovered hard work and hardship instead of adventure.

The shirt is worn without the detachable collar. It might be white, unbleached, red, blue, green, or black or in stripes or plaid as in Figure 29.

Front-flap breeches called railroad trousers were still seen everywhere although the button fly front was commonplace.

The hat is the traditional hat of rural people. It was made of either felt or straw. Boots of all styles were worn.

This man is smoking an Irish pipe.

Figure 85

Minstrel artists adapted the familiar attire of the period to their entertainment form. The high-waisted pantaloons of Figures 28 and 87 were made up in calicos, stripes, flower stripes, polka dots, and other colorful patterns. They were often of bright-hued satins and brocades.

At first the minstrel shows were performed by blacks, but as the shows' popularity grew, more and more of the performers were whites impersonating blacks. The music had its roots in both black and white culture as did the costumes. By 1860 there were 150 traveling minstrel groups in the United States. Some troupes even played before European royalty.

This man wears the fancy, embroidered suspenders or braces which remained the vogue throughout the century, seen again in Figure 195.

Suits like those of Figures 22, 23, and 90 (right) were made up in bright satins and calicos, too.

The "Uncle Sam" suit was often made in satins and cottons at this time. It consisted of a vest, tailcoat, top hat, and striped trousers.

For other minstrel clothes see Figure 47.

Figure 86

Before the Civil War, Cyrus McCormick's harvesters and reapers had revolutionized farming. When the war started the Confederate Congress asked southern farmers to stop planting cotton and plant food crops instead. In 1860 over five million bales of cotton had been produced—by 1864, only 300,000.

Pantaloons were often worn over shirts and trousers to protect them. This man's trousers can be seen at the ankles. Eventually called overalls, these pantaloons had developed pockets on the sides and straps of matching fabric. They were usually of blue or brown canvas.

His full, drop-shouldered shirt has the collar open and the cuffs unbuttoned and turned back. Sometimes a loose-fitting, satin-back vest like that of Figures 7 and 62 was worn over these garments.

Top hats, shakos, wide-brimmed straws, and all the hats of the '50s and '60s were common. The cap illustrated here has flaps that could be pulled down over the ears for warmth.

Figure 87

The war did not stop the prospecting; instead, it created a demand for gold and silver for both the Union and the Confederacy.

The dangers and the exorbitant prices, though, prevented men from moving their families to the mining areas until the end of the decade. Since few miners had anyone to sew for them, they bought the new manufactured clothes even though they were often of poor quality. "Store-boughten" clothes were better than nothing.

Not only miners but factory workers and farmers back east belted their shirts and smocks as shown here. Notice that the shirt is split at the sides and longer in back than front. The front has a waistline seam hidden by the belt with the shirttail slightly gathered onto it. The front panel is tucked. This man wears a large red bandanna around his neck.

His universal checked trousers are tucked inside his Wellington boots with their turned-down knee guards. Canvas-lined boots with turned-down tops like those of Figure 7 were frequently worn.

His wide-brimmed hat served many purposes. It might be used for a drinking vessel, wash bowl, ore carrier, fan, or pillow as needs arose. It may have been an early stetson.

One pony express rider was photographed in similar clothes. Abraham Lincoln was depicted in such attire on one of his campaign posters in 1860 with the shirt tucked into the trousers.

Figure 88

65

The frontier was an imaginary line dividing the country into areas with two people per square mile and areas having fewer! The 1860 census showed that about fifteen million people were living west of the Appalachians. The first cowboys were miners and trappers who settled down on homestead lands and became ranchers.

The deerskin hunting smock or coat was familiar on both sides of the frontier although in the East it was reserved primarily for hunting and farming. It was often dyed light blue.

This version of the buckskin was probably a winter one with its attached hood. When pulled up the hood would prevent wind and rain from going down the neck. In the mountains where rain is almost a daily occurrence this fringed coat would offer maximum protection. Fringe diverts water as it breaks it up and makes it run off in droplets.

The Indian leggings worn over trousers had fringed outer seams. Leather breeches were sometimes worn but more often cloth trousers were simply protected with boots or Indian leggings.

The shoulder pouch holds ammunition and other necessities. The Spencer repeating rifle was used in the West. The U.S. government used it as a trading gun for the Indians also.

Figure 89

Figure 90

Newspapers in 1863 reported that one thousand immigrants were coming into New York each day!

By the time of the Civil War America had 31,246 miles of railroads. After the war construction resumed full speed. The rails going west were being built by Irish workers. The east and west lines were joined in 1869.

Irishmen came to the United States wearing their native clothes which they continued to wear out of preference and/or necessity. On the left, the striped shirt, short vest, and kerchief (tied in back) illustrate Irish rural clothes of the period. The man's pantaloons have the front flap of earlier years. Possibly these were worn by so many railroad laborers that this is why they came to be called railroad trousers.

On the right, a man wears clothes of the early 19th century which became traditional clothes in Ireland. This tailcoat, knee breeches, and flared top hat make up an Irish folk costume today. Many immigrants arrived in such attire and continued to wear it for varying lengths of time.

Railroads going east were built by Chinese workers who were coming into California seaports. Chinese immigrations continued to increase until they peaked in 1882.

The Chinaman on the left wears the loose breeches, cap-sleeved coat, and coolie hat that he brought with him.

The man on the right has adopted the American boots and spurs. His coat sleeves were cut all in one piece with the body. He wears a pillbox cap. The full breeches are tucked inside his boots. Some pictures show these men barefoot.

One painting owned by the New York Historical Society shows Mexicans, Chinese laborers, and gold miners all standing together in a San Francisco saloon with the immigrants in their native costumes. It was not an unusual sight at this time.

Figure 91

As the war worsened, southerners encountered hardships that few Americans have experienced before or since. They gave until there was no more to give. When their government called for metal to be melted for cannons they brought in even their church bells and candlesticks.

Ministers of the time dressed much the same as they had since the beginning of the century. This preacher wears the fashionable collar of early colonial days which developed into a clerical collar. His dark robe and outer cloak evolved from 17th century ones, too. His whole outfit was one that grew out of our early history.

Only his hat is more recent. The early 19th century flared top hat came eventually to be associated with Quakers.

One circuit riding preacher of the time was described as wearing protective leather "overalls" (worn by the Mexican of Figure 33) over his trousers to shield them from the rain. He often wore an oilcloth slicker like that of Figure 128 (left) as he rode around his circuit.

Figure 92

American Costume

When police uniforms were first introduced the officers had to take a great deal of ribbing and abuse because of them. The buttons, badge, and belt plate were made of copper, thus the name "coppers."

This policeman wears the uniform seen in most U.S. cities. It is of similar design to the military attire of the period.

His hat is the stiff shako described in Figure 34. His uniform is, in fact, much the same as that of the California vigilante of a decade before.

His trousers are worn over his boots.

Figure 93

For centuries sailors were the only people to wear ready-made clothes. When in port a sailor did not have time to wait for a tailor to make his clothes so some enterprising shop owners learned to have them made up in advance in a range of sizes. Since the wide-legged sailor trousers had been called "slops" these shops were called "slop shops."

Until the Civil War merchant and military seamen looked much the same because they all assembled their own outfits. During the conflict a common uniform was prescribed for the Union navy and standardization began.

Merchant seamen remained the individualists they had always been. This seaman wears a belted middy which buttons at the neck. It has a dark blue collar. His tie is red.

The trousers or slops have a flap front. His jacket, like that of Figure 73, is the forerunner of the pea jacket. The black cap dates back to ancient times, being worn by Chinese and then Dutch sailors.

Figure 94

The Indians of the plains were immigrants, too, coming from the north woods during the previous hundred years. They gave up farming to become nomads dependent on the buffalo. Before the Civil War only a few isolated clashes between Plains Indians and the white man had been recorded.

These Indians, the Dakotas, wore the long fringe and handsome warbonnet which became famous the world over. The man on the right shows the tunic with neck and shoulder quillwork decorations. Although the tunic appears to have sleeves, it actually was usually caught at only one point at the side. Sometimes it was only a large rectangle worn like a poncho.

Every single feather in the dashing warbonnet was notched so that it became a record of the warrior's coups (times he touched the enemy). The notches were coded or slanted to show the degree of the coup.

The leggings illustrated on the left are shown without the tunic—as worn in warm weather. A belt around the waist holds the legging straps and the breechcloth, which goes between the legs and then folds over the belt. It does not hang as long in back as in front. Both the leggings and the breechcloth are decorated with quillwork which later became beadwork with traded beads. This headdress is simpler than the other warrior's.

These Plains Indians added thick leather soles to their moccasins, the only ones to do so at the time.

Figure 95

Figure 96

Plains women wore a short oval or circular deerskin tunic around the shoulders; it was decorated with beadwork and long fringe.

Skirts were wraparound and left open on one side as shown. The fringe around the hem continues up the side. The skirt shown is decorated with animal teeth and leather strips.

Leggings were fastened with leather garters just under the knees. This woman's leggings have leather ties and beadwork down the sides. She, too, wears moccasins with thick leather soles.

A wooden board with head posts supports a deerskin papoose carrier tied at several points up the front with leather strips. It is decorated with beadwork and made so that it forms a little protective canopy. In winter the baby was fastened in securely so that he could only peep out, but when the weather was warm his arms were sometimes left free as in Figure 39.

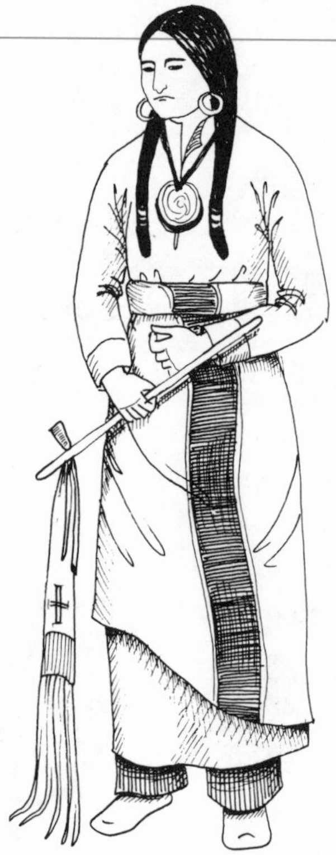

During the Civil War in 1862 there was trouble between the U.S. cavalry and the Santee Sioux Indians, in 1864 trouble with the Southern Cheyenne.

This warrior is dressed in the costume shown in actual photographs rather than in the more traditional one usually shown in paintings of the time. By the middle of the century many Indians had adopted the white man's shirt as shown here.

Most tribes had adopted the white man's machine-woven blanket which was available to them in trade. They wore it wrapped around the middle, a little above the waist, and secured by folds or rolls at the top. Tan blankets with red bands, as well as solid red ones were worn over leggings and breechcloth similar to those of Figure 95. Leggings became less full after the war.

This man wears a large medallion around his neck and loop earrings. He holds a peace pipe with decorative streamers.

Figure 97

In 1865 the Sioux, Northern Cheyenne, Arapahoes, and the Southern Cheyenne joined forces. In 1866 Fort Reno was enlarged and Fort Phil Kearny and Fort C.F. Smith were built. There were other serious fights with Indians in both 1866 and 1867 along the Bozeman Trail.

In 1867 the cavalry had breech-loading rifles but by '68 the Cheyenne had repeating Spencer rifles and Colt revolvers.

The warrior shown here has his white shirt buttoned at the neck and wears a white man's dark vest with his blanket, leggings, and breechcloth. He displays a notched feather in his hair and a medallion around his neck. Instead of a peace pipe, he holds a Spencer repeating rifle.

U.S. cavalarymen used to say that the Plains Indians were the "best light cavalry in the world."

Figure 98

70

The larger American fashion magazines made arrangements with European publications so that the new designs were published simultaneously in the United States. This naturally created great interest in fashions.

Formal gowns were elaborate and immensely full—up to ten yards around the hem! This ball gown has a white bodice and overskirt over a blue skirt edged with a white ruffle. The bodice has full lace sleeves topped with blue satin bows. Narrow lace edges the neckline with a pink rose in the center front. A full, sheer overskirt has shirred swags which are edged with narrow black lace. Similar dresses at this time had ruffles covering the skirt. On some gowns fancy ribbon sashes hung over the skirt as in Figure 42. The skirts of Figures 40, 42, 101, 102, and 106 can each be substituted for this one.

The lady's middle-part hairstyle is puffed out on the sides with long sausage curls behind the ears. Flowers and ribbons decorated the side and back of this style.

Figure 99

Figure 100

Clothing became so scarce in the South during the Civil War that by 1864 a lady's new bonnet cost up to $250.00! Resourceful women created their own from cornhusks, palmetto leaves, and straw. They adorned them with flowers made of shavings from cow's horns and dried wild flowers.

This woman wears a straw bonnet with a lace ruffle around the back where it is decorated with flowers. It is held in place with ribbon ties.

The princess dress with the plain sleeve was very fashionable. The tailored look, sometimes even a bit military, was new. This simple but elegant princess frock is of lavender with black dots. It has a white collar and cuffs with a black ribbon tie.

A hint of the military is seen in the black braid loops and tassels on the shoulders. Braid and tassels on the cuffs and around the hem match those on the shoulders.

Princess dresses were occasionally belted or topped with a corsage bodice or Spanish jacket like those of Figures 101 and 102.

71

American Costume

The idea of separate blouses, skirts, and jackets was here to stay although some people considered them mannish.

Waistlines were tiny and skirts over hoops were enormous. Flounces around the hem gave still more fullness!

This three-piece costume consists of canezou blouse (seen more clearly in Figure 107), skirt, and corsage bodice.

Corsage bodices might be hip- or even knee-length in back. One pictured in Godey's *Lady's Book* was like this one at the top but ended above the waist in an Empire length. Some were short and curved in front like the bolero jacket of Figure 102, others stopped at the waistline. Great individuality was shown where this bodice was concerned, which makes it particularly valuable for the theatre. A basic skirt and blouse could be inexpensively changed with extra corsage bodices or boleros.

The bodice was sometimes black with black braid or lace trim like this one. The slits in the flared sleeves repeat the design of the peplum.

Skirts were bedecked with braids, appliqués, embroideries, and ruffles in a manner that was almost architectural. This one has black grosgrain ribbon and appliqué used for a Greek key effect.

This lady's hair style is described in Figure 99.

Figure 101

The blouse was often linen because cotton production ceased during the war. Red was now as familiar a color for blouses as white. Ruffles on the cuffs often came down onto the hands as shown here.

Boleros, sometimes called Spanish jackets, were the rage. They might be crocheted, knitted, or sewn of wool or silk. They were adorned with heavy trims such as loops, tassels, braids, pleated ruffles, and crocheted edgings. This bolero has a pleated ruffle around the neck and edges topped with braid. The caps or epaulettes are cord loops with heavy braid. It ties at the neck.

The full skirt over a hoop has pleated ruffles and black ribbon designs around the hem. Black appliquéd bows are accented with jet button centers. Skirts were often bright colors with black trim. Wide belts were worn, sometimes with fancy or jewelled buckles.

The lady's hair bun is held in a net while a poufed ribbon wreath with streamers forms a halo on her head. (The plain net hair covering shown in Figure 107 was worn with dresses also.) She holds the universally popular parasol.

Figure 102

Many American businessmen and merchants attended the International Exhibition in Paris in 1867 with their families. When they returned, their wives and daughters had their steamer trunks filled with French fashions!

The coat or jacket was worn in many lengths and shapes. The popular princess line was particularly well suited for coats because its gores allowed it to flare out over the full skirts. The coats were sometimes belted like Figure 41.

This lady wears a black velvet paletôt coat edged with ribbon and decorated with silk embroidery and jet beads. Caps accent the shoulders. The split sleeves, in the style of the 17th century, are caught at the wrists. Sometimes they were flared and left open like those of Figure 42.

The coat was worn over bright-colored dresses or skirts which were very full and long in back, clearly forecasting the bustle of the near future.

As skirt fullness moved to the back, hats began to move forward and dip over the forehead. It was a natural balance for the skirt and for the large chignon hair styles. Bright colored feathers and plumes often matched the skirts of poplin, silk, or wool.

Figure 103

Figure 104

In 1867 three hundred million dollars was spent on dry goods in the United States!

There was a variety of coat fashions at this time which were given exotic names and made in bright colors. On the left is one in the burnous style called a "Cordelière Cloak." It appeared in colors like violet or fuchsia ornamented with cord and tassels. The point with tassel in the back was a characteristic of the burnous.

The coat on the right was a "Metternich" sack coat. A braid-decorated shoulder yoke ended in tassels giving the look of epaulettes. The same trim covered the back seam for a way, then ended with three tassels where the coat flared out with set-in gores, adding to its fullness. Sleeves had decorated cuffs.

Bonnets were accented with ribbon bows and flowers. Ribbon bows and bonnet tie ends were cut in interesting shapes with slanted, pointed, or rounded ends as shown. Muffs or colorful gloves were worn.

Shawls and stoles were the vogue as well as coats and jackets. Shawls like the one on the left were often fringed. They might be half circles and triangles, or full circles and squares which were folded and warmer as a result. Some were embroidered, some bordered, and others were in paisley designs. Pictures sometimes show the fringe so long that it touches the floor.

On the right is the stole which came in assorted sizes from dainty to floor length. In winter stoles might be fur or fur-trimmed. They often had ribbon or braid trim as shown. Plaid wool in winter and plaid taffeta in the summer were the mode as well as lace or velvet. The stole is easier and less expensive to make than a coat and offers limitless design possibilities for theatre.

Bonnets continue to move forward where they will remain during the coming decade as the interest in skirts continues to focus on the back.

Figure 105

Women were spending more and more time out of the home. By 1866–67 the walking costume with looped-up skirts was seen on the sidewalks, in parks, and at vacation resorts. Somewhat reminiscent of 18th century walking dresses, the costume gave a sense of motion even while the wearer was standing still. Always long in back, the skirt was sometimes up to the ankles in front.

By '68 and '69 skirts were flared or gored with little or no fullness in front while becoming more complex in back. This dress clearly demonstrates the transition from the hoop to the bustle.

Military-like braids and tassels were still the fashion. Sleeves on the very new dresses were fitted as they would be in the coming decade.

There was no actual bustle yet, just back fullness and large bows. The outer skirt was full and shaped like the skirt underneath. Later it would be pulled around to the back in a decided drape as in Figures 135 and 139. It would be divided in front and take on more complex shapes eventually, as in Figures 136 and 137.

Figure 106

Although the "old-fashioned" pantalets were not worn by women anymore they were retained by little girls. The practical advantages of the pantalet were beginning to be realized in sports clothes.

This girls' and young ladies' dress was worn in girls' schools in Germany and England. It was at this time beginning to be accepted in America. There is no question that it was influenced by Amelia Bloomer's daring creation of the 1840s as seen in Figure 15.

This canezou blouse with its radiating rows of lace between rows of shirring was the same as those worn under the jackets and boleros of Figures 42, 101, and 102. The bodices of Figures 43 and 109 are its tucked counterparts.

The skirt is much the same as long skirts of the decade. In fact, this costume can be made in full length.

Her hair is held in place with the modish hair net. Her shoes are leather and canvas high-tops.

Some skating dresses had trousers as part of the costume but they were still a bit shocking. Riding outfits had trousers, too, but they were concealed under the skirts.

Figure 107

Figure 108

By the late 1860s bathing suits were timidly featured in most summer issues of fashion magazines. Pictures were always accompanied by carefully worded captions making it clear to the reader that the magazine did not suggest that men and women bathe (swim) at the same spot. Advice was always given to readers about the proper "watering places" to visit and proper supervision of their daughters while there.

A cotton shirtwaist of blue or gray over full pantalets or trousers was considered proper attire for ladies. Both trousers and shirtwaist were trimmed with white piping. The waist was belted with a matching belt.

This young lady carries her long cape which she will wear to the water's edge and remove just before going into the water. Her hair is contained in a net with a bow on top. She wears bathing slippers.

Clothing became so scarce in the South during the Civil War that women resorted to making clothes out of mattress ticking, sheets, and old draperies. When dresses were available they were exorbitantly priced.

This woman might be a southern woman during the war or a rural woman in any part of the country. She wears the familiar blouse of the decade with her sleeves rolled up.

Her skirt is pulled up and tucked over her petticoat band or belt. It is artistically and meticulously arranged in the style of the 17th century. Every fold is placed so that the design is perfectly balanced. Although the purpose of the draping was to lift the skirt out of the way during work it was most assuredly an aesthetic expression as well. It was tradition, too, passed down from mother to daughter through the years in small towns and rural areas of the British Isles and Europe and then the United States.

Her petticoat is red and she wears a red kerchief knotted around her neck. She either wears a small hoop or several petticoats to hold the skirts bouffant.

The center front is caught up at the hem while the sides are caught at the hips and then tucked into place.

Figure 109

Seen from Pennsylvania to California, this dress was a familiar sight. It appeared on women going west in wagon trains, at a scutching bee, a barn raising, or in church.

Its high neck and small collar are folded under with the resulting opening filled in with a kerchief. Although the kerchief was often tied on the outside, or held under the belt, this method of tucking it into the neckline seems to have been the favorite one.

Although this straw bonnet was seen on the prairie as well as in town, the bonnets of Figures 17, 43, 45, and 46 were commonly seen with this dress also. The plain straw hat of Figure 44 was worn in rural areas, too.

Sometimes the kerchief was white but it was just as customary to wear a bright-colored one. Red was a favorite color as well as turquoise, rust, green, and yellow. Frequently the cloth sunbonnet and kerchief were coordinated. The dress and bonnet ribbons or sunbonnet might match and the kerchief be a contrasting color or white.

The size of the kerchief was as varied as the color; sometimes it was hardly bigger than a collar, sometimes almost a shawl.

This simple dress can be made in any fabric from taffeta to calico to flannel for any age woman.

The lady wears high-top shoes and carries a folding fan.

Figure 110

76

Another dress of infinite variety was this cotton, linen, or wool two-piece interpretation of the suit of Figure 41. It appeared on the prairie, in seaport towns, up and down the rivers, and in rural areas throughout the nation. It was worn in munitions plants in the North during the Civil War as well as on plantations in the South. It was usually home-sewn in simple fabrics.

Working women sometimes wore this dress in an ankle-length but it was often floor-length, too. It was always held out by several petticoats or a hoop.

Both black and white women were portrayed in such apparel. Black vendors in the deep South and along the Mississippi River were sketched in such dresses. Occasionally left unbelted, giving the appearance of a smock, the dress may have served as a maternity smock in longer lengths. It definitely was a part of the American scene.

Bandannas and sunbonnets were often part of the costume as were aprons and shawls.

Figure 111

Figure 112

Girls' dresses were gored now, like women's. Shoulder interest and fitted sleeves followed grown-up styles.

This charming dress in a soft white muslin has pink silk bows. Lots of tucks, insertion, lace, and rosettes are integrated into the total design achieving a complex but most tasteful result.

The forward-tilting hat with streamers down the back is the very latest fashion. Cloth was combined with leather for boots and shoes. Canvas, wool, and velvet were used with patent leather as were grosgrain and satin.

The canezou blouse and skirt as well as all the other women's clothes of the decade were worn, in shorter lengths, by young girls. The coat styles of the adults were all worn by girls, too.

Boys were dressed in European smocks much like those of farmers and factory workers. They might be worn belted, as shown, or tucked inside the trousers. During this decade it was the mode to belt them on the outside. Colors were usually subdued such as gray-blue or gray-green.

This young boy is outfitted in a smock of very plain design, its only adornment being a large bow tied under the soft collar. These bows were usually either red or black. The shoulder line is dropped down on the arm where the sleeve is gathered on.

His trousers are loose, ankle-length pantaloons. Boots of canvas and leather were worn by men and boys as well as by girls and women as described in Figure 112.

Hair was arranged in a slicked-down style, probably with oil, with the sideburns ending in spit curls on the cheeks. When caps were worn, they were tam-o-shanters or shako-type caps called "forage caps" as shown in Figure 49.

Figure 113

As familiar on the American scene as the men's clothes of Figures 84 and 90 was this little boy's outfit. It was seen throughout the country on all classes and races of children. In summer the shirt was muslin, linen, calico, or gingham. In winter it was linen or flannel.

The drop shoulders, full sleeves, and full body of the shirt were the same as those for men. Sometimes this shirt had the standing collar of Figures 29 and 85 indicating that at times the child wore a detachable collar and tie with it. It was often red or blue and just as often, flowered calico or striped muslin.

Pantaloons sometimes buttoned onto the shirt as shown. Some pantaloons had the front flap of the railroad trousers while newer ones had the fly front. In summer, children of the rural South might be barefoot.

The simple play clothes of city dwellers might be much the same as the garments worn by rural children.

Girls usually were dressed in aprons or smocks to protect their dresses. This apron is much like the wide-necked lacy one of Figure 115 (left). It has a tuck around the hem which can be let down as the child grows.

This little girl wears a sunbonnet with a neck ruffle so large that it forms a cape around her shoulders. Although she wears a high-necked dress, this cape would certainly offer protection to her neck were she wearing the off-the-shoulder neckline of Figure 115.

Her shoes are black lace-up shoes called half-boots. Her pantalets show a bit beneath her skirts.

Figure 114

Figure 115

A fancy or Sunday frock had its own lacy apron to match. An apron took much less time to wash and iron than the complicated dresses.

The girl on the left wears a pastel-colored, off-the-shoulder dress with ruffled lace sleeves. The skirt has two groups of tucks around the hem. Her white apron repeats the wide neckline edged with narrow lace. A lace ruffle goes across the low shoulder line to the waistband. Lace and ruffles surround the apron skirt, which is gathered onto the waistband.

Even her pantalets are her Sunday best with lace edging. Her boots are canvas and patent leather.

Large straw sailor hats were adorned with ribbon bands, bows, and streamers cut with fancy-shaped points. Points might be cut slanted, rounded, or as shown.

Little girls (right) were dressed in high-waisted aprons and dresses with yokes. This unusual apron has ruffles around the armholes which are cut with petal points edged in braid. The same braid edges the square neckline and pockets. Two rows of tucks trim the skirt allowing it to be let down as the child grows. With this dress she wears plain pantalets and side-button boots.

Her hairstyle of long braids with ribbon bows is a simpler one than the older girls' of long corkscrew or sausage curls. She might wear either the sailor hat or the sunbonnet.

Very little boys wore dresses of muslin or linen, somewhat plainer than those of little girls. This toddler's dress has a simple collar, cuffs, and one hemline tuck. Its only decoration is the ribbon tie and brooch at the neck.

His shallow, rolled-brim, porkpie hat has a velvet ribbon rosette on the side. He is wearing short stockings with his black patent-leather shoes.

On the right an older boy wears a zouave suit probably inspired by the zouave uniforms of the state militias. The bolero has two rows of braid on the rounded corners, neck and tapered sleeves. Underneath, he wears a white cotton waist with a little collar, which can be turned up or down, and pearl buttons.

His knee-length breeches are full at the hips, then tapered to the knees where they button. They have no kneeband. The waistband has a point in front. Several rows of braid follow the side seam. Some zouave breeches were wide at the knee instead of tapered.

Velvet was a fashionable fabric for these suits. Brown, gold, and green were the customary colors. One popular fashion magazine suggested a buff suit with coral braid trim.

He wears high side-button boots with scallops for each button. His stockings were similar to present-day tights or panty hose, being the new knit drawers with feet in them!

His hair is parted in the middle with waves and curls bunched over the ears. The caps of Figures 20, 21 and 49 were worn with this outfit.

Figure 116

Figure 117

Little girls' coats were often flared like this one to fit over the very full skirts and petticoats. This coat is gray with a stand-up collar and tapered sleeves. Bands of blue velvet go over the shoulder almost to the hem and end in three points. A tassel accents each point. Three points of velvet also decorate the cuffs. The coat fastens with a double row of buttons on a panel underneath.

This girl's felt hat is also gray, trimmed with blue velvet. It has the new forward tilt of adult hats. Her boots are gray wool and black patent leather, her gloves gray. Her plaid dress is similar to the little boys' dresses of Figure 151.

The baby's off-the-shoulder christening dress is made of fine handkerchief linen or batiste. The sleeves are split, giving them a similar appearance to the drawn-up ones of Figure 50 (right). A front panel is elaborately constructed of alternating rows of lace and shirring. Lace also borders the sides of the panel. White satin is used for the sash and bow. Satin bows were sometimes used down the panel sides and on the sleeves, too.

Rows of lace sewn together form the dainty cap. Tiny gathered lace frames the face.

CHAPTER 7

1870s

The Economic Revolution and the Styles It Influenced

We were becoming a nation on wheels, and the railroad engineer was a hero to young boys. People who weren't willing or able to go west by wagon or foot could now go on the train.

America had great prosperity in some areas and hard times and suffering in others. Southerners and urban immigrants would endure hardships throughout the century. Settling in the West had its problems and discomforts too. Postwar history must consider the economic revolution and the people who participated in it from the southern farmer to the "robber barons" and from the train robbers to the freed slave and the immigrant.

By 1871, one-half million sewing machines were produced a year bringing about another new idea—the paper pattern business. The mail order business founded in 1872 made clothes available to people on farms and frontier. The typewriter was invented in 1868 and by 1873 had created many job opportunities for women. Whether at home or at one of the new jobs, women's work would never be the same again.

The '70s saw the rise of professional sports which would influence clothing. It also was the decade of the American Centennial which inspired styles reminiscent of those of 1776.

As the white man moved west the Indian became aware of his nudity and began to cover himself. He adopted the clothes of the white man, becoming quite flashy in his approach to dress. The white man had adopted some of the Indian's clothes, so times they looked much the same.

More and more people were going west because of the railroads. Many who had not wanted to go in wagons or on foot could now go in relative comfort.

The sack coat, which has no waistline seam and goes from shoulder to hem in a relatively straight line, was the latest thing for traveling and all informal wear. It began as a lounge jacket (Figure 83) but was commonly worn within a few years. Tweeds and pin-stripes were favorite fabrics.

These four-button sack coats were both double-breasted, as shown, and single-breasted as in Figure 190. When single-breasted, they were fastened with the top button only.

The ascot tie, which could be purchased on a clip neckband, the jewelled stickpin, and the handkerchief in the breast pocket, established that this man was a dapper gentleman!

His hat, much like that in Figure 25, is worn high and round instead of pushed in. He carries an umbrella to complete the effect. His vest is like that of Figure 119.

Although elegant gentlemen favored this suit, at least one outlaw was known to have worn it, too. Black Bart, who held up twenty-eight stagecoaches between 1875 and 1883, was photographed in a tweed outfit of identical line, ascot, and jewelled stickpin. His hat was pushed in to become a bowler.

Figure 118

Figure 119

Those who followed the prospecters and miners to the West usually made more money than the first group. They were bankers, mill owners, succeeding mine owners, stockjobbers, gamblers, lawyers, doctors, merchants, and barkeeps. Back east there were the usual natty men and those who were becoming the new millionaires.

Gentlemen liked the studied look of this long sack coat. It, like the short version of Figure 118, had four buttons. Although it was occasionally worn open all the way, a man of fashion never fastened more than the one button at the top.

The stiff collar, ascot tie, vest, and checked trousers complete the suit. A handkerchief in the breastpocket and a watch showing on the vest were stylish as was the walking stick. These sticks with silver and ivory heads sometimes had umbrellas inside!

This man wears the new derby hat. His mustache and pointed cheek whiskers are appropriate to his fashionable clothes.

At least one western town marshall was photographed in the same outfit including the derby and jewelled stickpin.

With the growing popularity of sports, it was only natural that the tennis shoe should be introduced at this time. Rubber-soled tennis shoes with tops of buckskin or canvas were worn for tennis or boating.

This sailing suit was worn by sportsmen and college students. It is navy blue with white braid around the middy collar and cuffs and white stitching on the front pocket. The shirt underneath is white with blue buttons.

Although the blue sailor breeches have matching blue buttons, those on the middy are white to coordinate with the white braid.

The Union naval officer's hat of the Civil War was probably the inspiration for this white sailor cap. This man wears the same pointed cheek whiskers as Figure 119 but without the mustache.

Figure 120

Figure 121

In 1869 the first professional sports team was started. At first the players wore loose pantaloons and overblouses but before long they were wearing baseball suits not too different from those of today. Our first pro team took their name from their costume: they were the "Cincinnati Red Stockings."

This ball player wears a red and white striped shirt with a small, soft collar. His rather stiff cap is made of matching fabric.

The knickers are especially noteworthy because they had a belt loop on each side and one in the back. The belt loop was not to become a standard part of men's trousers until after the First World War. It was used only on baseball and football uniforms and the "crash suit" of the 1890s (Figure 192). These knickers have a fitted kneeband.

His baseball shoes are black high-tops with elastic insets on each side. The stockings, of course, are red. His belt is black.

Dressing gowns and smoking jackets still had shawl collars but now instead of having button fastenings they just wrapped around the body. They were held in place by a cord and tasselled belt.

This gown is of a flower-striped wool with a blue silk collar, cuffs, and lining. It predicts the blanket cloth bathrobe of the turn of the century as well as the terry cloth robe of today.

His shirt which shows at the neck has the detachable collar removed. His railroad trousers have a stripe down the side. The legs curve down in back until they touch the floor as in the previous decade.

Long nightcaps with a tassel on the end were called "jellybags." This one is striped silk with a silk tassel.

Figure 122

Figure 123

Although the railroad engineer was now competing with him, the fireman was still a hero to young boys. Fire companies still tried to outdo each other with dashing uniforms and equipment.

This fireman wears the short fitted jacket worn by some of the pre-Civil War militia regiments. It is double-breasted and bright red. (Men's coats had not yet settled on the standard left-over-right method of fastening and might appear buttoned either way.) He wears a white shirt and large black tie.

His black trousers are tucked inside what appear to be either oilcloth or early rubber boots. The canvas-lined tops are turned down.

A large metal plate, with the name of the fire company embossed on it, stands up on the front of his black fireman's hat. He carries a brass fireman's horn.

The mail order business was founded in 1872. Clothes could be mailed to people on farms and in remote towns. The new factory-made shoes and clothes for men were commonly seen at this time. It is interesting that the cash register was invented by the end of the decade. It would facilitate recording all those sales of the new ready-made clothes!

This man wears the typical work clothes and apron of the period. The apron had not yet developed the specialized pockets which it would have by 1900 (Figure 233), but it had arrived at the same general shape it was to retain until today. He wears a red union suit under his full, drop-shouldered shirt. His collar is open but the tie was commonly worn.

This apron can be worn over the work clothes of Figures 7, 29, 31, 85, 87, and 88.

Labor groups were beginning to organize because of the often dangerous or unhealthy working conditions in some industries and the low pay.

Figure 124

Utilitarian coats were cut on the same lines as fashionable coats and lounge jackets such as those in Figures 2, 24, and 83.

Such coats were made of denim or twill and then painted by the cattle drivers on the prairie to make them windbreakers!

The earliest cow-herd breeches were very fitted leather ones called "shotgun chaps" because they were said to look like gun barrels. They were fringed at the outseam.

Similar to English riding boots, those of the early cowboy had canvas tops. Later ones had scalloped, pierced, and stitched decorations. The slanted heel was to facilitate removal of the boot from the stirrup in case the cowhand was thrown. Getting one's foot caught and being dragged was something to be avoided!

Hats served many purposes such as a sunshade in summer and snow and rain shelter in winter. The indispensable kerchief served many purposes, too, like holding the hat on in wind or keeping the head and ears warm as shown.

Railroad crimes reached a peak in the 1870s and the robbers were looked upon as heroes at first. Eventually, of course, they came to be viewed as lawbreakers. One famous photograph of the James brothers shows one of them dressed in a coat similar to this one but longer.

Figure 125

Cattle drivers eventually became known as cowboys. The first cattle drives were for rounding up cows which had strayed from Mexico so that they could be sold to the gold towns.

What few farmers there were in the West were plagued by grasshoppers during the period 1874–76. Not only did they kill the crops but the turkeys and chickens, too—these fowl would eat themselves to death on the insects! Beef became more important than gold to a lot of folks.

Earliest chaps were the leather Indian leggings with fringe on the seam. At first snug-fitting as in Figure 125, they grew wider in a few years. Two separate pieces, these leggings had to be slipped on over the feet so the boots and spurs had to be removed each time. Since the chaps were rarely worn when the cowboy was off his horse, this meant a lot of trouble. Eventually they were made to snap on like those in Figure 162. The chaps shown here are cut almost down to the knees in back.

Shirts were white, colored, striped, checked, or printed muslin. Old pictures reveal a great deal of individuality.

Hats took on regional characteristics by the way they were shaped. It was said you could tell where a cowboy was from by the way his hat looked.

Bandannas were blue, black, or the favored red. Since it served many purposes including washing with it and wiping sweat, the kerchief was referred to as a "wipe."

The cowboy wears a gunbelt with a holster which is tied around his leg.

Figure 126

Cowboys refused to wear denim at first because miners and laborers wore it, but eventually they accepted and finally gave it its American folk identity.

The cowboy actually preferred a vest over a coat whenever the weather permitted it. It left one's arms free. It gave added pockets for the tobacco and cigarette makin's, too. The cowboy carried a little book for recording his time, comments about the trail, and what brands he had seen each day. Vests were sometimes satin-back, but many were deerskin or fur-lined. A plain shirt and bandanna are worn with the vest shown here.

Leather, denim, or twill jackets were worn more for protection from briars than from cold. As a result the fur-lined vest was worn in the north and the jacket in the Texas brush country.

Fur chaps of bear or goat were used on the northern ranges. Cowboys called them "hairpants." They were never worn if it looked like snow or rain because they smelled so bad when wet! Fringed leather chaps were the favorite most of the year. A belt held the chaps on while a gunbelt held the holster with Colt "peacemaker" pistol. The denim breeches had no belt loops.

A leather hatband or string went through holes in the side of the hat to become the "bonnet strings" to fasten under the chin. This cowboy has fastened his bonnet strings at the back of his head. The famous cowboy hat was designed by an easterner who toured the West—John B. Stetson of Philadelphia.

Gloves were a necessity because they protected the hands from rope burns.

Figure 127

The fisherman's oilcloth slicker became part of the cowboy's costume and was referred to as a "fish." He was never without it; he kept it rolled up and tied to his saddle to protect him from sudden cloudbursts.

The "fish" was usually yellow. The young or "green" horse was frightened by the sight and rustling sound of it and had to be taught that it was friendly.

Two versions of the slicker are shown here. On the left is the poncho which any cowhand could make himself from a few yards of oilcloth. (Soldiers during the Civil War had used oilcloth piano covers.) It was large enough to cover the man and fall down over the horse as well to drain the water off. The large hat protected the head while the kerchief caught any water that ran down the neck. Leather chaps were worn underneath as shown.

On the right is the cowboy slicker coat which is split high in back in order to go over the horse. His collar is turned up to keep the rain out. A rain slicker designed especially for cowboys (Figure 200) was later sold through mail-order catalogs.

Winslow Homer's paintings of fishermen often show them in the slicker and rain hat.

Figure 128

Figure 129

The American hunting smock was, by this time, recognized the world over as our native costume.

The utilitarian cowboy boot had been perfected so that any changes now were embellishments for aesthetic reasons. Fancy boots like the ones shown were advertised in mail-order catalogs by the end of the decade.

Although the buckskins were worn throughout the century they were more for show than function as the frontier disappeared.

Some town marshals wore buckskins or cowboy clothes but most wore "city clothes" while actually in office. Those who later toured with circuses and Wild West shows wore buckskin coats patterned more after 18th century styles than the most recent 19th century ones. This was only natural because by the '80s many men of the West were looking back and glorifying the "old days." Also America's Centennial was celebrated in 1876.

Wild West novels were the rage back east as the western pioneer and the cowboy became the newest idol of young boys. Even though the frontier was said to have no longer existed after 1890, westward migrations have continued well into the 20th century.

From the Civil War to 1900 less than 950 skirmishes between the U.S. Cavalry and the Indians occurred, making a little more than two skirmishes a month in an area of over a million square miles.

There was trouble in California with the Modocs in 1872–73, the battle of the Little Big Horn (Cheyenne) in 1876, and fights with the Nez Percé in Oregon in 1877.

After the Civil War we had a well-equipped and well-trained cavalry whose uniforms were much the same as those during the war. The addition of the gunbelt and holster with the Colt .45 Peacemaker pistol and the kerchief were the main changes.

This trooper wears the standard kepi, blue trousers with yellow stripe, and riding boots.

His side-button union-suit shirt was sometimes red, sometimes cream. Jackets and shirts were omitted during the heat of the day.

The yellow kerchief was essential to the cavalaryman. He pulled it up over the face to keep dust out of the nose and lungs. It also was used around the neck to absorb perspiration. It had many uses as described in Figures 125, 126, and 128. This famous yellow scarf was retained right up until 1948 when the U.S. Cavalry was discontinued.

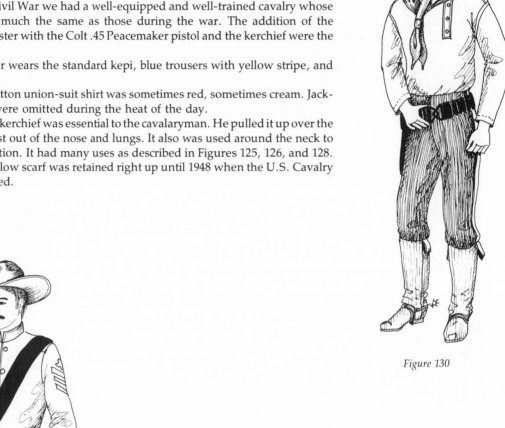

Figure 130

Figure 131

The First Regiment of Dragoons troopers made $11.00 a month before the Civil War (Figure 35). By 1870 the pay was $13.00. Many of the men were recent Irish and German immigrants. The buffalo soldier companies were black men, mostly former slaves who had moved west.

Officers went to the plains wars direct from West Point. For a time there was a surplus of second lieutenants waiting in line for promotions.

According to engravings and paintings of the uniforms, jackets varied some in length from that shown here to barely below the waist. This length was the most familiar.

The dark blue uniform had the traditional yellow (for cavalry) trim on the collar, insignia, gloves, and trousers stripe. The neckerchief of Figure 130 was yellow also.

The belt, shoulder strap with pouch, and hat were black as were the riding boots. The pistol was the Colt .45.

Many men of the West had discarded the buckskins by this time as discussed in Figure 129. The more remote the areas a man traveled the more likely he was to wear leather clothes.

Although this civilian scout wears a cotton shirt he has retained the Indian leggings and moccasins—it could be that his boots had worn out and he either made these or received them from the Indians. The style of his clothes is a mixture of civilian, army, and Indian cultures.

His shirt shows the new natural armhole and shoulder yoke still worn today. The front has a horizontal seam at the waistline with the lower part or skirt slightly gathered onto it. (Figure 133 shows the shirt on the outside.)

His hat is black, his trousers are blue. The army belt and strap are black. He holds an 1873 Springfield rifle and carries a Colt .45 in his holster.

Figure 132

There were still over 200,000 Indians in the high plains and Rocky Mountains at this time.

During the years that the white man had been adapting Indian clothes to his way of life, the Indian had been absorbing things from white culture. Notice the similarity of dress between this man and that of Figure 132. Years ago he had added the white man's shirt to his clothes. Next he adapted the kerchief, then the trousers, vest, boots, and finally the hat as shown in Figure 167.

This man shows the shirt that still only buttoned to the waist and had to be put on over the head. He has added his own bracelets over the sleeves. He wears his gunbelt buckled in the back, presumably so that he can get to the bullets quicker! His own knife and case are under his gunbelt.

He, like the white man of Figure 132, wears Indian leggings over his dark trousers and moccasins.

His hairstyle is noteworthy with its topknot and short-cut sides in front of the ears.

Figure 133

This man, probably of the Nez Percé, demonstrates the Indians' further acceptance of white man's clothing. He wears the vest over his shirt, which is on the outside. He also wears bracelets and several necklaces.

His trousers appear to have been fashioned from a blanket because of their bold stripes and rather heavy, stiff look. (They could be of handwoven Indian cloth.) He wears the breechcloth, either because of tradition, or because his trousers are actually Indian leggings like those of Figure 95, making it a necessity. The blanket he carries was probably a trade item.

One of the most startling things to appear suddenly at this time is the Indian's acceptance of the side-part hairstyle. Several contemporary photographs show it quite clearly. Interestingly, the hair is usually somewhat bouffant giving it almost a pompadour look! His long braids are wound with strips of fur. Large silver earrings are worn.

Figure 134

Figure 135

Not only the designer houses of Paris but our own theatre inspired the fashions of the 1870s. Most cities in the United States had town halls or opera houses for theatre companies traveling by railroad. Ladies saw the elaborate costumes worn by the actresses and singers and copied them.

The bustle, so apparent by the end of the '60s, had reached huge proportions by the early '70s. Since the early bustle was basically only the full skirts swept around to the back, it naturally started at the waistline. The addition of extra drapery and bows built it up rather high in back, producing a high-waisted look apparent in Figures 136, 137, and 139.

Formal bodices were heavily boned, coming down over the hips and ending in rounded points in front. Elaborate as they were, there was a certain daintiness about them with their little puff sleeves, low necks, and tight waists. This bodice and the first overskirt swag are pale green.

The second overskirt, also pulled back into a swag, is white lace and tulle. The full skirt, which often went into a train in back, was sometimes the same satin, peau-de-soie, or taffeta as the bodice, sometimes a plain white or cream. A large bow decorates the bustle. All the skirts are edged in pleated ruffles of lace or tulle. Fringe was used on many gowns. When invited to dance, the lady picked up the train and held it with a ring or loop on the side of the skirt.

Hairstyles of the '70s were swept up and back, the curls cascading down the back repeating the design of the skirts. This lady has flowers across her head matching the larger ones on her dress.

She wears a cameo or brooch on a ribbon around her neck and drop earrings. She carries a folding fan, probably lace.

America celebrated her Centennial in 1876. New clothes at the time reflected the styles of the Revolution. The hoop was still worn but it curved out at the sides and back only, with the front left flat.

The overskirt of this dress is split in front and turned back to show the lining while separate back overskirts reflect the panniers of 18th century dresses. A bow on top of the overskirt forms a bustle.

The bodice, too, is like the earlier bodice but, instead of having lacing in the front, it is filled in with a tucked blouse. These sleeves with their large cuffs reflect men's fashions, rather than women's.

Ruchings edge the bodice and the overskirts. One also is used at the top of the small ruffle above the skirt flounce. A ruffle edges the overskirts below the ruchings. Ruchings were a favorite dress embellishment during the Revolution.

This woman's hair is pulled up on the sides with curls on top and down the back, ending in a chignon. Curly bangs fringe her forehead.

Figure 136

The newly invented typewriter that was creating job opportunities for women depended on the sewing machine, for the first typewriter table was a sewing machine table and the foot pedal returned the carriage.

This dress might be worn to the office without the detachable train which fits up under the bustle. With the train it was a tea or house dress, without it a walking dress.

Reflecting 18th century styles during the Centennial celebrations, this dress had split overskirts and flounced sleeves. The bodice also resembled those of the colonial period.

Flat ribbon braid edges the sleeves, bodice, overskirt, skirt flounce, and the train hem. A tucked blouse with ribbon stand-up collar is worn underneath. These blouses were omitted in favor of a dickey and false sleeves in hot weather.

Made in poplin, taffeta, or wool for winter, they were of piqué for summer.

This lady wears the hairstyle described in Figures 135 and 136.

Figure 137

By 1871 a half million sewing machines were being produced a year. Although most dresses were so complex that they required an experienced seamstress to make them, this morning dress could be created by most housewives.

Worn over a blouse, it fastened down the front with buttons. The bodice had a wide cape-like collar over a shoulder cape edged with a ruffle. The sleeve cuffs were also edged with ruffles.

Skirt fullness was all at the sides and back, with a flat front. A skirt flounce always creates a pleasing motion as a woman walks. This morning dress could be worn on the street while doing the day's errands and must have made a pleasant impression. Fringe was often used on these dresses, adding to their motion.

The whole dress is trimmed with a dark braid which is also used for the belt. A hanging pocket attached to the belt matches the dress.

A little lace cap and gloves complete the ensemble.

This design is appropriate for a wrapper or dressing gown as well as a dress. Some coats of the period were similar in design, too, so it can be adapted to a coat as well.

Figure 138

The early bustles were so high that jackets had to begin to flare out a few inches before they reached the natural waistline, resulting in a high waist. Bustles were so large that the jacket flared out until it became horizontal as shown in this side-back view.

The separates of the '60s continued to be worn in the 1870s. Jackets of varying lengths were worn with skirts of either matching or contrasting fabrics. Sometimes these jackets were worn with a skirt and blouse, sometimes over a dress. A dark braid trims this jacket. A ruffled blouse shows at the bosom.

Whereas the overskirt of Figure 106 was full and flared, this one is straighter in front and pulled around and up toward the back. This draping of the overskirt pulled the skirts in close to the knees.

Hats were placed on top of the head with a forward tilt and a dip in the brim. This simple, tasteful hat has a feather in front. It is tied with narrow ties at the back of the head above the chignon.

One fashion print shows a walking suit in yellow with fancy black braid; another one is beige with blue embroidery.

Figure 139

Riding habits increased in popularity as horseback riding became more a sport than a necessity. Traveling could be done in carriages of all sorts, trains which went all the way to California or Montana, and steamboats up and down the rivers. There were steamships to take one to sea also. Not only would the horse soon become a luxury rather than a necessity but interest in sports and physical exercise would continue to increase.

Riding habits always follow the silhouette of the decade. The main changes through the years were usually in the sleeves and skirts. Jacket bodices had remained much the same for a hundred years as illustrated here. This habit can become the 1880s vogue with the sleeves and skirts of Figures 172 or 173. To create a habit of the '90s, use the skirts and sleeves of Figures 211 or 214. Riding dresses can be created for any period in history by using this jacket and substituting the prevailing sleeves of the period.

Riding hats have always been a feminine version of the current male hat worn forward on the head. Plumes and veils were always added. During the last part of the century women's hats were the brimmed styles somewhat similar to men's hats, and all hats were being worn with the forward tilt.

Figure 140

Figure 141

The paper pattern business was established after the Civil War and the demand for patterns was huge. In order to compete with pattern companies fashion magazines printed patterns in miniature with detailed instructions for using them.

A *Peterson's Magazine* of the '70s offered this unusual but practical apron. The editors suggested that the reader use "brown Holland with scarlet braid."

Bibs were still pinned afore, as shown here, to protect the dress bodice. The most unusual feature of this apron is the manner in which it ties around the bustle giving protection to the sides of the dress as well as the front.

This woman wears a little house or morning cap consisting of a double-ruffle over the head and old-fashioned lappets hanging down in back.

Her dress is a simple one, somewhat similar to that of Figure 136. When wearing this dress out-of-doors she would probably wear a cloth sunbonnet or rural straw hat like those of the '50s.

93

The bustle dropped to a lower position toward the end of the decade as illustrated by this dress and in Figures 143 and 144.

The skirt train was seen out-of-doors and at vacation resorts as well as in the home or ballroom. A special ruffled lining was always attached underneath the skirt ruffles to protect them from the dirt of the street or ground. It was called a dust ruffle and could be removed when dirty and worn. Not only dust but tobacco stain was a problem, too, since chewing tobacco was a common habit among men. Rings or loops slipped over the wrist to lift the train for walking, dancing, or whatever was necessary.

This polonaise is of white wool over a green-striped dress. It has buttons and tabs down the front allowing the dress to show through. The full, flared back is caught up into a bustle by a wide band and bow trimmed with the same braid as that around the skirt hem.

Especially interesting is the very new open collar, giving it a modern 20th century feeling. The cuffs of the dress are the same braid as on the polonaise.

The hat is very shallow with the brim down in front and curving up in back. It has ribbon streamers in back and a bird on top.

Because the weight of the dress moves back, the hat goes forward to balance the total design.

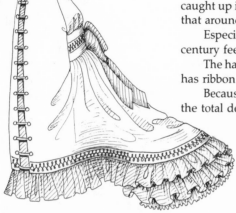

Figure 142

By the end of the '70s skirts had become so restrictive that movement was limited only to walking. Getting in or out of carriages or railroad cars took a bit of doing! Bands were used on the outside of the skirts partly for looks but partly to prevent the skirt from being torn.

There was a characteristic center panel down the back of many dresses at this time. Although it changed according to the decoration and draping on each dress it was always basically the same as shown here.

This overdress, a polonaise type, is fastened in front with a button tab at the waist. The skirt is pulled around on each side in a swag pannier toward the back where it joins the center panel. The center panel, flat at the torso, falls into a swag at the hips and knees. Two ruffles attached to the hem form a train. A third ruffle, barely visible, is the muslin dust ruffle underneath which protected the train. The lower part of the train was often detachable so that it could be removed for outdoor wear.

The dress is edged with velvet braid and a small ruffle. A double ruffle adorns the sleeve cuffs.

This dress, of fawn-colored cashmere, is worn over a black velvet bodice. The braid on both overdress and skirt is of embossed velvet. The fashion magazine which offered the pattern and directions suggested that twelve yards of cashmere and two yards of velvet be purchased.

See Figure 144 for hat.

Figure 143

94

All the coats, stoles, and shawls of the '60s continued to be worn during the '70s and '80s.

Coats are always designed to conform to the dresses underneath. As the bustle dropped, the coat fullness dropped also.

At the end of the decade new coats developed sleeves like wings which were attached at the side-back as shown on the right. They varied in length and in the decorations but were all of much the same construction. There was usually a box pleat at the center back to allow fullness for the bustle.

When collars were used they were usually pointed in back. Sometimes buttons, bows, or braid trim were used at the seam where the sleeves joined the coat.

Pleated ruffles, heavy fringe, fur, gathered ruffles, and braid were used on these coats. Some were fur-lined while others were of light, dainty fabrics for summer.

Seams were curved in to fit the back, then flared out over the bustle. They were never straight. As the bustle grew to enormous proportions in the '80s the coat curved out over it.

Hats at this time sat on top of the head. They might be tilted to the front as in Figure 142 or slightly to the back as shown here. The hat of Figure 143 is tied at the back of the head, this one under the chin.

Figure 144

Figure 145

The sleep dress of linen was a 19th century style. In the 18th century the chemise which was worn under the dress was also used for sleeping. When the blouse and pantalets or drawers became the vogue, the chemise was no longer used.

When a woman married she received a fine linen sleep dress which lasted for many years. It was often of the finest needlework.

The sleep dress shown here has a standing ruffle around the neck, front opening, and cuffs. Some had only small ruffles, some had flat ungathered lace trim, and still others were scalloped or embroidered on the edges.

Dressing gowns were knee-length or floor-length versions of the coats of Figure 144 made in linen, calico, muslin, or lawn. They looked much like the bathing cape of Figure 179.

Some combing capes like those of the '80s (Figure 179) were already being worn by fashionable women at this time.

Boys dressed much like men of the previous decade (see Figure 82). Not only are this boy's clothes made much the same but they are worn in the same manner. He fastens his coat with only the top button and tucks his trousers into gaiters.

Boots were worn at times, as were lace-up shoes and dark stockings. Red stockings were often worn, possibly as a result of the pro baseball players who made them famous (see Figure 121). Boys sometimes wore the high-top shoes with elastic insets like baseball players.

This boy's hat is a rolled brim sailor. His gaiters are of canvas worn over black lace-up shoes.

Figure 146

Figure 147

Roller skating was immensely popular during the '70s and '80s among grown-ups as well as children. Roller rinks were built even in small towns with grown-ups skating in the evening and children in the afternoon.

Women's skating dresses were ankle-length, worn with boots and hats.

Young ladies' and girls' dresses were the same as women's walking dresses. This girl wears a boned bodice that comes down on the hips with a rounded front and then curves down into a long bustle in back. There are two pleated flounces around the hem and a swag around the thighs.

She wears boots with points at the top. Her skates are fastened with a strap across the toes and another one at the instep which crosses over, goes round the ankle, and buckles. Skates were not attached to the boots yet.

Figure 148

Young boys wore jackets that looked much like the lounging coats of gentlemen as in Figure 83. They were of wool or velvet with fancy bound edges and facings.

The young boy's jacket on the left is bound with quilted satin all around the neck, front, and hem. The cuffs have a tab which goes up the arm a bit. The double-breasted jacket has satin tabs connecting the buttons. Although this jacket is belted, jackets were worn unbelted as well.

The matching knickers have tabs at the sides of the knees like those on the sleeve.

He wears tall gaiters over his shoes. Sometimes shoes and stockings were worn without gaiters. His hat is a matching Scottish tam.

This outfit was suitable for both roller and ice skating. Sometimes it was fur-trimmed.

On the right, a young boy wears the waist. It comes just to the waistline where it has a fitted band. This one has a stand-up collar and buttons down the front but one now in the Brooklyn Museum has a turn-down collar and a fly front. Sometimes they were tucked in front and had ruffled collars but they always had the waistband as shown. The cuffs are turned back.

His trousers are full pleated pantaloons which taper to the ankle. They are short and cuffed, revealing his side-button shoes.

He wears a broad-brimmed straw sailor hat with ribbon band and short streamers.

All classes of children wore this waist and pantaloons in a wide range of fabrics from homespun to fine linen.

Young girls wore dresses that were elaborately constructed like this one. It is silver gray poplin dotted with magenta and trimmed with panels of black and gray velvet. The panels go over the shoulder and down the skirt, becoming smaller at the waist. A bustle bow is made of the same chevron-designed velvet. The neckline, cuffs, and hem are banded with black velvet. The flared skirt is fuller in the back than the front.

The hair ribbon and sash are magenta velvet matching the dots of the dress.

This young girl wears a guimpe (blouse) with tucks in front and lace around the neck. The cuffs show at the dress sleeves.

Boots were made of cloth and leather. These are gray wool and black patent.

Her middle-part hairstyle has bunches of long curls held close to the neck. The hair ribbon is worn like a headband on top of the hair instead of going underneath.

Figure 149

"A prettier walking dress for a little girl could hardly be designed," stated *Peterson's Magazine* in the 1870s when describing the dress on the left, to be made from their pattern and directions. "The bottom is scalloped in buttonhole stitch, and braided above in a very simple pattern as shown, which needs no tracing, as any expert needlewoman can carry it by her eye."[!]

This little girl's charmingly elaborate dress with its tabs, overskirt, skirt, and bodice, is buttonhole stitched and embroidered of white piqué. Her matching pantalets are embroidered, too. The magazine suggests long sleeves "for the street."

Her bonnet has a shirred ruffle around the face and buttonhole stitched petals and leaves on top and back. It has a little neck ruffle to protect her from the sun.

In the center is a cloak with sleeves and scalloped shoulder cape. Appropriate colors were white, blue, or pearl-colored wool with braid trim or black-and-white plaid flannel trimmed with blue velvet.

One very interesting part of this little girl's costume are her crocheted gaiters. They are scalloped on the top and bottom with a strap under the foot and a drawstring at the top. The crocheted drawstring has tassels on each end. (Her right leg has the pantalets and skirts raised in order to show the top of the gaiters.) She has a fur muff and wears a flat little hat like those worn by women.

On the right a very little girl shows the hood and wrapper (cape) most often worn by babies and toddlers. The younger the baby, the longer the wrapper. Infants' capes were christening-dress length.

Sometimes short capes, like this braid- and tassel-edged one, were used on longer ones. Some wrappers consisted of as many as three capes of short to long lengths. Beige with blue trim was a popular combination but gray with red was worn, too.

Figure 150

Scottish outfits for very little boys were the mode after the Civil War and plaid fabrics were so popular they were used for dresses of all styles.

On the left a little boy wears a bias-cut plaid wool dress of black and white. It is trimmed with black-and-white silk and jet buttons. White was used for the collar, cuffs, and skirt band onto which was applied the black braid. The cuffs also were adorned with buttons. The sash, also bias-cut, is edged with black-and-white fringe. The dress fastens on the side-front.

He wears matching pantaloons, dark stockings, and side-button shoes. His hat is a curled brim sailor.

The little boy on the right wears a Scottish kilt, jacket, and vest of a blue, green, and black plaid. Black velvet trims the jacket, cuffs, and skirt. A little fringed sporran hangs in front while matching pantaloons are worn underneath.

His hat is noteworthy, being a tam with chin ties. A tassel on a cord is attached to a center button on top. His low-cut slippers have rosettes at the front.

Figure 151

CHAPTER 8

1880s

Troubled and Extravagant Times and the New Folklore

The '70s had seen the use of electricity in industry; the '80s saw it move into the home. There was great interest in architecture. Women's fashions reflected architectural design, upholstery, and drapery. The times were troubled but extravagant—perhaps the assymetric designs in womens dresses reflected this.

Tourism became an industry in this decade. Sports and their accompanying equipment and clothing became an industry too. Biking was so popular that bicycle clubs worked to pressure Congress to improve roads. They issued the first road maps, handbooks, and organized tours. Of the two hundred thousand miles of railroad laid during the 19th century more than a third was laid during the '80s.

The popularity of tennis, boating, and swimming brought about the use of rubber in shoe manufacture. By the middle of the '80s the United States was on the way to world leadership in oil, iron, steel, textiles, and shoes. The average factory worker worked ten hours a day, six days a week, for five hundred dollars a year. Even though shoes could be purchased for two dollars a pair they were too expensive for a laborer's family.

The floodtide of immigrants brought many tailors from Europe who worked in the clothing factories or started their own factories and stores. Many poured into the West to become homesteaders. By the end of the '80s there were hundreds of towns with European and Scandanavian names and at least one hundred newspapers in the United States printed in languages other than English.

The phonograph was here to stay while the buffalo was vanishing. The frontier was almost gone but the folklore concerning it was big-time entertainment.

By the beginning of the '80s the United States was on the way to world leadership in production of iron, steel, oil, textiles—and shoes! American-made shoes were prized items in other countries.

A new idea in footwear was the collar worn around the ankle. It was a short variation of the spat, only three inches high with just three buttons on the side.

Another new idea was the crease in the trousers. At this time it was used primarily only by very fashionable men and for formal occasions.

Straight coats with capes were important at this time. They were sometimes of plaid wool. When made of water-repellent fabric this coat was called a Mackintosh after the man who originated the idea. Mackintoshes were always lined with plaid cloth as many raincoats continue to be in the 20th century.

Bowler or derby hats were worn with this coat as well as the helmet hat of Figure 153. This hat is gray with a black band.

Figure 152

It was bicycle enthusiasts who first worked to persuade Congress to pass legislation to improve the roads around the nation. At this time roads were hardly more than muddy, rocky paths. Biking was becoming a major sport or pastime even though the tall bikes called "bone-shakers" had no brakes or chain yet. Bicycle clubs still included only a few women because of this.

This man's belted sports jacket was cutaway at the front corners to allow freedom while pedaling. He wears a white shirt, tie, and sometimes a vest underneath.

Knickers at this time were not as flared as those to come later. This man wears wool socks with fancy knit fold-down tops. His shoes are lace-up oxfords.

The hat, called a summer helmet, has a brim which is narrow on the sides and wide in back and front to shade the eyes and protect the neck. It sometimes had ear flaps which tied under the chin or on top.

A shoulder strap and pouch holds maps, first aid kit, and binoculars.

Gentlemen also used this outfit for participation in other sports.

Figure 153

Not only did bicycle clubs bring about government-improved roads but they also issued the first road maps. They even issued handbooks on organized tours.

The safety bike had been invented in 1877 and was being mass-produced by the late 1880s. It had a chain, brakes, and two wheels the same size—much the same bike we know today.

This wheelman wears clothes like those of Figure 82, fastened in the fashionable manner. The sport suit was given a special club identity by the addition of a neckerchief and matching sash of a bright color such as red, blue, or yellow.

His long trousers are tucked inside leather gaiters with little metal clips or buckles up the sides. His shoes are lace-up oxfords.

The watch on a chain in the watch pocket was an important part of his equipment as was his new map.

The visored cap is similar to a conductor's cap.

Men's mustaches now were waxed and turned up at the corners like handlebars.

This outfit was worn for fishing, shooting, and other sports as well as for biking.

Figure 154

Figure 155

Although men and women bathing (swimming) together was still frowned upon by some, seaside and lakeside resorts were booming. In fact tourism became an industry in the 1880s.

Early bathing suits were of wool knit in two pieces. The shirt often had short sleeves although occasional pictures do show sleeveless ones. Navy was the most familiar color with red or white bands around the legs, shirt, and sleeves. Suits could be ordered from the new mail-order houses.

The rubber tennis shoe was introduced and soon afterward the rubber bathing slipper. Caps like that of Figure 156 were sometimes worn for bathing.

Part of the reason for the tremendous rise of the clothing industry was that many of the immigrants pouring into America were tailors. Large numbers of these German, Polish, and Russian workers sought employment in textile and clothing factories. Many of them started their own factories or clothing stores.

This boxer wears dark, rather plain, knee breeches and a rubber cap to keep his hair out of his face. He wears no shoes. Boxers in the '80s still fought with bare fists, but boxing gloves and shorts were used by the '90s. These shorts would be much the same as the bathing suit shorts of Figure 155.

The knee breeches shown here were used for boxing as early as 1860, according to one folk painting in the Chrysler Museum which shows a boxing team clad in yellow breeches with black polka dots while their opponents wear red with white dots. They have on wide belts, high button shoes, and white stockings but no caps as this man does.

In 1877 Teddy Roosevelt boxed in an outfit like this one when he tried for the lightweight crown at Harvard. He lost.

Figure 156

Figure 157

Early baseball players used neither mitts nor field gloves but by the '90s both were advertised in mail-order catalogs.

Caps of the '80s were softer than the earlier ones as in Figure 121 although they still had a sewn-in crown. (The baseball player of Figure 228 wears the gored cap of the 20th century.)

This player shows the new lace-up shirt of the '80s with short sleeves although shirts of the '70s were still favored by some teams. The name of the team was written across the front as indicated on this one.

Knickers at this time had one belt loop in front and one in back for the dark belt. High lace-up shoes and colored stockings were worn.

Pictures show many players sporting mustaches but some are clean-shaven.

The new interest in travel brought about the two-piece sleeping suit eventually known as pajamas. The name came from India, from the loose trousers of cotton or silk worn by both sexes called *pāejāmah*. Women's pajamas were first advertised around 1919.

They were designed because of the Pullman car and were considered more dignified for travelers than the old nightshirt!

Sleeping suits came in madras plaids or blue, lavender, or pink stripes. They were of Indian or Chinese design with cord loops or frog fasteners as shown. As might be expected, they were considered a startling novelty!

Figure 158

An interesting step in the evolution of the overalls, these high-waisted pantaloons were worn over one's other clothes. They are similar to the farmers' pantaloons of Figures 28 and 87 but by the 1880s they were commonly seen on carpenters, repairmen, painters, and laborers.

This man wears the folded paper hat that came to be associated with carpenters and then plumbers. The caps of Figures 7 and 121 were seen on workers, too.

Often blue in paintings and lithographs, the pantaloons were probably denim. They were also made of white or unbleached canvas. This man's checked trousers show underneath the short pantaloons.

He wears a red undershirt which was sometimes double-breasted as in Figure 130. White, checked, or plaid shirts were frequently worn over the undershirt. Familiar also was the vest.

Figure 159

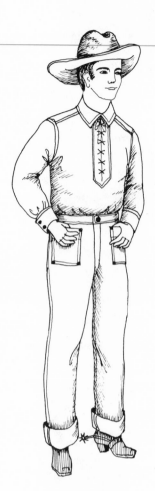

After several years of herding cattle and living the bachelor life, many cowboys decided to settle down, become ranchers, and raise a family.

By the 1880s homesteader farmers numbered in the thousands as German, Russian, Swedish, and Norwegian immigrants received government lands. In some American towns at this time languages other than English were spoken most often.

Shirts had, by this time, developed the shoulder yoke and a natural shoulder line at the armhole, as shown, but they still opened only at the chest or to the waist instead of to the hem. Most work shirts were flannel, in bright colors or plaids.

The new denim jeans were double-stitched and riveted at the points of stress. They have a waistband and front fly much the same as the jeans of today. It is believed that miners developed the idea of the metal rivets to prevent the heavy ore samples from tearing off their pockets. This man wears his jeans folded over at the hem over his cowboy boots. He wears spurs.

His hat is the large felt stetson manufactured in Pennsylvania for use in rural areas of the East as well as in the West.

This shirt continued to be sold by mail-order houses into the 20th century.

Figure 160

Before 1890 there would be over four hundred towns in Minnesota with Swedish names while some towns in the Dakotas had Norwegian for their principal language. Immigrants continued to pour in from Denmark, Iceland, Germany, Finland, Scotland, and Wales.

Many of these immigrants wore the double-breasted shirt shown here. It was the everyday or work dress for lumbermen, miners, firemen, some cowboys, farmers, mill workers, and young boys in all parts of the country although the North and West are usually more closely associated with it. Its similarity to the old European double-breasted shirt of Figure 31 should be pointed out. It was often blue wool flannel but was seen in black, red, green, and gray as well. The shirt shown here has white piping and white pearl buttons.

This man's trousers are blue denim with double stitching and rivets like those of Figure 160. They are tucked inside his canvas-top black boots, a favorite footwear during the last quarter of the century.

His cap is the shako described in Figure 7.

Figure 161

The large hat at this time was described by its content potential, such as two-gallon, five-gallon, or ten-gallon. This was not as farfetched as it may seem since the hat was actually used for a wash basin or a water container for a horse.

The new batwing chaps could be snapped on or off so that the spurs and boots did not have to be removed each time as with the older shotgun chaps. A real cowboy always removed the chaps when he got off his horse after working. Only a dude would wear them around town. Each of the large scallops had a metal snap or clip under the decorative metal disks.

This cowboy wears a checked shirt with a shoulder yoke and natural shoulder line at the armhole. It fastens only at the chest on a front panel. The fringed buckskin shirt was sometimes worn as was the vest. The coat of Figure 125 or a fur vest was worn in winter.

It was said that a man who could sing had a good chance to be hired as a cowhand and if he could make up verses "out of his head" he was sure to be hired. When the cows were tense they could be calmed by singing and guitar playing.

Figure 162

The Great Basin included the area between the Sierra Nevada Mountains and Rockies on to the Pacific Ocean.

The Paiute Indians of the Great Basin started their "ghost dance" religion in 1870 which spread eventually to the Sioux in the 1880s and finally to the Cheyenne and Arapaho. It ended at Wounded Knee Creek in 1890.

Paitues were wandering desert Indians whose culture included only the barest physical necessities while their spiritual life was complex.

Ghost dance Indians wore shirts which each man painted himself after seeing the designs in a vision. The mystic designs were believed to protect the wearer against the white man's bullets.

With the shirt this man wears a breechcloth which hangs below his shirt; his leggings are made of small animal skins. He wears moccasins and decorative headband. For winter he fashioned a cloak of rabbit skins which he holds in his hand.

In summer, Great Basin Indians wore little or nothing as shown on the right. A breechcloth of woven sagebrush bark was suspended like a skirt. Thong sandals fashioned from yucca fiber were much like Roman sandals. This man wears several strands of small beads, one of which holds a large round pendant.

His basket is for the roots, insects, and seeds he gathers for food.

(For U.S. Cavalry uniforms see 1870s.)

Figure 163

105

Indian women of the Great Basin were weavers and food-gatherers. This woman wove her tunic from small strips of sagebrush, and her little peaked cap as well. She wove basket bowls and pots and covered them with pitch to waterproof them.

Her leggings and moccasins, like those of Figure 163, were made of the skins of small animals. She, too, wore a rabbit skin cloak in winter.

Because of her foraging way of life the basket was a constant part of her costume as she wandered over the desert looking for food such as seeds, roots, insects, and small animals.

Figure 164

Indians of the Southwest lived from central Arizona east and north to New Mexico. They included the Hopi, Zuni, Navajo, Pueblo, and the Apache. The last great fighter, Geronimo, finally surrendered in 1836. He was an Apache.

By the time of the Indian wars the Southwest Indian had adopted the white man's shirt and neckerchief as shown here. It was worn over the very long (usually white) breechcloth seen hanging from beneath it here. Sometimes a leather belt was worn, sometimes just a twisted fabric around the waist.

Soft leather fur-lined boots such as these were favored over the white man's riding boots. Black riding boots and trousers were occasionally worn.

This man not only wears a kerchief but a cloth headband too. Many Southwest Indians are shown with their hair parted in the middle and unadorned.

Figure 165

Women of the Southwest had by this time adopted the clothes of the white woman as shown here. Dresses were most often two-piece but occasionally they appear to be one-piece.

This woman wears a calico blouse on the outside of her skirt. It has a small white collar and cuffs. Her skirt is plain white with a flounce at the hem. Sometimes the skirt matched the blouse, sometimes not. One old photograph shows a checked gingham skirt with a calico blouse.

Her boots are like those of Figure 165. Her hair is worn long with a middle part here but it was occasionally worn in a bun at the back of the neck.

Most photographs of this decade show little or no jewelry but silver necklaces were worn at times. Little girls dressed in the same manner.

Figure 166

Figure 167

Plateau Indians of the Northwest lived in western Montana, Idaho, Oregon, and Washington. They included the Shoshone and Nez Percé.

With the exception of the breechcloth and moccasins this Plateau Indian has accepted the white man's mode of dressing almost completely.

His shirt is held in with a fur belt while bracelets form puffs at his upper arms. The shirt has the small neckband of a dress shirt with a detachable collar. The collar is eliminated in favor of a bright colored kerchief.

He wears a long breechcloth either out of tradition or necessity, depending on whether he is wearing trousers or Indian leggings. (Legging construction is shown in Figure 95). The trousers or leggings are made of either a blanket or a handwoven textile.

One of the last items of white man's dress to be accepted was the hat, but by 1890 the Indian had adopted it too. This one is buff-colored with notched feathers decorating it.

His side-part hairstyle is described in Figure 134.

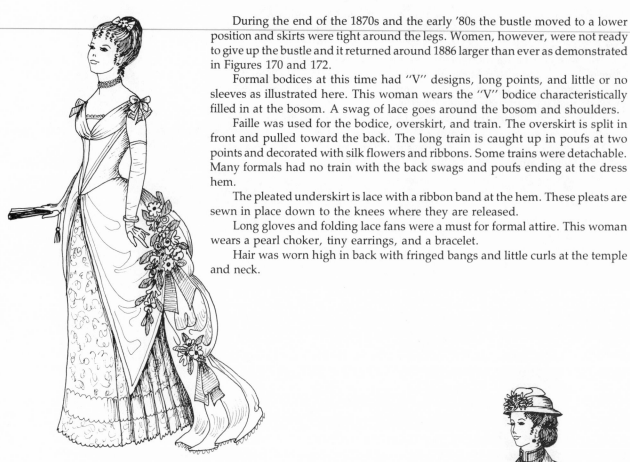

During the end of the 1870s and the early '80s the bustle moved to a lower position and skirts were tight around the legs. Women, however, were not ready to give up the bustle and it returned around 1886 larger than ever as demonstrated in Figures 170 and 172.

Formal bodices at this time had ''V'' designs, long points, and little or no sleeves as illustrated here. This woman wears the ''V'' bodice characteristically filled in at the bosom. A swag of lace goes around the bosom and shoulders.

Faille was used for the bodice, overskirt, and train. The overskirt is split in front and pulled toward the back. The long train is caught up in poufs at two points and decorated with silk flowers and ribbons. Some trains were detachable. Many formals had no train with the back swags and poufs ending at the dress hem.

The pleated underskirt is lace with a ribbon band at the hem. These pleats are sewn in place down to the knees where they are released.

Long gloves and folding lace fans were a must for formal attire. This woman wears a pearl choker, tiny earrings, and a bracelet.

Hair was worn high in back with fringed bangs and little curls at the temple and neck.

Figure 168

Women had, since mid-century, been leaving the home to work in the mills. In the '70s the use of the typewriter lured them into offices and in the '80s women were going West to become teachers. The era of the school marm was here.

The Ulster coat shown here was worn by all classes of women in all parts of the country. It was made of a variety of fabrics from white pique or flannel to tweeds, checks, and water-repellent cloth. It was seen on riverboats, trains, and coaches as it was especially appropriate for travel.

This lady's Ulster has several box pleats in back allowing it to flow out over the bustle of the dress. It has a hood, large enough to go over the hat, attached under the collar.

Capes of assorted lengths from the small ones of Figure 174 to the longer one of the men's coat in Figure 152 were often added. One coat of the period had a water-repellent cape as long as the coat. (A similar coat in the author's collection is made of black brocade velvet.)

The stand-up collar of the dress underneath shows at the neck, while its pleated flounce shows at the hem of the ankle-length coat.

Her hat is a small sailor adorned with flowers and ribbons.

Figure 169

In the early '80s the knees were so constricted by their skirts that women could take only the tiniest steps. In order to prevent ripping the skirt, bands or even small chains were sewn inside at the knees!

Asymmetric designs became the vogue for a time as illustrated by this dress. The pointed, diagonal front of the bodice is accented with a heavy braid to point up the asymmetry. The same braid is used on the cuffs.

The pleats of the skirt are stitched in place to the knee before being released. A flower-printed fabric is used for a diagonal drape across the skirt, held in place by braid down each side. A very low bustle in back is of matching fabric. It is edged with a heavy upholstery-like tassel fringe.

This lady wears a soft blouse underneath with cuff ruffles and a jabot at the neck predicting the neck interest to come.

A pillbox hat with ribbon loops adorns her head. She carries the universal lacy parasol decorated with a tassel.

Figure 170

Sleeves of the early '80s were so tight that they, along with the tight bodices, restricted movement to a large degree. Those of Figure 170 are equally tight.

The new bodice of the decade was quite long, often with a point in front. It was at times squared or rounded. The look was full-hipped and full-bosomed. Mail-order houses and clothing stores offered hip and breast padding for ladies who needed it.

Dresses at this time gave a decided impression of drapery and upholstery with fringe, tassels, drapes, and swags as shown. This interesting dress has a collar of crochet or macramé and beads around the neck. Each point ends in a tassel. Matching fringe edges the asymmetrical hip drapery.

Skirts began, by mid-decade, to become less restrictive to the legs. This skirt has the pleats released at the thighs rather than the knees, giving more freedom to the wearer.

A blouse shows at the neck and sleeves.

Hairstyles were becoming higher again after the long curls of the '70s. This middle-part coiffure is pulled up into a large bun at the back. Fringed bangs and side ringlets frame the face.

Although women were becoming more and more active in sports, their dresses made no more allowance for movement or a specific function than before the interest in sports occurred.

Figure 171

By 1887 bustles were huge again as in the early '70s. Those early bustles (Figures 136, 137, and 139) had sloped down from the back on a raised waistline, giving an integrated silhouette. The result was that the bustle seemed to belong to the person. In contrast, the new bustles of the late '80s seemed more like something apart from the body being pulled around as if on wheels. They were sometimes described as looking like horse's tails because they went out from the waist, then rounded up and over before falling down the skirt.

This jacket of striped wool opens to the waist where it is then fastened and belted. The gored and pleated back flows out over the bustle into coattails. It has the front fullness which will continue to round out in the '90s. Sleeves have a new fullness at the upper arm now with gathers at the shoulder.

The bodice underneath is the same fabric as the two overskirts which cross over in front forming two deep points. They are draped up toward a back overskirt which cascades down over them. The underskirt is the same fabric as the jacket with braid around the hem.

Hat brims for a time turned up in front and down in back, giving the appearance of a bonnet. Brims were wider in front. Crowns were high and then decorated on top, adding still more height. This lady wears the ribbon ties behind her ears.

This skirt and the sleeves can be used with the jacket of Figure 140 for an 1880s riding habit.

Figure 172

Sporting dresses were worn for hunting, boating, tennis, and cycling although the huge bikes were unsafe for children and women. Safer was a three-wheeled contraption which had one small wheel in front with a seat in back between two enormous wheels—a kind of tricycle in reverse. Both men and women are pictured pedaling it like a pedal boat.

This simple and elegant flannel suit-dress has a single-breasted jacket with edging on the lapels, pleated coattails, and pockets. The lady wears a tucked blouse underneath.

Her skirt has alternating large box pleats with two small single pleats, producing a scalloped effect around the hem.

White was used for boating and tennis dresses while dark colors like brown, black, or gray were appropriate for hunting and biking.

Her hat is a narrow-brimmed straw sailor with a wide grosgrain ribbon band.

This dress can also become a riding habit when made in black. Long muslin trousers and boots should be worn underneath and the hat should be cocked to the front.

Figure 173

Capes became the vogue toward the end of the decade although the coats of Figures 144 and 169 were still worn throughout the '80s.

This cape is flared rather than straight. Three small cape-collars flare out over the shoulders. A small double loop fastens two buttons at the stand-up collar.

The hat is the high-crowned one of Figure 172 with the front of the brim turned up into a bonnet effect and decorated with looped ribbon. It has small plumes on top.

Sometimes these caps were wool and sometimes of a lightweight or water-repellent fabric.

The lady holds the very popular parasol.

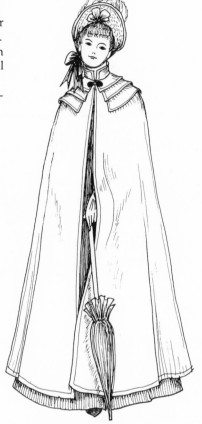

Figure 174

Figure 175

The design of sports outfits at the end of the '80s began to permit more freedom of movement although the corset was still worn. Skirts were a little shorter on all dresses, sports outfits being slightly above ankle-length.

This hiking or cycling dress has a jacket which fastens only at the chest and hangs free from there down. It has a stand-up collar that folds over. Sleeves are gathered into the armhole at the shoulder as on all dresses at this time as they move toward the huge sleeves of the '90s. Back seams, similar to those shown on the bodice front, end in box pleats at the waist allowing the jacket to flow out over the bustle. A tucked blouse with a stand-up collar is worn under the jacket.

The large pointed belt is separate from the skirt and laces in the back. Although the skirt is shortened it still has the bustle and back fullness. Bands of velvet encircle the skirt at the hem.

Gaiters of jersey or canvas were worn over shoes. They were of various lengths going to the calf, knee, and even up to mid-thigh.

This woman wears a hat much like a man's homburg. Her binoculars were usually carried in a strapped pouch as in Figures 24 and 153.

American Costume

A woman wears the Spanish-style riding chaps originally for men but adapted for women at this time in the West. Actually a skirt-like leather garment, this laces in front and back for a few inches and then opens the rest of the way down in order to fit over the horse. These chaps are worn over knickers or trousers held by canvas gaiters as shown here.

An old photograph of a group on a western expedition into Indian territory in 1886 shows a woman wearing dark chaps and a white shirt with white canvas gaiters over her shoes. She also sports a black Spanish or Texas-style hat, a bandanna kerchief around her collar, and gloves with flared gauntlets. Around the turn of the century the chaps developed into a divided skirt with pleats in front and back, giving much the same appearance as the chaps shown here.

Boleros and vests were sometimes worn as were the jackets of Figures 173 and 175.

The divided skirt developed as a riding outfit in the West about the same time that it was first worn for bicycling in the East after the safety bike came into popular use.

Figure 176

Figure 177

One amusement that may have been enjoyed at tea time during the '80s was listening to the phonograph as it played the early cylinder recordings.

Tea aprons were appropriate for entertaining at home, for walks in the garden or country, and for picnics. Out-of-doors a large straw hat (like Figure 44 or 45) decorated with ribbons and flowers was worn.

Unusual in construction, this apron has a gathered or drawstring neck which ties in back. It has ribbons attached at the sides at a point about 1⅓ yards from the neck, then pulled up around toward the back and tied. The upper part falls out in front as shown.

These aprons were usually of a sheer delicate fabric, lace, or satin. They were trimmed with lace edging or embroidery and pastel satin ribbons.

Dresses underneath were much like those of Figures 170, 171, and 173 without the jacket. A basic skirt and blouse or a simple dress like that of Figure 178 can be changed inexpensively from one scene to another in the theatre by the use of a work apron and then a tea apron over it.

1850s. Uniform of First Rhode Island militia (Fig. 60); two-flounced, hoop skirt with bodice jacket (Fig. 42); frock coat (Fig. 22)

1860s. Play outfit (Fig. 114); Confederate coat and cape (Fig. 71); walking costume with looped-up skirt (Fig. 106); Confederate infantry uniform (Fig. 69)

1860s. Sunday frock with lace apron (Fig. 114); tailored princess dress (Fig. 100); Union cavalry uniform

1870s. A Centennial inspiration with detachable train and bustle (Fig. 137); sportsman's sailing suit (Fig. 120)

1880s. Biking suit (Fig. 154); tight skirt with assymetrical design (Fig. 170); box-pleated skirt over extreme bustle for young girls (Fig. 182)

1890s. Softly gathered dress with very large sleeves (Fig. 209); tennis or seaside coat (Fig. 190); little boy's sailor middy (Fig. 218)

1900s. Blue denim bib overalls with jacket (Fig. 232); simple tucked-and-pleated dress (Fig. 246); delicate dress with scalloped lace yoke and high neck (Fig. 236)

1910s. High-waisted chemise with lace overdress (Fig. 267); army aviator's uniform (Fig. 260)

In the 1870s electricity began to be used in industry. At the same time that electricity created jobs for the woman outside the home, it was beginning to help to make her work easier in the home.

The apron was, of course, used while cooking and cleaning but it was worn while at work on a job away from home, too. One old photo of the new telephone operators called "Hello girls" shows them wearing aprons like this one over plain dark dresses like the one shown here.

Starch was important in the 17th century, then lost favor during the 18th and early 19th centuries. It came back into vogue after the Civil War to reach a peak in popularity in the 1880s.

This linen apron is embellished with cutwork embroidery and pull work. It is edged with cutwork eyelet. The neat fold creases show clearly in photographs and paintings at this time and are therefore characteristic of the costume of the period. Little girls' aprons were stiffly starched, too.

Figure 178

There was a strong similarity between the capes and robes used for lounging and those for beachwear.

Bathing capes and dressing gowns were constructed like the coats of the '70s (Figure 144) with bows or cords and tassels at the back to serve as bustles, as shown on the left. This cape has the batwing sleeves, front, neck, and hem trimmed with braid. For beachwear the cape covered a swimming suit like that of Figure 108 except that the pantaloons came to just below the knees in the '80s. They were sometimes gathered in at the knee like bloomers on the most recent suits. This lady wears a ruffled mobcap over her hair and the new bathing slippers on her feet.

As a dressing gown, this batwing-sleeved robe was made in varying lengths to slip on over the nightgown.

On the right a young woman models the combing cape which was worn over the nightgown for dressing or lounging.

Capes edged with ruffles like this one in longer lengths also doubled as bathing capes. Although there was a great variety of detail, the basic construction of these robes and capes changed little from one to the next. They were usually variations on a theme and offer many possibilities to the costume designer.

Figure 179

113

A young lady wears the youthful version of the swag and bustle. The dress is dark with a white pleated swag, cuffs, and collar. The front, below the waist, is shirred with the fullness released above the waist. This bodice is amazingly prophetic of women's dresses in the '90s.

Instead of buttons, the dress has laces down the back. It would have been virtually impossible for the young lady to have dressed herself without assistance! Although longer than little girls' dresses, it is shorter than those of grown-ups.

In summer a ruffle was fastened in at the neck and cuffs but in winter a blouse was worn underneath. Black high-button boots are shown.

The youthful hairstyle is pulled up at the sides to the crown with a fringe of bangs at the forehead. The back hair hangs down in soft curls.

Roller skating was a favorite amusement for all ages. This dress is typical of those worn for skating.

Figure 180

Tennis aprons were the vogue for a short time during the '80s. Some had bibs, as does this one, some had Tyrolean straps, others only waistbands. This apron has a pinafore bib which has no straps and is literally pinned to the dress bodice as shown. The waistband fastens with a button in the back instead of ties.

The dress under the apron is of a print fabric with a solid color swag around the skirt. The bustle matches the swag. Fringe edges the swag while chenille ball fringe trims the skirt at the hem.

Interesting little swags decorate the sleeves at the lower arm in imitation of the skirt swag. A double ruffle of sheer fabric edges the neckline while single ruffles edge the cuffs.

This young girl wears high-cut slippers with rosettes. Her tam has a yarn pompon at the crown.

Without the apron this dress was worn for roller skating.

Figure 181

Figure 182

The extreme bustles of this decade were worn by girls as well as women. Bodices dipped down in front giving a swayback appearance.

This girl shows a dress with a pointed yoke at the shoulders with a stand-up collar. The long sleeves are fitted at the shoulder but gathered in at the cuffs. A wide belt matches the yoke and cuffs.

Two skirts, with large box pleats, curve out over the petticoats underneath. The bustle holds the skirts out at the back giving a feeling of movement.

She wears dark stockings and high boots with side buttons. Her hat is a high-crowned one sitting on top of her head. Even a bird wing on one side adds to the sense of motion about the costume. Her hairstyle is like that of Figure 180.

Figure 183

Boys wore, at this time, an interesting metal tap on the toes of their shoes. It was under the sole and also curved up over the end of the shoe, protecting the toe. These taps were called "blakeys."

A young boy on the left wears a blue sailor suit with white braid, buttons, and tie. The knickers button all the way down the outseam.

He wears boots and short stockings or socks. His hat is a rolled-brim straw sailor with ribbon streamers.

On the right a little boy displays the universally popular Norfolk suit worn by males of all ages. Its main characteristic is the tucks down each side in front and in the center back. The Norfolk was always slightly long-waisted and belted as shown here. These suits were linen in summer, tweed in winter.

Knee breeches with side buttons were worn over dark stockings. These stockings were sometimes combined with the knit drawers to form a garment much like the knit tights of today.

His boots are black kid. His hat is a flat sailor with short streamers.

115

Little boys' coats were much like those of girls. This double-breasted coat is straight in front with side pocket flaps. The back is gored to curve in at the waist and then out at the hips where box pleats are set in. A tab is fastened horizontally with buttons giving the coat a bustle.

This little boy wears stockings and high-button shoes. In winter he would wear leggings to match the coat like those of Figure 185.

His rolled-brim straw sailor hat is worn on the back of the head. His hair is curly.

Figure 184

Little girls' fashions followed the fashions of their mothers as illustrated by these coats. On the left is an extravagantly decorated one of velvet with braid and lace ruffles all around the front, collar, cuffs, and pockets. Burgundy and dark green were favored colors with white or cream lace. A large satin bow forms a bustle.

Leggings might be knee-high or full length. They sometimes matched the coat or were cream-colored flannel. Her hat is like the woman's hat of Figure 169.

This coat was sometimes trimmed with white fur instead of lace.

On the right is a more tailored coat for a little girl. It is double-breasted and straight in line with a bias-cut flounce at the hem. Around the top of the flounce is a festoon caught up and gathered at intervals. The collar, cuffs, and festoon are made of the same fabric. The pleated ruffle below the coat flounce belongs to the dress underneath.

This child wears white stockings with high boots which come to a point in front. Her hat brim dips in at each side. It is adorned with cord rosettes and tassels.

Figure 185

An interesting apron frequently worn at this time by very little girls is shown in two versions. On the left it is seen from the front, on the right from the rear. The front is all one piece, sometimes rounded at the corners, sometimes not. It has a wide neck and little cap sleeves. The back comes down to just below the armholes. It buttons in back. Sometimes pockets were added.

The apron on the left is a fancy one with a scalloped ruffle and braid. One fashion magazine which offered a pattern for such an apron suggested that the ruffle be buttonhole-stitched at the scallops. It is a gray linen over a dark red dress. The apron is embroidered with white thread and trimmed with red braid.

Gray socks are worn with black high-top shoes. Her hat is like the woman's hat of Figure 172 with the brim wider in front than on the sides and back.

The baby wears a white apron over a dark blue dress.

Figure 186

117

CHAPTER 9

1890s

New Sports, New Jobs, and New Problems

The 1890 census showed that the frontier was gone. Any land with two or more people to a square mile was considered settled and that meant all but a few isolated areas. Washington, Montana, Wyoming, Idaho, and the two Dakotas were now states. Northern and southern railroad lines were joined and one could not only ride the train to California but to Canada as well.

American shoes were outselling French shoes in Europe and England. The United States invented basketball, volleyball and figure skating. The mushrooming interest in sports meant still more new shoe designs.

Bicycling was a national sport and brought to American clothing such classics as turtleneck sweaters, skirts and blouses, divided skirts, and even pants for women. The

sports craze included not only women but children as sports were beginning to be taught in schools. Street lights in many cities, by the end of the '90s, made walking and biking safe at night as well as another new sport—automobile riding.

Slums existed in large cities. This, together with new waves of immigrants from Italy, Bohemia, Greece, Syria, and Poland brought new prejudices and problems. Child labor and poor working conditions were just two of those problems to be improved in the coming decades.

The cash register of the previous decade and the adding machine of the '90s would eventually be used by women who were leaving home to take jobs. A few men were now going to work in a new building called a skyscraper.

Changes in the morning coat since the 1850s (Figure 23) have been minor. The shawl collar has given way to a notched one and the breast pocket has been added. The morning coat of the '90s was of somewhat straighter lines although on some the hips were still padded. The construction of the back seams is like that of Figure 188.

During the '90s the coat was always buttoned only at the first or top button as shown. Edges were sometimes bound with a narrow satin binding. It was fashionable to wear a handkerchief in the breast pocket at this time.

Solid colors for the coat were black, navy, gray, and brown. Popular fabrics were gray pin check, gray hairline stripe, and a rough textured gray worsted. Also important was a black background with blue and red threads, and a dark gray, subtle plaid.

A crease down the front was the most outstanding development in trousers at this time. The crease was commonplace now, being worn by men of all classes.

This gentleman wears spats over his shoes. His hat is a homburg with a wide ribbon band and bow. It has a decided 20th century look about it.

Figure 187

Figure 188

The frock coat, now called the Prince Albert, has remained fashionable since the 1840s. (See Figures 1, 22, and 81.) Both single-breasted and double-breasted, it was usually of black broadcloth of various weights with black satin lapels. Men of all professions wore this coat the year around in all parts of the nation.

The image of the pot-bellied millionaire depicted in fiction was based on certain facts of this time. It was an extravagant era with elegant dinners often having eight or ten courses during the evening.

Double-breasted vests of black or light gray were worn while trousers were most often dark. Spats over the shoes were the mode. Top hats were coming to be considered for formal wear only at this time.

A fashionable suit was called an English walking suit. It was identical to this coat in the back as seen on the left. The front differed only in that the front corners of the skirt were rounded. It was worn buttoned to the waist like this one.

Walking sticks often served more than one purpose. Some concealed swords, pistols, vials, or tiny drinking goblets inside!

120

By 1890 railroads had joined South Dakota, Montana, and Minnesota with St. Louis, Kansas City, Omaha, and Denver. One could ride the train all the way to Canada.

Chesterfield coats with velvet collars were worn in the city and for travel. They were most often black with the new fly front covering the buttons. Pockets had flaps and there was a small pocket on one side for one's watch. The more people traveled the more important the watch became.

Gray and black striped trousers, with neat creases pressed in, were worn over shoes covered with spats. The derby or bowler hat was usually seen with the Chesterfield but the black silk hat was worn, too.

Walking canes at this time might have silver, gold, or ivory handles. One popular cane for the city had an umbrella inside in case a gentleman should be caught in a thundershower.

This coat has remained in fashion up to the present time. It has been made in water-repellent fabrics to become a raincoat as well as an overcoat.

Figure 189

Sometimes referred to as a tennis or seaside coat, these black-and-white striped sack coats were shown in the most elegant fashion magazines as well as in the Sears Roebuck and Montgomery Ward mail-order catalogs.

Lapels were notched and four buttons were used down the front. Patch pockets were sewn on carefully with the stripes directly in line with those on the coat. Front coat corners were either squared, as shown, or round like those of Figure 227. Although stripes were the most common, other combinations were used. Stripes soon varied in size, too, with broad and narrow stripes used together.

Flat-brim straw hats with wide bands were considered the proper accessory for these coats.

When the coat was worn for tennis or at the seaside, shoes of white buck or black canvas with rubber soles looked smart with it.

The small bow tie and stiff, turned-down shirt collar completed this classic outfit.

The double-breasted suit of Figure 118 was still worn at this time.

Figure 190

Sport suits for biking, golfing, or hunting were made of checks or tweed for cool weather, of flannel or linen for warm. The lighter, warm weather ones were called summer suits.

This Norfolk suit has a yoke along with the characteristic pleats and low belt. Some Norfolk jackets were pleated all the way to the shoulder seam without a yoke but all had the pleats and low belt. (In the 20th century after belt loops became fashion on men's trousers, the belt on the Norfolk jacket ran through the pleat as in Figure 253.)

Knickers had narrow kneebands and were not as full as they would be a few years later.

Of special interest here are the wool socks with little loops through which ran leather straps with buckles. Although loops were used on baseball uniforms and sport socks, the idea was not applied to regular trousers yet.

The soft sport cap constructed of small sections and having a visor was the latest thing. It would still be worn in the 1930s.

A stiff-collar shirt and tie are shown here but the turtleneck sweater was worn with this jacket also, as was the cap of Figure 192.

Figure 191

The invention of the automobile would have as important an effect on clothing as the trains had had several years before. The crash or outing suit shown here was worn for driving and for all kinds of travel.

Often made of light gray linen, the coat was longer than that of Figure 190. It came to just above the knees. The more expensive crash coats had fancy piping trim. Some mail-order houses offered them in heavy textured Russian linen or in tiny checked linen. Although long, the coat still had the customary four buttons.

Trousers had the now familiar crease and the new cuff at the hem as well as the fly front, giving them a present-day look. The black belt was worn on the outside of the trousers but no belt loops were used yet.

Vests were occasionally worn over the white shirt and small bow tie. The cap was usually either white or navy.

Buckskin oxfords with tips were the very latest shoes. The tips were not perforated but they would be in a few years as shown in Figure 223.

Figure 192

With the duster coat, men carried a black bag, which looked much like a doctor's bag, for tools, binoculars, first aid, and other things essential to driving the automobile.

White linen was the fabric for the calf-length coat which was belted in back. The patch pockets included a small one for a watch. The eight buttons down the front were pearl.

The hat was outstanding because it was the forerunner of the aviator cap of the First World War (see Figures 260 and 261). The automobile helmet shown here is of silk shantung with a stiff visor and holes over the ears. The separate goggles were of buff leather with glass lenses. They came down onto the cheeks and curved up over the nose. Other hats such as the top hat and the caps of Figures 192 and 194 were worn with the duster also.

Gloves were always worn for driving. Sometimes they had fancy flared gauntlets which covered the sleeve cuffs, keeping dust out of the sleeves.

Figure 193

Ten million Americans were riding bikes by the early '90s. Bikes now had rubber tires, brakes, pedals, and two wheels of the same size.

The turtleneck sweater was designed in England for bicycle riding but was soon taken up by golfers and schoolboys. Sweaters with other collars were designed for biking, too. Some had collars which laced at the opening while some had open necks and plain collars.

Sweaters were usually wine, black, navy, or tan. One popular style had white bands knit in at the wrist and hips. Mail-order catalogs labeled all pullover sweaters at this time "bike sweaters." Anyone who has ever ridden a bike on a brisk day knows how comfortable a high-necked pullover can feel.

Thick wool socks and knickers were worn with the sweater at this time. High top shoes were especially designed for biking and other sports. Hiking and golf shoes had spikes in the soles.

There was a cyclist's cape similar to the oilcloth slicker of the cowboy in Figure 128. It was only thigh-length and came in a leather case which could be fastened to the bike.

An old photograph of a football game in 1889 shows the men of one team playing in outfits much like this one but with stocking caps on their heads. Their opponents are wearing snug-fitting shirts like the football shirt of Figure 228. Some of them also wear knit stocking caps.

Figure 194

Collars and cuffs could be purchased separately. These new celluloid-lined collars and cuffs would not wilt and they were waterproof, according to advertisements at this time. They came in a number of shapes and styles which could be buttoned onto the shirts. Extra shirt fronts could be had in starched cloth or celluloid also.

The collarless shirt shown here was also available with a flowered, checked, or striped "bosom." This bosom or front panel had a buttonhole tab at the waist so it could button onto the trousers as shown.

Plain braces or suspenders were usually red, brown, or black. Many were beautifully embroidered in silk, needlepoint, or cross-stitch on a black, cream, red, or pastel background. The two braces were now usually joined together and fastened onto buttons on the trousers as shown.

Hair was worn in a high side part by young fashionable men at this time while older men retained the middle part.

Figure 195

Smoking jackets had only one braid fastener during the '90s and until 1910. The shawl collar, pocket flaps, and wide cuffs were usually made of striped, plaid, or checked silk. Hip pocket and one breast pocket held the things needed for smoking. Often a dark satin binding outlined the jacket as shown here.

Hair was parted in the middle and oiled with oil of Macassar. In order to protect the furniture from this hair oil, napkin-like covers called anti-macassars were put on the chair and sofa backs.

This man wears creased trousers and oxfords with the new tips and squared toes. By the mid '90s American shoe manufacture became so important and admired that American shoes were sold in Europe and England. They became more sought after than French shoes.

Figure 196

The first electric lights were installed in the White House in 1891 and before long people in homes across America would enjoy being able to turn on a switch and light up a room at bedtime.

Although the new pajamas of Figure 158 were favored by dapper gentlemen and dudes, the old-fashioned nightshirt was preferred by more conservative and older men. Mail-order catalogs still featured them. Made of soft muslin or flannel, these nightshirts came in stripes or flower-stripe designs. Finer ones were embroidered around the collar, front, cuffs, and pocket in red, baby blue, rose, lavender, or black.

The bathrobe of Figure 122 was still worn at this time. It might be made of silk, wool, or blanket cloth.

Figure 197

Figure 198

Considered proper attire for professional men, this stand-up collar Prince Albert coat was advertised for doctors, ministers, lawyers, and others. The regular Prince Albert with lapels of Figure 188 was advertised also.

A variety of hats were worn with this coat depending on what one's profession was. After the turn of the century this coat was used primarily by members of the clergy. The coat was usually made of black, sometimes gray, broadcloth.

Men, at this time, started wearing the new brown shoes and stockings. They soon became so "everyday" that black shoes, as a result, were reserved for dress or formal wear.

Of interest to professional men of means during the '90s was the building of America's first skyscrapers—the office building of the future. The elevator invented in the 1850s was improved in the 1870s, thus making the new tall buildings possible.

125

An oiled cape coat of the '90s was advertised as appropriate for "motor and grip men, drivers, teamsters, miners, and farmers." It came in black and the cape was detachable. An outstanding feature of the coat was that it was flannel lined. Metal clips instead of buttons were used to fasten the front.

A sou' wester hat had ear flaps for winter protection and a wider brim in back than in front for keeping water off the neck. The hat came in either black or yellow.

This man wears boots, possibly of oiled leather or rubber. Coats similar to this one but without the cape were made of black rubber. They had pockets and flannel linings. One dressier model was a black lightweight rubber coat with a velvet collar and plaid lining.

For a policeman's coat see Figure 234. The ones of the '90s were the same as those of the 1900s.

Figure 199

Figure 200

Any land having two or more people per square mile was considered settled land. Only a few areas here and there had fewer than two people per square mile by this time, according to the 1890 census, so essentially there were no more unsettled territories—therefore no more frontier. Washington, Wyoming, Idaho, and the Dakotas had become states. The end of the frontier did not mean the end of the cowboy by any means, however.

The pommel slicker or saddle coat was designed especially for cowboys, deliverymen, circuit riders, and any horseman who had to be out in all kinds of weather. Cutaway corners at the front fit over the horse and the rider's legs. Extra zinc snap fasteners allow the front to lap over further, making the riding coat into a walking coat. There is a split in back. Shoulder caps and pocket flaps divert the rain and give extra protection while elbow patches help to prolong the life of the coat.

This rider wears a cowboy hat and leather riding boots.

A jacket-and-trousers set much like that of Figure 201 was available in black rubber or oilcloth also.

126

The average factory worker at this time worked ten hours a day, six days a week for five hundred dollars a year. The American Federation of Labor was formed in the mid-'90s and was composed of a number of small craft unions.

The "blue collar uniform" of the tradesman, repairman, and deliveryman evolved into our company blue and gray outfits of today. The tradition of blue and gray for factory workers goes back many generations in Europe. It came to America with European immigrants. The clothes shown here were blue denim but they were available in different fabrics for different occupations. Pockets were reinforced with metal rivets.

Mail-order catalogs offered this jacket in blue, black, gray, white, or striped. Newspaper ads and catalogs always gave suggestions as to who should wear which color and fabric such as white for grocers, cooks, waiters, butchers, bartenders, painters, and paper hangers. Black also was sometimes suggested for waiters. Engineers' outfits were blue-and-white checked or striped while cowboys and construction workers were offered blue denim.

One catalog of the decade referred to this denim jacket and jeans (called overalls) as riding clothes for anyone riding a horse and suggested black for those riding bicycles.

This man's cap was called an engineer's cap. Most of the caps and hats of the period were worn with these clothes. His brown brogans were called "hard-knock shoes."

Figure 201

The denim breeches of Figure 201 were called overalls because work clothes were still often worn over other clothing. This newly invented garment first manufactured in the '90s in Wisconsin was called "bib trousers" or "apron overalls" in the mail-order catalogs.

This garment, eventually just called overalls, had rivets on the pockets and other points of stress. The narrow shoulder straps were riveted onto the bib and had to be dropped down instead of unbuckled or unbuttoned.

Blue overalls were recommended for horseback riding, black for bike riding. (Denim and twill have always doubled for sports and work clothes as they do today.) Apron overalls of white were suggested for painters and blue for carpenters and mechanics.

Hats were bike caps, cowboy hats, engineer's caps, and any other appropriate for the occasion.

In 1906 the construction crews working on the Panama Canal included men dressed in the new overalls and dark shirts with wide-brimmed cowboy hats. Some members of the crews were dressed in the clothes of Figures 62 and 66.

Figure 202

Naval officers at Manila Bay in the Spanish-American War of 1898 wore this all-white service coat and trousers. Because of the heat they did not wear the navy blue uniform of identical design which was used in cooler climates. This coat style had been regulation since 1877.

Occasionally a belt was added and a few officers wore the dark coat with white trousers and hat even in the heat.

The frock coat of Figure 72 was still regulation wear for high officers in the Spanish-American War. The open collar and the belt as well as the cap continued to be worn as shown.

First-class petty officers sometimes wore navy blue double-breasted sack coats like that of Figure 118.

Chaplains wore the regular frock of the clergy with a navy cap with strap but no ornamentation.

Figure 203

For the first time in our navy's history the middy was officially worn outside of the trousers in the Spanish-American War. This classic sailor suit for enlisted men is much the same as that worn today. It has a wide collar which was sometimes blue, sometimes white. Two rows of braid trim the collar and sleeves.

The whistle was part of the uniform and a special pocket was provided for it. Notice how this influenced children's clothing in the little boy's suit of Figure 218.

All white was worn in battles at Cuba. Many men just fought in white V-neck shirts with short sleeves and white sailor trousers with black belts. No belt loops were on the trousers. Some sailors wore no shirts at all. In colder climates this uniform in navy blue was used.

The hat is somewhat like the sailor hat of today except that the brim is flared. The hat was white canvas with rows of stitching on the brim.

Petty officers are described in Figure 203.

Figure 204

1890s

The U.S. Army used the new khaki uniforms for the first time in 1898 during the Spanish-American War. "Khaki" comes from the Hindu word meaning dust.

Uniforms were still blue in 1894 (see Figure 131) when the U.S. Cavalry was called in during the Pullman strike in Illinois. (Strikers dressed like the men of Figures 62 (right) and 84.)

Officers wore khaki jackets with a blue collar and epaulettes. The jacket was a bit shorter than civilian suit jackets. Two pleated breastpockets had flaps and buttons. A scarf or bandanna was often tucked inside the collar as shown here or simply knotted on the outside.

Khaki trousers were tucked inside leather gaiters with metal clips down the center front.

Wide-brimmed hats were battered and floppy even on the highest officers. Crossed sword insignia decorated the brim as shown here. Tan gloves with flared gauntlets were worn.

In cold weather a turtleneck sweater was worn under the jacket.

Figure 205

During the Spanish-American War only 460 Americans were killed while 5,200 died of malaria, dysentery, typhoid, and other diseases.

In hot climates no jackets were worn over the blue shirts of enlisted men. Shirts fastened only at the chest, and necks were open with blue kerchiefs tied inside. Occasionally a red bandanna appeared. Pockets had button flaps but no pleats.

Khaki trousers were tucked inside natural-colored canvas gaiters which had buttons down the side. A dark belt was worn on the trousers but no belt loops were used yet. Some men chose suspenders instead of the belt and some wore both. A large floppy tan felt hat was rolled or pressed into an individual shape for each man.

When in battle soldiers like this man wore gun belts and holsters. An ammunition pouch hung from a strap while a canteen hung from the belt.

Although the Krag rifle was regulation, many men actually used the old Springfield of the 1870s and '80s.

Figure 206

129

At the beginning of the decade sleeves were growing still larger at the shoulder and upper arm while remaining fitted at the lower arm. This dress with a caftan robe has the full rounded bodice front and the high boned collar which held the chin up.

Velvet was used for the dress with white lace cut-outs appliquéd on the sleeves, collar, and hemline. Several pleats give fullness to the center of the bodice. A satin sash ties in front.

The caftan, made of a lighter weight fabric, is very full in back, ending in a small train. It is worn wide out to the sides in order not to conceal the body underneath. This dress and caftan combination is particularly versatile for theatre costumes.

This woman wears her hair in a chignon at the crown of her head and small soft curls around the face.

Figure 207

By 1893 the hourglass figure was the vogue and skirts widened to make the waist seem even smaller. There was no separation at the breasts and the resulting look was referred to as the "monobosom." Sleeves continued to balloon out as shown here.

This woman wears a formal gown of moiré. Velvet, satin, tulle, silk, brocade, and lace were also used for gowns at this time. The bodice has pleats giving fullness to the bosom. The belt is curved with ribbon streamers hanging from it.

Trim for this gown consists of lace, crystal beads, ribbons, flowers, and appliqué. Feathers, ruffles, braid, and embroidery were also favorite trims at this time.

She wears long white gloves and several small bracelets. Very little jewelry was needed with the decorative dresses. When earrings were worn they were tiny. Necklaces were rarely worn. Her hair is pushed into a wavy pompadour with a bun at the crown.

Figure 208

130

Sleeves eventually became so large that they flopped downward. The bodice fullness moved out onto the shoulders, instead of just originating at the neck as in Figure 207, and was gathered into the center of the waistline.

Ruffles at the shoulders and elbows add to the sleeve interest. The neckband and the belt are both gathered on this soft white dress.

Skirt fullness was all at the sides and back where several large pleats were sewn in on this flared skirt. Sometimes skirts were longer in back than in front, but the extra back fullness always gave an appearance of extra length even when there was none.

Hair was parted in the middle and pouffed out at the sides before being twisted into a bun at the back. Sometimes large straw hats like the "old-fashioned" ones of Figures 17 and 45 or the new one of Figure 212 were decorated with flowers and ribbons to be worn in the country or the garden.

Figure 209

Figure 210

The skirt and blouse became an American classic to remain with us until the present, with minor changes. The tucked full-sleeved blouses might be made of sateen or percale of stripes, flowers, or dots on dark backgrounds. Black-and-white or blue-and-white were popular striped combinations. Many blouses at this time had detachable collars and cuffs. This was not only practical for a working girl but also for theatre design. A costume change can be made with new collar and cuffs on a neutral blouse.

A tie was often worn as shown in Figure 214. Skirts were advertised as having a "four and a half yard sweep" or more. The ankle-length skirt shown was advertised as "canvas lined" and "velvet bound" (around the hem). Skirts were often plaid, dotted, checked, striped, or jacquard. They might be of taffeta, moiré, or wool.

Belts of alligator, seal, black silk, patent leather, embossed leather, or grosgrain had silver or jeweled buckles.

This lady wears the flat wide-brimmed straw sailor hat on top of her head. Her high-top shoes lace up. The bonnet of Figure 46 was still commonly seen in the '90s. It was sometimes worn with a simple skirt and blouse such as this.

Women wore reefer coats (like that on the young girl in Figure 220) over the skirt and blouse in cold weather.

Sleeve protectors like those of Figure 244 were worn by some office girls and factory workers as well as for house work.

American Costume

Suits were proper for walking, golfing, office work, and all casual occasions. The sailor influence was seen in women's and girls' clothes as well as little boys'.

This woman wears the short-jacketed walking suit with large sailor collar. The collar, cuffs, and skirt hem are trimmed with braid. Bands of velvet or satin were frequently used for trim also. Sleeves were ballooned at the upper arm, close fitting at the lower. This jacket can be used interchangeably with those of Figures 213 and 214.

Skirts were fitted at the waist and flared at the hem wich much fullness pleated in at the back. Mail-order houses and newspaper advertisements offered "skirt retainers" and "skirt anchors" for holding the skirts in place. A retainer was a wide belt worn around the waist; it had large hooks in back. Loops on the inside of the skirtband fastened onto the hooks taking the strain of the heavy backs off the waistband and keeping the skirt in place. The full back of the skirts gave a pleasing silhouette.

Blouses were tucked and very high-necked. Hats were flat sailors worn at the front of the head. They were trimmed with feathers, ribbons, flowers, plumes, tulle, lace, buckles, and beads. Wide belts were worn over the skirts as in Figure 210.

Figure 211

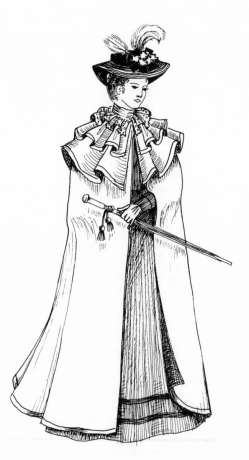

For daytime shopping trips the new adding machine, combined with the cash register of the previous decade, now speeded up sales. They also opened still more jobs for women outside the home.

Clothing design was focusing more and more on the shoulder at this time. Full capes of all lengths and sizes were for both daytime and formal wear. The flared cape shown here has two small shoulder capes over a full-length one. Lace neck ruches were separate and therefore optional. A velvet binding edged the capes. Bindings might be satin, lace, braid, or fur.

Many combinations of these capes were worn, such as the long one with only the middle shoulder flounce or, in warm weather, only the three short ones. One cape of this decade in the author's collection consists of only the largest size of the three small capes with a neckband and a ruffle standing up at the neck. The neckband is boned for stiffness and a large bow ties at the neck. The cape has a full gathered lacy ruffle at the edge. It is made of black silk with ecru lace and lace appliqué. The ties are quite long with a ruffled lace flounce at the ends.

These capes were never gathered in at the shoulders, they always flared being cut in circular or half-circular shapes.

The lady wears her large hat cocked. She carries a tailored black umbrella with ivory handle and tassels.

Figure 212

132

Cycling had been steadily increasing in popularity since the 1860s—now with the new safety bike it was the rage. (For details see Figures 153, 154, and 194.) It was bicycling, in fact that made pants or trousers acceptable for ladies. Amelia Bloomer's costume was finally respectable for sports and physical education.

These full bloomers sometimes advertised as "Turkish trousers" were, as the ads said, "so full that the division is not noticed." Even though they were the fashion, conservative people still considered trousers shockingly anti-feminine and even anti-family! In spite of this they were here to stay and even the *Ladies Home Journal* of 1895 had several advertisements for these very full, pleated biking bloomers and gaiters. The leg band is just under the knee with the fullness dropping down lower before curving up.

This jacket has the same sailor collar as Figure 211; in fact the jacket is the same except for the length. This one has pockets with flaps at the hips and a split in the back. The jackets, blouses, and bodices of this decade can be mixed and matched.

Jersey gaiters buttoned up the side, as shown here, sometimes with a tab at the top for adjustment. The blouse is like the bodice of Figure 209 with plain sleeves.

Men's caps were made in feminine versions for sports wear. The sailor and the engineer's caps were also worn.

Figure 213

Many cities and towns had street lights by the end of the '90s so it was safe to go for a ride or walk after dark. The continued craze for biking and other sports brought about more new ideas in clothing comfort and freedom.

The divided skirt of Figure 176 which was just that—a divided or split skirt—eventually was combined with the bloomers to become what is known today as culottes. They were available in either calf-length or ankle-length. The long length was used for biking as well as the shorter one.

Jacket bodies were much the same as 20th century ones. This lady shows a double-breasted jacket edged with braid or velvet. The button-flap pockets have matching edging.

Her blouse is quite mannish with its stiff detachable collar and man's tie. Softer blouses were also worn.

"Glove-fitting bicycle leggings made of jersey" were advertised. They were available in black, blue, tan, and light or dark gray. The engineer's or jockey cap was worn on top of the head toward the front as shown. The golf or touring cap of Figure 213, the wide-brimmed sailor, or the yacht cap of Figure 120 might be worn with this suit—depending on the sport the lady was engaged in. Gloves were a must for biking and golfing in order to protect the hands.

Figure 214

The nightdress (not yet referred to as a gown) was of muslin or linen with plain or fancy yokes. The sleeves of sleeping garments always reflect the fashion of other attire at the time. Nightdress sleeves of the '90s were huge although not fitted at the lower arm. Yokes were round or square of varying sizes with some coming to the waist in the center front. Round collars were used as were standing ruffles as shown here. Occasionally a ruffle was added around the edge of the yoke.

Flounces around the hem were sometimes added but the July 1895 *Ladies Home Journal* gave some insight into how fashion editors felt about them. It said, "The fancy which existed at one time for having a ruffle on the hem of the nightdress had the short life it deserved."

Dressing gowns and combing sacques like those of Figures 179 were worn over nightdresses but the combing sacque of the '90s had slits for the arms. They were of varying lengths.

Figure 215

Figure 216

Corsets of the '90s achieved the fashionable posture by pushing the rib cage forward. The head, as a result, was held back in order to compensate for balance. Steel and "unbreakable French wire" were used for support. Bust and hip pads were available for ladies who hadn't enough padding of their own.

Fine cambric drawers had up to seven rows of tucks with fancy openwork ruffles or handmade lace at the hem as shown by the lady on the left. Her corset is the longer length, coming down on the hips. It hooks in the front and laces down the back. She wears the chemise without sleeves.

On the right a lady models the short corset which comes to slightly below the waist. Her chemise has dainty puff sleeves. Corsets were advertised as in "white, black, or drab."

Petticoats were cotton, silk, or flannel, the silk one on top and the cotton or flannel underneath depending on the weather. In winter the flannel petticoat was worn underneath for warmth and at least one fashion magazine of the decade suggested that a flannel petticoat be worn all summer long "on the advice of physicians." In addition to all this, any skirt of quality was fully lined.

Two slightly different variations of the "French twist" hairstyle are shown here.

The sweater became a classic item of clothing for children almost immediately after its appearance and especially for boys. Both turtleneck and open-collar styles were seen on the golf course, at school, and on bikes in all parts of the country.

Physical education and sports were now taught in schools and the sweater was ideal because it kept one warm without restricting freedom of movement.

Most boys wore knickers gathered onto a knee band, as shown here, or the knee breeches of Figure 218 with their sweaters. Suspenders were worn underneath.

Long wool stockings or footed long linen drawers covered the lower legs. They were always in dark colors. High top lace-up shoes had pull straps at the back. The golf or touring cap was often worn with this outfit but the yacht cap and the wide-brimmed stetson were worn too.

The young newsboy was a popular hero of fiction at this time so it seems appropriate to mention here that newspapers now had comics as regular features.

Figure 217

Boys' suits now came with two pairs of pants and many were advertised as having "double seats and double knees."

The suit on the left is of "hard twist cashmere" in a dark gray diagonal pattern. The jacket is a double-breasted sack coat like those worn by men. It has a handkerchief and a watch pocket as well as two pockets at the hips. A shirt with stiff collar and a pre-tied tie are worn underneath. The turtleneck sweater was sometimes worn with the suit for sports.

Knee breeches are straight with just a slight taper and neatly creased. Three buttons fasten at the side opening. The little boy on the right wears the same knee breeches.

Dark stockings and high lace-up shoes with pull straps were worn with the suit. The derby was for older boys while little boys usually wore the sailor hat with this suit.

Little boys wore sailor middies almost exactly like those of navy men in the Spanish-American War (Figure 204). The whistle and its pocket were always a part of the costume. Both sleeves and body had more fullness than adult middies. This little boy has a high-neck blouse on under his full middy.

Both boys wear the fashionable side-part hairstyle.

Figure 218

A really new development in children's clothing was the play overall called the "brownie suit" (left). It came in blue denim or gray stripes with clip fasteners at the shoulder. Advertisements advised, "Let your child play in the healthy outdoor air," or proclaimed, "They are being worn everywhere this season." Although not until well into the 20th century would children's overalls become standard play wear, this little suit was destined to revolutionize attitudes toward children's clothes. The invention of rubber diaper covers meant that trousers could now be worn by toddlers.

On the right a little boy wears a suit that was familiar in all parts of the country for boys three to eight years of age. It was flannel in blue, tan, slate, or brown with middy braid trim. Stripes were popular as well as solid colors. Blue-and-white pin stripes with navy collar and cuffs and white braid were advertised as well as a red-and-blue striped combination with blue braid.

A drawstring or elastic gathered the middy in at the waist where it then bloused out over the hips as shown. A bow was worn at the collar.

Braid matching that on the middy was used down the outseam of the breeches.

A navy flannel or white duck sailor tam had "U.S. Navy" on the band. Dark stockings were worn with high-cut slippers with bows.

Figure 219

The nautical look was as prevalent in girls' clothing as in women's and boys'. The "reefer" or sailor jacket became the rage for girls as a result of the pea coat becoming regulation naval attire in 1886. The large sailor collar was squared in front as well as in back and trimmed with middy braid as were the cuffs and pocket flaps. Coats were navy, red, tan, or green with navy, white, black, or gold braid trim and pearl buttons. They varied in length from slightly below the waist to a few inches above the hem of the skirt. Some reefers had epaulettes like those on the toddler's coat of Figure 221.

Tams of either Scottish or naval feeling were worn with the reefer. Dark stockings and high button shoes completed the outfit. Girls wore gaiters like those of Figure 213 in winter at the end of the decade.

Dresses underneath were like women's skirts, blouses, and dresses shown in Figures 209 and 210. Dresses like that of Figure 221 but with a natural waistline were worn also.

Figure 220

Figure 221

Very little girls wore full coats with lace-edged collars over dresses like that of Figure 222. Shoulders were broadened with epaulettes over the full sleeves. Buttons were huge and fastened the coat from a center panel underneath, giving an appearance of a box pleat in front. In summer, coats were white piqué, in winter white or cream flannel.

Large floppy hats decorated with ribbons and plumes were worn with the coats as were high button shoes and white stockings.

On the right a little girl shows the dress that was universally worn at this time. It was seen everywhere in many interpretations which varied only slightly from this one. The variation was usually in the collar which might be round, square, pointed, sailor, ruffled, cape-like, small, or stand-up. Advertisements always pointed out the large hems which could be let down as the child grew.

Fabrics were plaids, checks, stripes, and calicos, pink and blue being the favorite colors. Piqué, lawn, or percale were summer fabrics, flannel the winter one.

This little girl wears dark stockings and high-cut slippers with bows. Her hair is a middle-part style with fringe bangs. When she wore a hat it was like that of the toddler on the left.

Toddlers wore high-waisted, long-sleeved dresses with smocking or tucks. Actually they were rather plain, the quality being in the fabric, lace, and workmanship.

Slippers with one strap and a button were seen with short socks in warm weather. Hair was worn in curls all over the head as shown.

Babies wore long dresses with a yoke at the shoulders. The yoke was usually circled with a lace ruffle as shown on the baby in the carriage. Long sleeves had ruffles at the wrists while a ruffle stood up at the neck. Cape collars like that of Figure 221 (right) were familiar also. Baby coats usually had capes around the shoulders as in Figure 250.

Rubber diaper covers were used at this time so babies and toddlers enjoyed a freedom they had never had before—especially in cold weather.

The new rubber nipple was popular and sold through mail-order catalogs. The toddler holds the flat baby bottle with the new nipple. The baby holds a rattle.

Figure 222

CHAPTER 10

1900s

A Modern Sophistication, the Arts, and Ecology

Just as the railroads were completed joining all the major cities of the country, the automobile and the airplane came along. One era was completed and another begun. Before the '90s there had been only a few dozen automobiles. In the following decade there would be several million and new clothing styles to wear while riding. One in forty Americans had telephones and many homes in the city had indoor plumbing.

The West was calm now and Americans would have to find their excitement elsewhere. The modern art movement was on in the cities and modern architecture was here. Phonograph records were a national craze and the musician would soon take his place beside other heroes. In 1903 the first movie telling a continuous story was made. Both the musician and the movie star would eventually have an influence on American costume as would the new Olympic stars who gave us both sports clothes and underwear styles.

The idea of the assembly line revolutionized factory work and enabled mass production of needed items. By mid-decade nine out of ten men were wearing factory-made clothes called "ready-mades."

Our modern transportation, communications, and mass production were beginning to make the southerner and northerner, the easterner and westerner, the immigrant, and the Indian all look more and more alike. Men's clothing was becoming standardized.

As the 20th century swept America into a modern sophisticated era efforts were already being made to preserve our natural environment with parks and wildlife refuges.

By the 20th century men's clothing had become so standardized that a code of rules was developed much like military regulations. Changes in fashion in the 20th century would usually be minor such as the length or width of trousers, shape of lapels, number of buttons, manner of fastening, and the shape of the shoulders.

The sack coat was the style with the frock coat still being worn by some men, usually the older ones. At the beginning of the 1900s nine out of ten men and boys were wearing ready-made factory clothes.

Single-breasted round-cut sack coats were still worn with only the top one of the four buttons fastened as shown here. The watch pocket was still prominent. Edges were stitched or sometimes bound with braid. The straight vest matched the coat. Popular colors were blue serge, black, and dark gray. Small plaids of green and brown, tiny black-and-white checks, and herringbone tweeds of navy, brown, or gray were the customary fabric patterns.

Shoes had the newly invented extension soles with perforated tops, vamp, and lace stay. The fedora hat of soft felt had a curled brim with a creased crown. Canes or walking sticks were plainer although the extravagant ones described in Figures 188 and 189 were still used.

The tuxedo was introduced in England and soon came to the United States.

Figure 223

When the Wright brothers made their historic flight in 1903 they wore dark suits like this one with the cap of Figure 192.

The square-cut sack coat was a little longer than it had been a few years before. It always had four buttons with the top one high on the chest as shown. The handkerchief and watch pockets had flaps like the hip pockets. Favorite fabrics included a plaid of dark and medium brown mixed with olive. Gray pin checks as well as black-and-white checks were favored too.

The straw hat of Figure 190 and the derby of Figure 225 as well as the fedora were commonly seen with this suit. The tan-and-white shoe was new and fashionable for sports wear and spats were still worn. The stiff detachable collar stands high while the bow tie is quite small.

This suit was seen on college students, politicians, business men, and men of all walks of life in all parts of the country.

Figure 224

In 1903 the first automobile crossed the continent from San Francisco to New York in 63 days! The driving outfits of Figures 192 and 193 were still worn as well as the Ulster coat shown here.

For driving in bad weather, the Ulster could be purchased in either black or yellow rubber or oilcloth. A dressier raincoat was made of waterproofed mackintosh cloth with a plaid lining.

Slant pockets facilitated warming the hands in this handsome coat still worn today. Favorite colors for a heavy winter coat were navy, brown, black, tan, and gray.

This coat was available not only in a variety of fabrics but also in a variety of lengths. Some coats were thigh-length of corduroy with leather trim. There were also shorter leather ones with fur trim. This style lends itself to modification so easily that it has great potential for theatre design and individual characterization.

Figure 225

Figure 226

The Ulster of fur was worn in all parts of the nation which have a winter season. Gold had been discovered in Alaska in 1896 and enough settlers were attracted to qualify this area for territorial status by 1912. During this time of growth many of these coats were worn into the territory.

Some of the furs advertised included calf, "curly dog," bearskin, and Russian buffalo. Also popular in ads were coonskin, Norway seal, black seal, otter seal, Astrachan fur, beaver, and chinchilla. The quilted linings were usually waterproof. Some coats were wool or duck (waterproof) outside and lined with sheepskin.

The double-breasted Ulster of fur usually had fancy braid or cord fasteners but occasionally they were plain like the wool coat of Figure 225.

Hats were European style with flaps on the side which could be pulled down over the ears.

141

American Costume

A unique form of breeches that was destined to remain a classic appeared at the end of the '90s in England. The jodhpur was a combination of knickers with gaiters or leggings. It appeared at the same time in the uniforms of England's troops in India and Australia—the name coming from a state in northwest India. The jodhpur was designed for bike riding and well designed, for it solved the problem of the trousers getting caught in the bicycle chain.

The man shown here wears a matching round-cut sack coat with the new jodhpurs—a very natty outfit. Both are of tweed. He wears a high, stiff-collared shirt and small bow tie. A turtleneck sweater might also go with this outfit. His hat is the golf or touring cap and he wears leather gloves.

The practical design of jodhpurs made them suitable for many other sports as well as biking. They were soon used for hunting, hiking, horseback riding, and in a few years they would become famous as aviation attire. The U.S. Cavalry would eventually adopt them.

Figure 227

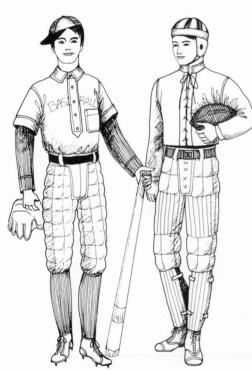

Figure 228

Uniforms and equipment were available for just about any sport by the beginning of the 20th century. Stores and catalogs offered the baseball outfit on the left. The short sleeve shirt has cuffs and a turn-down collar with piping on the edges. It was offered in a long sleeve version too. The name of the team was put on the front. Long undershirt sleeves show at the arms.

Knee pants were quilted in squares as shown and a webbed belt ran through the loops. Belt loops were used on baseball pants several decades before they were used on regular trousers as shown in Figure 121.

The cap called the "college cap" is that still worn today. This man wears colored stockings and the newly designed baseball shoes with spikes. The glove and ball bat are those advertised at the time.

On the right a player wears the new football uniform of the 1900s. His shirt has a stand-up collar and laces down the front. His knee pants also lace in front and the quilting is of a different pattern at the thighs. Catalogs offered plain quilted pants like those on the baseball player for football as well. They also have belt loops.

The football player wears padded shin guards over his stockings and lace-up football shoes—the beginning, along with the pants, of specially designed protective garments.

The most interesting part of the football uniform is the leather helmet. It is made of a band around the head with smaller bands going up to the crown. An open space after each band allows for ventilation. Ear flaps with a hole over the ear are fastened with a strap under the chin.

See Figure 194 for football clothes of the previous decade.

142

The revival of the Olympic Games not only caused interest in sports outfits but in men's underwear as well, inspiring the sleeveless undershirt and boxer shorts.

Bathing suits were available in two styles. The man on the left wears the one-piece style with buttons on the shoulders. It was of cotton knit and offered in navy blue, sometimes with white binding on the edges as shown, sometimes plain. Advertisements for this suit read "made like a Union suit."

Two-piece suits like that on the right came in cotton or wool, the wool model being more expensive. They were offered in black or navy with white or red stripes at the bottom of the shirt, around the legs, and sometimes at the neck and armholes. V-neck suits were available, as were sleeved suits like that of Figure 155. The more expensive wool suits were recommended in advertisements "to prevent chills."

Boxers and track athletes of all ages wore shorts coming to just above the knees, like those on the right. Some were gathered onto elastic at the waist and quite full while others fit more snugly like these. Some pictures show a shirt like the bathing suit top tucked inside the shorts.

Young boys wore swim suits like these; little boys wore only the shorts.

Both men wear their hair in the new side-part style.

Figure 229

The buttoned sweater became a favorite for casual wear, both away from home and for lounging or smoking at home. Fancy smoking jackets like that of Figure 196 were still worn by some men but, for the majority, the new sweater suited most of their needs.

Sweaters were advertised in gray, black, brown, or navy, and the more expensive ones were sometimes offered in fancy knits such as cable stitch and decorative ribbing.

Shirts and ties were always worn underneath the sweaters in advertisements but the plain collar was sometimes buttoned up without a tie. It was rarely, if ever, worn open at this time as the open or polo-shirt collar did not come into fashion until the '20s and then was filled in with a scarf.

Coat sweaters were literally coat sweaters in that they were single or double-breasted copies of the sack coat with collars and lapels like those of Figures 118 and 224.

Turtleneck sweaters (Figure 194) had by this time become fancy with horizontal stripes either all over, around the hips and sleeves, or across the chest. They came in cable stitch, ribbing, and other novelty knits also.

The side part was the very latest thing in men's hairstyles.

Figure 230

Men's pajamas were at this time quite oriental in design. (The origin of the pajama is described in Figure 158.) Expensive ones were made of silks usually in stripe or patterned stripe designs as shown. Flannel stripes were worn in winter and they, like the silk and cotton pajamas, were of oriental designs.

The cuff of the trousers shown here was the very latest style and predicted the fashion that would eventually be used on all men's trousers.

Bedroom slippers were also familiarly seen at this time. Felt ones of the shape illustrated here were shown in most mail-order catalogs. They often had a contrasting felt or leather binding on the edges. Slippers of the same design were called "carpet slippers" and were advertised as made of "genuine Brussels carpet." Some stores offered fine kid or alligator slippers of the same basic design, sometimes with elastic insets in the sides.

Nightshirts were still worn by older and more conservative men less interested in fashion.

Figure 231

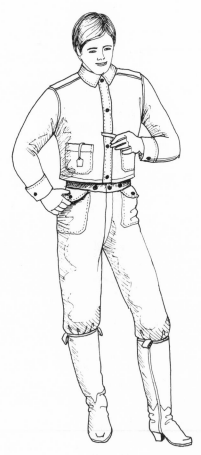

Figure 232

When the 20th century began the West was much like the rest of the country because the mail-order houses had enabled westerners to buy the same clothes as everybody else. Only Oklahoma, New Mexico, and Arizona remained territories and in a few more years they would become states.

The lack of the frontier now caused an interest in conservation. President Theodore Roosevelt set aside the first wildlife refuges, which were the beginning of our national park system.

Denim jeans were still called overalls while what we now refer to as just overalls were called "bib overalls" at this time. This man wears the overalls and short jacket that have come to be American folk clothing recognized and sought after all over the world today.

Overalls (without bibs) were sold in blue denim, tan denim, and black-and-white or black-and-gray striped denim. Solid black ones were advertised as "Texas Ranger overalls."

Mail-order catalogs recommended "black and white hairline checks" for lumbermen, grocers, farmers, harvesters, grain elevator operators, and others.

Blue denim bib overalls and a jacket the same length as the sleeves were recommended in ads for railroad workers, mail agents, miners, and carpenters. White duck bib overalls and short jackets were recommended for miners, paper hangers, and painters. Panama Canal construction crews wore an assortment of clothes including these dungarees and those of Figure 202.

The shirts of Figures 160–162 were usually worn with these American dungarees. "Dungaree" comes from the Hindu word *dungri* meaning a coarse cotton fabric for sailor or work clothes.)

Plenty of pockets were always included for the watch and "cigarette makin's" for roll-your-own cigarettes.

By 1900 one in every forty Americans had a telephone. Many of those phones were in general stores and grocery stores which served as community centers. Store owners who invested in telephones did not mind taking messages or lending the phone because it brought customers into the store.

By the start of the 20th century the work apron had developed adjustable straps and specialized pockets for the tools of various occupations. Instead of rivets as on the overalls these aprons had pocket corners reinforced with leather triangles and extra stitching. Machinists and carpenters wore this apron as well as grocers and retail clerks. Fabrics used were khaki-colored duck, white duck, and blue denim.

Heavy brown shoes with high tops called brogans were worn for work.

Plain shirts, suit coats, or long-sleeved union suit shirts were sometimes worn with the apron instead of the shirt, tie, and vest as shown here. Sleeve garters were commonly used to hold the shirt sleeve fullness out of the way instead of rolling them up. A cuff protector or gauntlet of celluloid could be worn over the white shirt cuffs to keep them clean.

Figure 233

Police uniforms consisted of double-breasted knee-length coats and trousers of very dark blue or black. A round, high-crowned hat with a metal plate was favored during the 1890s and 1900s instead of the billed cap of former years as shown in Figure 93. The billed cap or shako returned to use in the 1910s.

The black rubber policeman's coat shown on the right was worn over the uniform in rainy or cold weather. An extra flap in the back, across the shoulders, gave protection from rain as did the shoulder caps at the armholes. Straps at the wrists were used for adjusting the sleeves.

Mounted policemen wore the still-popular slickers and pommels of Figures 128 and 200.

The first movie film telling a continuous story was produced in 1903. These early 20th century policemen were immortalized in the movies as the old "Keystone Cops."

With the western frontier no longer in existence and no more stagecoach hold-ups, Indian fights, or range wars, excitement now would come from train robberies. It was no coincidence that that first movie story was the melodrama *The Great Train Robbery.*

Figure 234

Dress up occasions were not just parties but included going to see the vaudeville shows, romantic plays, and operas which were being booked in all parts of the country now. Practically every town had a music hall and many had elaborate opera houses.

Formal gowns were often of sheer fabrics and lace in delicate colors. The bosom still curved out from the waist and the posture was swayback. The cream-colored gown shown here has lace on the sleeves and in the "V" of the neckline. A soft fabric comes over the shoulders and bosom and then crosses over at the waist. Two large pink roses decorate the bosom. Waistbands and belts curved down in the front under the full bodice. Beads and sequins were used on many dresses along with lace.

Skirts were fitted at the waist and hips, then curved in below the hips before flaring out at the hem. This skirt has back fullness which goes into a small train. For formal wear, trains were very long.

The lady holds a large-crowned, soft-brimmed hat adorned with pink roses matching those on the gown. Hats were fashionable for garden parties at this time.

The "dog collar" or choker necklace consisted of several strands of pearls held in place by bands of diamonds or other stones as shown.

Hair was teased into a pompadour or side poufs and then twisted into a bun at the crown. Sometimes little ringlets hung in front of the ears.

Figure 235

Dresses were of delicate fabrics such as voile or lace with the new interest at the shoulders and neck. This soft dress has a scalloped lace yoke and very high neck on the soft gathered bodice. It buttons in the back. Many bodices at this time were tucked like that of Figure 244 (left) while other tailored styles opened in front like that of Figure 244 (right). Sleeves still have fullness at the shoulders but predict the fitted ones to come. There is new fullness at the lower arm.

The waistband and belts of the decade curved down in front accentuating the swayback look. Skirts kept close to the thighs down to the knees where they then flared out. This skirt has lace panels set in at intervals around the hips with extra fullness pleated in, adding to the hemline width. Many skirts of the period were just plain gores without decoration of any kind but having this general shape.

Favorite colors were pastels especially blue, green, lilac, and cream. Lots of white lace was used with these pale colors.

In contrast, one very familiar dress at this time was all black with lots of tucks and a brooch or cameo at the neck.

Simple house dresses and those of rural women and working girls sometimes had gathered flounces like Figure 244.

Hair was pushed toward the face and then doubled back to the crown where it was twisted into a bun. It was teased and coaxed into soft waves. Little curls often encircled the face and hung at the nape of the neck.

A 1908 photograph of women in the Navy Nurse Corps shows them wearing very plain versions of this dress in all white. The bodices were tucked like that of Figure 244. A description accompanying the photo read, "A dress like that generally worn by the civilian nursing profession."

Figure 236

Women's literary circles were popular and women were said to have been more widely read than their husbands and brothers. Women's clubs of all kinds were experiencing tremendous growth as women became concerned with social problems. A proper ensemble for a woman's club meeting or for any daytime affair was the suit.

Made of wool or moiré, such suits were often trimmed with satin, velvet, or braid. This jacket has lapels that go all the way to the waist where it fastens with a hook and eye. If the corset and a woman's own body did not produce the needed curves, she simply purchased extra padding for the bust, hips, or "bustle." Curves were essential to beauty during the 1900s.

The gored skirt was the most commonly worn skirt at this time. Flared flounces were usually added as shown. A variety of designs were used for attaching the flounce as illustrated in Figure 238.

Colors for these suits were black, tan, black-and-white tiny stripe, dark blue, gray, or brown. Black was a favorite color for trim.

"Rainy day suits" were made of water repellent cloth.

The hat shown here has the wide brim turned up high on each side and down at the front and back. It is worn toward the face, giving an upswept look. It is decorated with flowers, feathers, and ribbons.

Figure 237

Women were out of the home more and more for work and for volunteer work. The General Federation of Women's Clubs grew from 50,000 at the end of the '90s to almost 1,000,000 by 1910. Women were concerning themselves with public health, public safety, and social injustice.

Coats and capes for these daytime activities were heavily decorated with braid and fur. On the left a hip-length cape has a flared standing collar edged with fur which continues down the front. The cape is flared but less so than the capes of the '90s. Each of the horizontal braid or velvet bands ends with a button. Favorite trims were strips and bands of plaid fabric, velvet, fur, braids of varying widths, and beads.

The coat on the right has a bodice like that of Figure 237, which opens to the curved waist. The coat skirts are flared only slightly more than the skirt. Three rows of narrow braid enhance the lapels, cuffs, and skirt flounce.

Fur scarves and "collarettes" were extremely fashionable. They might be of large pieces or made up of several sizes of animal tails as shown. Furs came from chinchilla, opossum, stone marten, bear, muskrat, and lamb. Less expensive ones were made of imitation fur. The lady wears a matching muff.

Brims of the large hats were curled and cocked into many shapes but always decorated lavishly with ribbons, flowers, feathers, and tulle.

Figure 238

American Costume

High-fashion clothes inspired by those of Paris were already taking on the looseness of the decade to come. This elegant walking suit in bright red has several rows of matching red braid on the edges for a decorative yet subtle look. The coat is full and flared. The sleeves are so full that they hang in a vertical line at the wrists when the arms are bent. The coat edges are trimmed with a loop braid giving the impression of scallops.

The skirt, although looser than those of Figures 237 and 238, still has the hem fullness that flips out below the knees. This was partly achieved by the cut, partly by the petticoat.

The white fur scarf and the large white muff are adorned with ermine tails. The ends are fringed with small white tails.

Her hat predicts the huge styles of the 1910s as seen in Figures 264 and 268. It is black with large swathes of white tulle completely covering the crown.

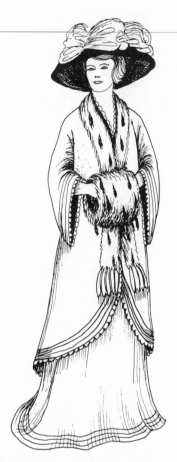

Figure 239

Some people were alarmed at the spread of motoring. Some were even more alarmed that women were learning to drive. Even though more and more people were driving, it was still considered a sport and a pastime. It would be a while before people began to think of a car as a necessity.

Dusters or automobile coats were just long versions of suit jackets as seen in Figures 237 and 238. They often had velvet collars and piping on the lapels, cuffs, and yoke. Sometimes they had a waistline seam and sometimes they were princess-style. Pockets were always important so that a lady had places to keep items needed on a trip.

This woman's coat has a fly front with hidden buttons, but buttons were used on top as well. Some coats were double-breasted. Black, brown, tan, gray, and dark blue were favorite colors.

Her blouse has a mannish stiff collar which stands high. She wears a tie.

Automobile hats were always draped with large veils usually of chiffon. Few roads were paved, with the result that the motorist had to cope with mud in wet weather and dust in dry. The veil was necessary and gloves always protected the hands.

Figure 240

Public bathing was still considered shocking by some and therefore was engaged in with clothing that was much like that worn for other occasions. Even for golf and bike-riding clothes were still basically dresses with only slightly more freedom than dressy clothes.

Swim clothes were called bathing suits by the mid-1900s. This bathing suit was popularly offered in stores and mail-order catalogs. A sailor style of dark blue or black, it has a white duck sailor collar, tie, and wide band at the hem. The tie is embroidered with anchors. The dark dress was advertised as available in "granite cloth or mohair which shed water well and do not cling."

Full bloomers were worn underneath the dress and were attached to the waistband. The cap sometimes worn with the suit was like a 20th-century shower cap. It could be purchased in rubber, lined with cotton, or in "oiled silk" which was not only waterproof, but transparent. One advertisement suggested that the cap was "also useful during housekeeping for dusting."

Black stockings and heavy canvas slippers of either black or white were worn. The canvas slipper had tape trim and ties.

A rubberized cloth bathing suit bag of blue or black held not only personal articles but also the popular inflatable water wings.

Figure 241

Figure 242

Kimonos became popular during the Art Nouveau period. They were available in "fancy figured Japanese challie" or "fancy fleece-down flannel." Solid bands of coordinating color edged the neck, front, and sleeves. There was usually shirring at the shoulders as shown. If a woman preferred not to wear her kimono loose, sometimes a cord and tassel belt came with it. These lounging robes came in an assortment of lengths. Short ones were worn over skirts or nightgowns.

Similar robes had high necks with collars and tie belts. They were advertised as "eiderdown bathrobes or lounging robes." One fashion print shows a sailor collar like that on the bathing suit of Figure 241. Otherwise the robe was the same as this one.

The lady holds a curling iron to help achieve the hairstyle she wears. Waving irons with several small prongs were available as were kid hair crimpers, "aluminium hair pins," celluloid imitation tortoise shell hair pins, combs, and "rats."

Women in Colorado had obtained the right to vote before 1900 while those in some more eastern states still could not legally make wills. Being freer of some of the old restrictions than those in the East, women west of the Mississippi seemed less shy about asserting their independence.

Although the name "culottes" would not be used until after 1910, women were openly wearing the full divided skirts for riding both the horse and the bicycle by the end of this decade. This was especially true in the newer states.

This garment is an interesting combination of a skirt and the chaps of the 1880s as shown in Figure 162. The main difference is that while the chaps were two separate pieces, this riding skirt is made in one piece. It does, however, wrap around the legs in a similar manner and fasten with buttons all the way down to its hems.

Gloves with gauntlets and fancy stitching were always worn to protect the hands. The blouse opened over the chest and fastened with pearl buttons. Both the blouse and divided skirt are of khaki or gray. In brush country in the West they might be leather.

This lady has the wide brim of her western-style hat turned back against the crown in front and down in the back. Her hair is arranged in a long braid.

Figure 243

It is a subject for debate whether the new gadgets eased woman's work or just speeded it up—allowing her to do even more. At any rate the stores and mail-order catalogs had the most marvelous array of gadgets. There was no recipe or household task so small that someone hadn't designed a new implement to do it with. A large number of homes in the cities had indoor plumbing by the early years of the decade.

Advertisements at this time show a great variety of aprons as well as household gadgets. One apron (left) was recommended for when "You want to work in the kitchen in your good clothes." Called the "allover apron," it was seamless with armholes that fit loosely over the dress as shown. It tied in the back at the neck and the waist. A lady could have her choice of blue or brown checked gingham.

The bib apron on the right was most fashionable as it had the fullness gathered in at the waistline and caps or "epaulettes" on the shoulder straps. The skirt was gathered onto a waistband which tied in back in large sashes. These aprons were usually of solid colors with dark braid trim as shown. Expensive ones had tucks and insertion or embroidery.

Some ads show this same style apron with ruffles at the shoulders. Many had rounded skirt corners with a ruffle all the way around. Advertisements in 1902 showed aprons identical to this one but without the epaulettes. Plain gathered skirt aprons without any kind of bib were worn, too.

The woman on the right wears gathered sleeve protectors with cuffs over her long fitted dress sleeves while working. For dust cap see Figure 241. She holds a wire carpet beater. The woman on the left holds a 1903 "revolving egg and cream beater."

Figure 244

Dresses (not yet called jumpers) were worn over a guimpe (blouse). They usually had low necks and full short sleeves. They were often of plaid wool in winter and gingham in summer. Fabric bands of coordinating colors were used for trim and belts. Dressy ones might be of "pearl" or cream-colored flannel.

Bodices were full in front and curved at the waistline like women's dresses and skirts were almost always pleated. This dress has an appliquéd band around the neck which imitates the crossed belt.

The guimpe was fine linen or soft cotton. It might be silk for very expensive dresses. This bodice is tucked and the neck is high.

Dressy oxfords tied with ribbons were a favorite shoe for girls. They were of black patent leather or white canvas.

The young girl holds a large hat like that seen from the side in Figure 250. It has flowers around the gathered crown. Coats were still the reefer of Figure 220. Older girls wore the sailor dress also.

Figure 245

A charmingly simple dress of the period was this tucked and pleated one. The bodice is tucked from shoulder to the curved waist giving the fashionable fullness in front. Pleats go all around the full skirt. The high neck and cuffs are plain. In fact, the dress is completely unadorned; its beauty lies in its construction. One example was pale blue with a white leather belt. Checked or plaid ginghams and practical colors like gray or brown were worn for school and play.

Oxfords tied with ribbons were the mode as well as the high-top shoes of Figure 220. The reefer coat of the '90s was still worn in cold weather. This girl's sailor hat lies on the floor beside her but she might also wear the hat of Figure 250 or a sunbonnet.

At least 1,700,000 children under age sixteen were employed in factories and fields during this decade. Laws were passed in 1907 prohibiting young children from working more than 66 hours a week and from night work! Photographs show some of these children working in dresses like this one with an apron added and the "allover apron" dresses of Figure 248. Boys often worked in clothes like those of Figure 247 (right), made usually of coarse cloth and dull colors without trim. Although plain and often somewhat rumpled, they were of the same basic lines as fashionable clothes. Virtually all photographs show dark stockings and lace-up high-top shoes like those of Figure 247 on both girls and boys.

Figure 246

151

Both the ice cream cone and chewing gum were introduced in this decade.

The sailor look, already a classic, was to remain a favorite right up to the present. Almost every little girl had at least one sailor dress. The middy dress shown here came in linen or chambray. Colors were blue, tan, or red with white soutache braid trim. The dickey was white piqué as was the tie.

This little girl wears ribbon-tied oxfords but the boots of Figure 220 were still commonly worn. Her hair is parted on the side and tied with a large bow.

In cool weather, she wears the same reefer coat as that shown on the boy.

The sailor look was as important for boys as for girls as shown by this reefer (sailor) coat. A young boy wears the dark-colored coat over checked knee pants and suspenders. He wears a white shirt and tie but the turtleneck sweater was often favored. Some reefers had the "storm" or square sailor collar in back.

His shoes are heavy brown ones with rounded toes—the latest thing. They have pull straps at the back. He wears dark stockings. His cap is a golf or touring cap worn by all ages of men and boys.

All the boys' clothes of the '90s were still worn at this time.

For the clothing of child laborers see Figure 246.

Figure 247

Little girls wore the practical "allover apron" for play. It was usually put on over the dress but sometimes worn in place of a dress. Belted only in the back, the little apron on the left also fastens down the back with pearl buttons. These aprons were usually sold in either blue or brown checks or solid gray and trimmed with piping on the collar, cuffs, pocket, and belt as shown. Advertisements recommended this type for children two to eight years of age.

On the right is a belted apron usually worn by girls aged two to twelve. It was sold in either blue and white, red and white, or brown and white checked gingham. It, too, buttoned down the back. Piping was used on the belt, collar, cuffs, and pocket of the finer quality aprons; cheaper ones had no trim of any kind.

Both children wear large ribbon bows in their hair. The little girl on the left has two bows of a striped ribbon. Both have bangs.

High button shoes were usually preferred with the apron as shown. Heavy lace-up shoes like those on the boy of Figure 247 might be worn with plainer ones.

For clothing of young children employed in factories and fields at this time see Figure 246.

Figure 248

Figure 249

The two basic styles of suits for little boys were still the Norfolk and the sailor suits of Figures 183 and 218. Both were worn the year round for dress-up.

The concept of comfortable, tough clothes for freedom in play had been evolving for several years. The "brownie suit" of Figure 219, recommended for both boys and girls, established the trend for sensible play clothes which continues today.

On the left a child wears "brownie overalls." Although recommended for both boys and girls they were advertised in separate ads. Those shown in the girls' section of advertisements and catalogs were usually enhanced with "fancy trims" such as lace, embroidery, or braid. Those for the boys were somewhat plainer with large bow ties at the blouse collar. Only very young girls wore them but overalls were recommended for boys aged four to twelve. Straps were crossed in back, and buckles and hook fasteners were used in front on the blue denim or gray-and-white striped overalls.

Advertised for both boys and girls, the "romper play suit" on the right was for ages two to eight. It came in either blue or red with white trim. The bodice was gathered at the shoulder yoke and at the low waist seam where it was belted. The legs were full at the hips and tapered at the ankles. They were sometimes gathered at the ankle. White piping was used on the belt, yoke, collar, cuffs and pocket as shown. One mail-order catalog recommended this suit as a "clothes saver."

Little girls wore full coats with large sleeves. They were made hip-length, finger-tip length, or dress-length as shown on the left. Colors were blue, red, or cream with black, white, or blue collars and cuffs. One advertised coat was black-and-white check with red flannel collar, cuffs, and buttons.

Sometimes a sailor collar was used with an embroidered eagle on the sleeves. Very dressy coats were of cream flannel with velvet trim. For spring they might be cream or white poplin, or white linen. For summer, white piqué was preferred with insertion and lace on the collar and cuffs.

The little girl's large hat is decorated with ribbons but sometimes plumes or tulle were used. In summer flowers encircled the crown. Her stockings are short, her low-cut slippers have one buttoned strap.

Babies wore long "wrapper" cloaks of cream or white with capes. These cloaks (coats) varied only in the style of the cape and the amount and kind of trim. They were shown in magazines, newspapers, and mail-order catalogs by the dozens with only slight variations. This one has a small flared cape yoke with a flounce gathered onto it. The cape and coat skirt have satin ribbon, lace, and braid trim as well as tucks. Cream-colored or white sateen was always used for the lining. Summer cloaks were of white silk or piqué.

The dress underneath is much like that of Figure 222. The fitted cap is made of cream flannel and lace.

One magazine suggested that the cloak could be shortened when the child grew older and wore shorter dresses.

Figure 250

CHAPTER 11

1910s

World War I and the Modern Woman

Alaska gained territorial status in 1912 as a result of the settlers drawn by discoveries in 1896.

Each of many new movie studios was turning out from three to five movies a week. An American president rode in an airplane. Art classicists were jolted by the New York art show of American Moderns and French Postimpressionists and again when the Metropolitan actually purchased a Cézanne! As if that weren't shocking enough, Isadora Duncan campaigned for women to do away with their corsets to enjoy the "natural figure."

The U.S. Public Health Service was bringing down the death rate in America while public high schools were doubling in number. Seventy-five million dollars were appropriated for road building by the Federal Highway Act of 1916. The income tax was introduced.

Montana elected the first woman to the House of Representatives in 1916, the same year that the military chased Pancho Villa back into Mexico.

War in Europe had been going on since 1914, the *Lusitania* was sunk in May 1915, and America declared war April 6, 1917. Corset manufacturers soon began converting the 8,000 tons of steel formerly used for ladies' corsets to ammunitions. The "natural body" would soon become the style as old corsets wore out.

When the war ended women were wearing lipstick and eye make-up, bobbing and bleaching their hair, driving cars, and even smoking. The war made the wrist watch, shorter skirts, and loose clothes the fashion. It was evident that the old ways were not to return; freedom, once experienced, is not readily relinquished. It was said that American women went into World War I still in the 19th century but came out of it in the 20th. The Nineteenth Amendment was ratified in 1920.

The tango became the rage in the United States before the First World War—after it went from South America to Europe. The dance appealed to all classes and all ages of people

This formal outfit was worn while doing the tango at elegant clubs, parties, and in the movies. The black tail coat had satin lapels and padded shoulders.

The waistcoat was always white and very low cut with rounded collars. The vest with points was introduced at this time and has remained in fashion right up to today.

Shirts had a stiff front and collar with pearl buttons or studs. A small white tie was worn.

Trousers were tapered in a little at the ankles. A braid or satin band followed the outseam and a crease was always pressed in the trousers.

A black opera hat, white gloves, and white spats were all essential to the look. The new hairstyle was oiled and combed straight back.

The morning coat of Figure 187 was still worn at this time also. The tuxedo was familiar, too. It had been introduced in England during the '80s and eventually was accepted in the United States.

Figure 251

Trouser cuffs came into fashion at the end of the previous decade and would remain popular to the present as would the crease.

Suit jackets were the sack coat with slightly rounded corners. Although the four-button coat was still popular the three-button one was now worn, too.

One outstanding new design in men's clothes was the vest with points at the waist—another feature remaining in style today. This whole costume has the look of today. Only minor changes have taken place in the decades since.

The touring or golf cap was favored for sports and all casual wear. Knickers were still in style and might be substituted for the trousers (see Figures 191 and 194). Sweaters of both previous decades were still advertised at this time.

The man shown here sports the latest hairstyle, oiled and combed straight back.

During the war farmers, factory workers, and coal miners could dress better than they had in the past. Farm families in general were able to purchase things they could not previously afford because they were getting fairer prices for their crops. This would continue until the depression and should be taken into consideration when designing costumes for this time.

Figure 252

In 1890 there had been only a few dozen automobiles in the U.S. By 1917 there were five million!

Sport suits for automobile travel (or riding locally), bike riding, flying, hiking, golfing, and country outings were an important part of the American scene. The jacket of the time was the Norfolk with the belt running under the pleats now instead of over them as in the past (Figure 191). The belt had also moved up to the natural waist instead of being lowered.

Jodhpurs were the rage and were worn for all sports on into the 1930s. (By World War II they would be reserved just for horseback riding.) By 1910 they laced at the side of the lower leg instead of buttoning as in Figure 227. They had double thickness on the inside of the legs and seat; it was sometimes suede, other times the same cloth as the jodhpurs. Knickers and wool socks were still worn and can be interchanged with them.

Lace-up boots were the latest in men's footwear, probably an outgrowth of the lace-up high-top shoes which had been used for sports for years. Heavy wool socks were sometimes worn over the jodhpurs in favor of boots. Made in a variety of fabrics, this sports outfit might be tweed wool, checks, or the new khaki.

Touring caps had no band and were no longer gored as in Figures 191 and 227. The visor is large and the front of the cap falls out over it.

Boys and men of all ages accepted this suit. The jacket of Figure 252, the coat sweater of Figure 230, and the turtleneck sweater can all be interchanged with this Norfolk jacket.

Figure 253

Figure 254

The khaki uniforms of the Spanish-American War (Figures 205 and 206) gave way to the greenish khaki or "olive drab" around 1902.

In 1916 U.S. troops were ordered into Mexico to capture Pancho Villa and his band. Army officers wore riding boots and jodhpurs as shown.

Jackets were curved in at the sides to fit the body. Collars stood up and there was piping at the edge of the cuffs. Four pockets with button flaps were always on the five-button jacket.

The "peaked" hat worn by officers would remain regulation up to the present. It was a shako with a wire running around inside the flared crown. This wire was bent so that the crown curved up in front in a peak.

Both naval and marine officers wore uniforms that were much the same as this. Naval officers usually wore no belt and their coats had no lower or hip pockets. They preferred the leather puttees of Figures 255 and 260 (left) to boots.

While actually in chase the army officers wore the shirt of Figure 255 with a dark blue tie, as did even General Pershing. It was probably because of the heat of the Mexican climate.

157

It was the cavalry troops that chased Villa back into Mexico in 1916. Their uniform consisted of jodhpurs (called "riding breeches" by this time) and shirt as shown. They wore leather puttees. Officers wore riding boots as seen in Figure 254.

Leather straps had been replaced around 1910 by the new heavy webbed ones. A kind of carry-all belt with pouches all around was supported by two straps or braces. It was referred to as the "Sam Browne" or British belt after the British general who designed it. It was permissible to wear only the right shoulder strap at times.

Shirts opened only part way down as shown. Some men were pictured wearing only the undershirt (Figure 130) during fighting. A tie was added for dress occasions.

A broad-brimmed felt hat was called a field or campaign hat. In 1912 the brim was stiffened and four "dimples" were pushed in instead of the two of former years. These formed what was called the "Montana peak." The cord around the crown was of the branch color or gold for officers. The famous yellow scarf remained regulation until 1948 when the U.S. Cavalry was no more.

The Krag army rifle was issued after 1890. The holster carried either a Colt .45 or a Smith and Wesson .38 handgun.

During Pershing's pursuit of Villa some airplanes were sent as observers and messengers. It was the first time the army had used planes! Since it was a cavalry mission the riding breeches were naturally worn by these first pilots and therefore became part of the air force uniform.

Figure 255

Figure 256

High naval officers still wore the frock coat of the 1860s (Figure 72) and the service coat of the 1890s (Figure 203). Officers of the navy air force, however, dressed more like army officers as described in Figure 254.

This chief petty officer's coat was regulation from 1913 and worn during World War I. (It changed from four buttons to three in World War II.)

His stiff collar and soft bow tie have a relaxed look more like the sailor kerchief than a dress tie. The blue cap has become soft and rounded with a patent leather visor.

The 1913 regulations ordered chaplains to wear single-breasted frock coats with six black covered buttons similar to the coat of Figure 198. These regulations also allowed dungarees to be worn. Men engaged in work that might be damaging to their regular uniform and men aboard submarines were permitted to wear them for the first time.

A typical uniform of enlisted men of the U.S. Navy of World War I consisted of middy and flared or "bell-bottom" trousers with a front flap opening.

The middy had a slightly dropped shoulder line and a pointed yoke at the chest. It was folded under at the hips. Sleeves were full and gathered onto cuffs.

A white undershirt showed at the neckline. The traditional black folded kerchief was tied in front in a horizontal knot as shown. A soft black sailor tam had the name of the man's ship on it.

Three white braid stripes on the cuffs indicated petty officers, ship's cooks, bakers, and hospital apprentices. Two stripes meant seamen second class while one stripe showed a man to be a third class seaman.

Enlisted men as well as officers were allowed to wear dungarees in order to preserve the uniform after 1913. The proper regulation hat always accompanied the work clothes.

Figure 257

The first time that jodhpurs were officially worn as military attire was by the British Imperial Volunteers and the Colonial Australian Lancer troops during the Boer Wars in 1900. The British wore boots, the Australians the new leg wrappings believed to have originated in India. By 1915 soldiers of Germany, France, Italy, and Russia were wearing jodhpurs.

The uniform of the U.S. Infanty in World War I consisted of jodhpurs and leg wrappings. (Puttees are defined both as cloth wrappings and as leather gaiters in dictionaries and military records. This book refers to the leather gaiters as puttees.) Photographs in army archives show soldiers wearing not only leg wrappings and puttees but also boots and canvas gaiters.

The basic jacket had a stand-up collar, five buttons, and four pockets with button-down flaps. The flaps rounded down into a point for the buttonholes. The entire jacket was tailored with top-stitching as shown.

The overseas cap could be folded flat and put into one's pocket when not worn. Men also wore the campaign or field hat described in Figure 255.

Records state that artillerymen wore leather puttees like those of Figure 260 (left), but Captain Harry S. Truman of the 129th Field Artillery was photographed wearing lace-up boots like those on the right.

Figure 258

159

American Costume

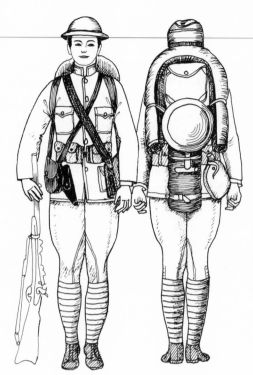

The field outfit of the American Infantry for active service was adopted in 1917. The uniform is the same as that described in Figure 258. Shown here is the equipment added to it for active service.

On the left a soldier wears the British steel helmet and carries a rifle which was either the Krag, used by the army after 1890, or the Springfield which was often used. A strap over his left shoulder holds his haversack for rations and provisions. The strap over his right shoulder holds his gas mask on the left hip. (Sometimes the gas mask was worn in front with the strap around the neck.) An ammunition belt is fastened around the waist with a holster and handgun suspended from it, shown under the haversack.

On the right a soldier wears the overseas cap. His helmet is fastened at the center of the pack. Directly under it can be seen the handle of the entrenching tool (shovel). The shovel in its canvas cover appears just above the helmet.

Under the shovel and helmet is the knapsack of either leather or canvas for extra clothes and the like. Strapped over the pack, in horseshoe fashion, is the poncho blanket and hanging on the right near the soldier's hand is the canteen in its canvas cover.

All this equipment weighed over sixty pounds! Climbing out of a trench with a full pack was no easy task, especially when a soldier was already fatigued.

Figure 259

The navy, army, and marine aviators all dressed in similar uniforms. On the left is shown a navy aviator uniform worn as early as 1914. Navy flyers wore their khaki jackets without belts. They usually had no lower pockets but the breast pockets with flaps were like those of the infantry as was the stand-up collar.

Jodhpurs buttoned at the outseam. They were worn with leather puttees which fastened in center front.

For dress they wore the peaked shako cap of Figure 254, for flying the leather helmet and goggles as shown here.

Marine flyers wore the same jacket with hip pockets and the field hat of Figure 255.

On the right an army pilot wears a jacket with an open collar and pleated breast pockets. The hip pockets are attached at the top and hang free at the bottom. He wears the brown leather belt and strap which the army favored.

His jodhpurs are worn with wool socks and lace-up boots.

The overseas cap was regulation; the leather helmet and goggles were used for flying. Aviators in all branches liked the neck scarf described in Figure 261.

Figure 260

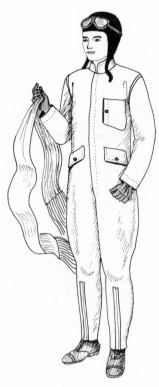

During the latter part of the war a rubberized canvas one-piece flying suit of khaki was designed for navy flyers. It was known as the "overall suit" and was put on over the uniform to protect it. It had plenty of pockets and zippers! The front and the tapered legs had the very new zipper closures. This suit seems to be the forerunner of our supersonic flying clothes as well as our space clothing of today.

This flyer wears the leather helmet with goggles and leather gloves. He holds the scarf which was used for cleaning the goggles, wiping the face, and keeping the neck warm. It was worn for aesthetic reasons too because it was so dashing while flying in the wind. The movies helped to popularize the scarf. A close-up of an aviator sitting in a plane had no movement but a scarf flapping in the wind gave the scene a sense of motion. Gentlemen bikers of the '80s (Figure 154) had used the scarf in the same way.

Figure 261

Although uniforms for nurses were not officially prescribed until 1924 they were worn several years earlier by navy, army, and Red Cross nurses.

The Norfolk style jacket of Figure 268 served as a uniform as well as the stand-up collar service jacket worn by men of the military (Figure 258).

An interesting cape of 1918 was worn over the uniform. It had a high stand-up collar and fastened with three buttons down the left side. Long slits went up in front of the arms almost to the shoulder. The arms came through the slits and the front was belted with a wide matching belt allowing the flared back to hang free. Pockets were added to the rather straight front panels. Buttons along the arm slits could be fastened so that the garment could be worn as a traditional cape. Service insignia pins were displayed on the collar.

The wide-brimmed hat, rather mannish in style, varied according to each individual. Some nurses had very flat, stiff-looking brims while others curled them up on the sides and down in the front as shown by this woman.

Women of the Naval Reserve Force were photographed in 1917 in blue suits almost identical to that of Figure 268 with their white blouse collars open at the neck. Their hats of similar design were white. They wore white suits in summer instead of blue.

The coat of Figure 269 as well as the cape were used by women in the reserve forces and nursing corps.

Figure 262

At the beginning of the decade the swayback, round-bosomed corsets of the previous decade were discarded in favor of the natural figure. The idea was helped along by Isadora Duncan who danced barefoot and campaigned for the natural body and freedom of movement.

This formal gown has the raised waistline popular during the early 1910s. A wide bertha around the shoulders is accented with a large pink rose in front. Sleeves under the bertha are edged with tassel fringe. An overskirt which laps over at an angle in front has the same fringe. The "peg top" skirt is full at the knees and tight at the ankles. The front of the skirt is pulled up, causing it to drape around the legs.

The lady wears long gloves and holds a folding fan. Her hair is puffed out at the sides and pulled back in a bun. Her headband has a plume which swirls around in a round shape. Slippers with buckles took the place of boots.

Figure 263

Figure 264

Peroxide was first used for bleaching the hair at the beginning of the decade and hats were huge, plumes and feathers making them even wider.

Waistlines went up as the natural figure image replaced the artificial corseted look. The sleeve underarm seam went directly from the belt with extra fullness pleated in. Lace was used on almost every dress at this time.

Skirts were draped in the most extravagant swags and pleats as shown. One fashion print of 1918 showed an almost identical design as this in the back of a dress.

The fur boa became the vogue as well as all kinds of fur scarves and collars. Boas of other materials were worn, too.

Carrying a purse was a mark of fashion as well as a necessity now that face powder was popular. By the end of the decade a number of cosmetics were used. The new slippers were worn with dark stockings, some of which had embroidered or beaded designs on them.

162

By 1914 women could vote in twelve states—all west of the Mississippi. While American women struggled for the vote, a designer in Paris, Paul Poiret, was producing what was called the "one legged woman" look, his dress designs so restricted women's legs.

Skirts were restrictive in design already, but to make them more so bands were placed around the lower legs limiting movement even more. This pale gray dress has a green satin band around the legs creating the "hobble skirt." Only small quick steps could be taken; thus stepping into streetcars or automobiles and going upstairs became difficult and sometimes dangerous. The "hobble" was reminiscent of the restrictive skirts of the 1870s as seen in Figure 143.

A redingote of the same pale gray is worn over this dress and left open as shown. The lower collars, cuff band, sash, and buttons are green satin. The dress underneath could be worn without the redingote.

Small hats and cloches came into fashion by 1913—hats often looked like flower pots at mid-decade. Long white kid gloves and small clutch purses were familiar. Muffs were popular as were umbrellas and ostrich fans.

Figure 265

At mid-decade before the war fashions were feminine and glamorous and seemed to be heading in the direction of the designs of the '20s. World War I would, of course, turn women's thoughts toward practical, comfortable, sports clothes.

Fur-trimmed coats were very full at the body and hips but became narrow at the lower legs. They often fastened with only one button or no button at all, being wrapped around the body and held in place. Poiret introduced kimonos of similar shape and in wild, exotic designs and brilliant colors.

Live models were first used by Poiret who traveled over Europe and America with nine mannequins to publicize his creations. His trouser-dresses which he named "culottes" shocked people and would not be accepted in America until after the war.

All ages of people enjoyed dancing the tango. Women danced in their close-fitting hats with the feathers reflecting their movements in a dance of their own.

Slippers developed straps at the instep at this time. A purse on a chain or strap was popular as one could hang it over an arm while dancing.

Figure 266

Hemlines went up to the top of the boots at mid-decade and the chemise with its high waist was considered "graceful, practical and very modern."

The overdress was often a part of the chemise with one, two, or three tiers but the chemise had just one skirt at times, too. Lace was used on many of these dresses. Some were Russian-style with fur trim. Serge was recommended for morning, velvet for afternoon, and satin and lace for evening. Some were even made of cotton and were washable. One fashion magazine suggested that a silk sash be used with a washable dress so that no one would guess that it was washable! This lace and satin chemise has an interesting ribbon and rosette hanging sash.

Hair was teased and frizzed with the curling iron so that it appeared very wavy and thick. It was pushed toward the face and then pulled to the back and fastened with a large bow as shown.

Umbrellas were either carried closed or used to protect ladies from the sun.

In May 1915 the *Lusitania* was sunk off the coast of Ireland. The war was to bring about many changes in women's clothing.

Figure 267

In 1916 Montana elected the first woman to the House of Representatives and the U.S. Cavalry chased Pancho Villa back into Mexico. The men who participated in that conflict wore leather gaiters (sometimes called puttees) with their jodhpurs.

Many of women's clothes at this time and during the war were inspired by the clothes of men. Gaiters or puttees were worn by women almost immediately. They were put on over the high top shoes as shown here.

Suits were mannish too but they were also comfortable and practical—and modern. This woman wears a suit which is similar to the Norfolk suit. It has lapels and an open collar. Her blouse is buttoned up to the neck. The stock tie blouse was sometimes seen (as in Figure 269) as was the frilly jabot blouse. Sometimes a man's tie was added for a very tailored look. Popular colors were blue, nile green, orchid rose, and oyster white for dressy suits. Dark or checked fabrics and khaki were preferred for casual wear, linen for summer.

Large flat-brimmed hats with rather squared crowns were commonly worn. Some had just a hatband, others plumes or flowers.

Figure 268

164

War was officially declared in April 1917 and women in America and England took over many jobs previously held by men.

Two coats worn by these women became fashion classics—the tailored boy coat and the trench coat. The trench coat at this time even had the shoulder panel, the button cover flap, and adjustable sleeve straps that it still has today.

The coat shown here was seen everywhere. It has wide lapels, epaulettes, and sleeve straps. The pockets are quite low on the hips and the wide belt is dropped slightly below the waist. It was usually of a dark color.

Hats were somewhat mannish too like this one. The blouse is a stock tie with a stick pin.

One very new item at this time was the wrist watch. Its importance was realized during the war as women worked at helping to run the country.

This coat was worn by women in the military services also, as described in Figure 262.

Figure 269

It was said that American women went into the war years still in the 19th century and came out of them in the 20th!

The knit dress of 1918 ushered in the 20th century style of soft casual knits. The success of sweaters for men inspired sweaters and sweater dresses for women, too.

This woman wears a two-piece sweater dress of wool. It has a large sailor collar and bands of color at the wrists, hips, skirt hem and collar. A cord tie with pompons is tied at the neck. Similar dresses sometimes had soft tie belts worn low and loose. There were one-piece sweater dresses of much the same design and the Norfolk style two-piece dress of Figure 277 was worn by women as well as girls.

Hats were knit, too, as is the one shown here. Some were cloches, others more like stocking caps. Shoes had very pointed toes and straps over the instep.

One startling thing to come about at the close of the war was the bobbed hair. Although shocking, short hair was here to stay. Lipstick was worn as well as eye make-up.

Corset manufacturers had converted to ammunition during the war. The eight thousand tons of steel annually required to make corsets would help the war effort. It was inevitable that once women experienced freedom they would not want to go back to the restrictions of the corset.

Figure 270

165

A metal-framed portable windshield was designed to protect a lady's face from wind and dust! Only a few of the more elaborate cars had windshields before the war, so this, at mid-decade, was a rather advanced idea. A frame fit over the head and rested on the shoulders while an adjustable support held the windshield in front of the face. A leather case for the windshield is carried in this lady's hand.

Coats were full and long. Many coats during the last half of the decade had chin-protector collars which could be pulled up over the chin, worn folded as shown, or unbuttoned and lying flat as a large collar. The design of this coat resembles that of the Norfolk jacket (Figure 191) with its pleats and low, buttoned belt. It has wide cuffs on the loose sleeves and large hip pockets.

Waterproof fabrics were used at times, making this a raincoat. This style was so popular that it was still advertised in the mid-twenties.

Hats for automobile riding still had large chiffon veils both for securing the hat in wind and for protection to the skin.

Figure 271

Figure 272

The war ended in November 1918 and a lot of people assumed that women would go back to the corsets, long skirts, and old ways of dressing. But women had experienced freedom in clothing and they certainly were not going to turn back the clock now. Bobbed hair, trousers, and make-up (including lipstick and mascara) were here to stay. The ladies had worn overalls, dungarees, and knickers during the war and they enjoyed their freedom.

Two sports outfits would be worn by women well into the '20s. On the left is a sports suit for hiking, camping, cycling, and other activities. It consists of a rather mannish thigh-length coat over knickers and wool socks with decorative tops. The young lady sports a man's shirt and tie under the coat. For women not ready to appear in the new knickers pleated skirts could be worn over them as shown in the girl's outfit of Figure 278. Wool tweed, khaki, and linen were popular fabrics.

Her hat has the brim turned up in front and down in back.

On the right is a sports outfit used primarily for horseback riding. It is knee-length and worn over knickers. (Jodhpurs for women would be worn during the 1920s.) It, like the coat on the right, has the new dropped waistline.

Note the khaki cloth puttees or gaiters like those worn by military men (Figure 255) and soon taken up by the ladies (Figure 268) for daytime wear as well as for sports.

The hat was inspired by the cocked hats of the Spanish-American War. The cocked brim is held in place by a button and buttonhole. Her blouse has a stock tie which is still worn for riding today.

Both jackets shown here were often worn in the casual unbuttoned manner of Figure 278.

166

Bathing suits at the end of the decade were made up of a chemise top and the newly respectable knickers.

A V-neck is filled in with tan on this black taffeta bathing dress. A tan sash is worn low at the hips. The sleeves are open at the shoulders predicting the new sleeveless styles to come in a few years.

Knickers, worn underneath, have a wide band which covers the knees.

Canvas slippers have ribbons wound around the ankles like ballet shoes. A kerchief is tied around the head, with the long ends hanging at the side.

The lady bather carries a beach bag for her towel and other items.

Figure 273

Women have always taken clothing styles from men but after the turn of the century it must have seemed to some men that nothing of theirs was to remain exclusive.

Another form of male trousers feminized by the ladies was the pajama—and feminized it was, deep peach being the favorite color. Even the trousers cuff was borrowed by the girls.

This soft jersey or silk top was thigh-length. Interesting sashes were attached at the sides, on the hips. They were pulled to the back, crossed and returned to the front where they were casually tied as shown. The sashes, cuffs, and neck facing were of a cream color.

Although pajamas would never be accepted by many women they would take the place of the long nightgown for the young and modern who were more daring.

This lady wears the new bobbed hair.

Figure 274

The new kimono which appeared at the end of the war was a somewhat more authentic shape than the one of the previous decade seen in Figure 242. It resembled the pre-war coats shown in Figure 266 with its narrow hem and full body.

Advertisements read, "Hand embroidered Oriental crepe de chine in flower designs." Favorite background colors were rose, pink, purple, and black with black or dark contrasting colors on the sleeve and front facings. Two large cord "frog" fasteners were used. Sometimes only one large button fastened it. Some advertisements show plain flowered kimonos without the facing bands.

This woman's hair is worn with the new side part and short bob. The ends are combed onto the cheeks while the crown is raised by teasing. This new hairstyle and the new clothes appeared at about the same time that the Nineteenth Amendment was added to the Constitution.

Figure 275

All the boy's clothes of the previous two decades were still worn at this time. Special clothes for sports activities for children were now a common sight.

One of the favorite outfits to appear was the boys' baseball uniform. Sold both for make-believe play and for actual team participation, it was usually of light gray flannel, with blue or red trim as shown. Belts were worn but pictures rarely show a buckle in front; this was apparently traditional with professional baseball uniforms as seen in Figures 157 and 228.

Baseball caps worn in imitation of professional players were jauntily placed backwards or sideways or worn with the brim turned up as shown on this young man.

He wears stockings to match the trim of the shirt, knickers, and modern-looking high-top tennis shoes. They were of white canvas with black rubber soles and binding and a round emblem over the ankles.

Figure 276

The Norfolk jacket of men and boys was eventually used as inspiration for women's and girls' clothes.

Two-piece dresses in the tailored styles were worn by women for career and daytime activities as well as by schoolgirls. This tunic top has the button front opening to one side. Top-stitched tabs come from the shoulder down to the hips. The collar and cuffs are top-stitched too. A wide patent leather belt is worn at a lowered waistline. The skirt laps over in the center front where it fastens with matching buttons.

These dresses were often of a solid dark fabric with checks or stripes used at times. Collar and cuffs were always a crisp white.

Hair was teased, pushed in waves toward the face, and then pulled to the back where it was fastened with a large bow. The hairstyle of Figure 280 was popular also. Slippers with insets at the toe were worn.

Jackets like that of Figure 278 were worn over these dresses in cool weather. Coats like that of Figure 271 were commonly seen on schoolgirls and young ladies.

Figure 277

An outing or sports suit for girls included three pieces: a jacket, knickers, and pleated skirt. The knickers were worn at times without the skirt, especially for summer camp, physical education, and other all-girl activities. When adults or young men were present the skirt was usually worn unless, of course, the young lady was very modern. The skirt is flipped up here in order to show the knickers.

The casual manner of wearing the jacket open with the belt fastened was most fashionable. The fact that such suits were often advertised as being of "London style" or "A London model" gives a clue to their origin. This young lady has added a tie to her blouse neck.

She wears long wool socks with fold-down tops. Oxfords were stylish for women and girls, being worn with casual dresses as well as sports clothes. Her hat has the brim turned up in the popular mode.

Figure 278

169

The most outstanding thing about boys' clothes at the end of the war was the belt loop. Loops were, at this time, incorporated into the design of new clothes although they would not be accepted by many men for another decade. They, of course, were never accepted by some men who preferred the braces they had become accustomed to.

The boy on the left wears his shirt and knickers for play. His sleeves are rolled up but he has kept his tie on. Plain stockings are worn with brown brogan shoes with rounded toes. His hat is a classic rural straw.

On the right a nattily dressed young boy wears a Norfolk jacket much like the adult version of Figure 253. This modern postwar version has the open collar which men and boys would prefer to the present time. His textured socks have fancy fold-down tops. His shoes are the dressier, more conservative pointed-toe style. Mail-order catalogs offered both the newer rounded or pointed toe. His cap is the seamless golf or touring cap shown from the side in Figure 253.

Figure 279

Young girls continued to wear dresses of the previous decade until the war when the waistline moved down. This double-breasted dress (left) has an extremely low waist with a very wide belt. It has interesting pleats in the skirt which continue the line of the buttoned panel of the bodice. Checked wool in winter and gingham in summer always had crisp white collar and cuffs. This girl's tie has two loops.

Her hair has been teased until it is quite bouffant at the crown with waves and curls around the face. A ribbon goes around the head on top of the hair and ties in back for a rather romantic effect.

Although she still wears side-button boots, both slippers and lace-up oxfords were familiar as well.

On the right is a coat of sophisticated design with the two large buttons like adult coats and kimonos. It has very wide cuffs and around the collar a little fur scarf with tails.

Her hat brim is fashionably turned up in front and she wears gloves. Her shoes are flat-heeled slippers with bows worn with stockings—a very dressy outfit.

Figure 280

170

Little girls' dresses were much like those of their big sisters with very low waistlines. The low and wide belt of the dress on the left is set into the side-front seams. The collar and cuffs are of lace. The entire outfit is very stylish with the new strapped "Mary Jane" shoes. The little lady also is very modern in her bobbed page-boy hairstyle.

Fur-trimmed coats pleased girls of all ages. On the right is a coat of the same basic style as that of the older girl in Figure 280. It fastens to one side with two large buttons. The little collar and cuffs are white fur with black animal tails. Very expensive coats might have real ermine, most were rabbit or some other white fur. The little girl wears a matching muff and a hat with a peak at the crown.

Leggings were all lengths and worn by both girls and boys. Although they occasionally matched the coats, they most often were of cream or buff. They had a strap under the instep.

Figure 281

Figure 282

Very little boys wore short knicker or romper suits.

On the left is a reefer coat and sailor tam worn over the sailor rompers. The tam has "U.S. Navy" on the band. The coat is double-breasted like the navy coats that inspired it. The little boy wears gaiters or leggings which come up over his knees to meet his rompers. They have a strap under the foot.

On the right is a one-piece romper in a sailor design. Romper suits sometimes were of a smock or apron design like the play suit of Figure 249. It has the new belt loops that "big boys" were wearing. The collar, cuffs, pocket facing, belt, and tie are of blue, the suit white or gray.

In warm weather or indoors the new short sock was the fashion. After the war socks developed colored bands at the top. Both little boys and girls wore the one-strap slippers.

Two different hairstyles are shown with the short side part on the left, the bobbed page-boy cut on the right.

Figure 283

Even before the war, children's clothes had become simple and practical for play. Both toddler and baby wear the popular smock which was made from a plain rectangle of cloth. Two crescent-shaped cuts were made forming cap sleeves and armholes in one operation. The piece was hemmed at the bottom and turned over at the top forming a casing for a drawstring. Not only was it simple to make but it was simple to wash and iron as well. Aprons might be hemmed like the baby's or edged with braid like the one on the left. Some were edged with lace and embroidered or appliquéd.

The toddler on the left wears a full-crowned hat with a wide brim like those of Figures 245 and 250. It is decorated with a ribbon band for play but might be more elaborate with bows and flowers with a lacy apron or dress. Both children wear short socks and black slippers.

The teddy bear and the "Raggedy Ann" doll were first produced before the war. Millions of the teddy bears were sold to both boys and girls—so many that they were almost a part of the costume of the decade just as a parasol, walking cane, or some other accessory became associated with certain periods. Teddy, of course, was named for President Teddy Roosevelt.

CHAPTER 12

Design and Construction

BASIC DESIGN PRINCIPLES

The principles of design must always be general considerations. Too many rules and charts result in formulas. Some general rules, however, can serve to help one to begin to analyze character and mood and to express them through costume design.

Line is contour or outline. In costume it might be an outline of a lapel or cuff. Line can almost be interpreted as seams because even a lapel has to be sewn around the edges before it is turned. A skirt gore or a shirt yoke are the lines of your design. The first stage of a design is your pencil sketch without tone or color.

Line is often more a matter of historic period than of character although period lines can easily be modified or exaggerated in order to express character or mood.

Basic lines are horizontal, vertical, and diagonal. These lines can be stright, curved, or irregular. Walt Disney movies are a classic example of the use of sharp or pointed lines for witches and other villains and of curved lines for heroes and other "good" characters. Irregular lines can be used successfully for unstable characters.

Form is area, shape, or mass. In costume design it is usually thought of as silhouette. The possibilities are the obvious geometric shapes such as the circle, square, rectangle, triangle, cylinder, and cone.

In advertising and packaging the shape of the container is usually round for feminine and squared for masculine products. This is especially evident in personal items such as cosmetics and toiletries. Manufacturers are so convinced of our subconscious symbolism that they spend millions of dollars appealing to it.

Usually angular shapes symbolize youth while sloping ones show age. Irregular shapes can show instability. For example, a young girl has narrow hips and small bosom, giving a more angular form than a matron with large curved bust and hips. Although both are curved one is much more curved than the other.

The symbols of age are very apparent in silhouette. The head moves forward and the back becomes rounded. The shoulders slope and the torso thickens in the middle. The ingenue should have a high bosom, an old woman a low one. There are so many symbols involving the bosom that by raising it, lowering it, flattening it, or padding it you can portray a wide range of characters in genres from drama to comedy to burlesque.

One very old set of symbols which many of us learned in elementary school is that a triangle with the point up and the base at the bottom is feminine while one with the base at the top is masculine symbolizing that a man's width and weight is in the shoulders while a woman's center of gravity is in the hips. (It probably has been eliminated from today's teaching as sexist propaganda but it can be useful in theatre design.) How often have you seen the stereotyped masculine camp counselor or

173

domineering wife in theatre and the movies as a large, broad-shouldered, narrow-hipped character. Just as often the effeminate male has been portrayed with narrow shoulders and curved hips.

For the musical production of *Tom Sawyer* I designed one basic costume for the women and girls in the chorus who served as townspeople, church congregation, and courtroom spectators. Their basic costume consisted of dress, bonnet, and shawl. For the early group scene they wore the complete outfit, the shawl held in place with the hands, giving a straight, solid, and "proper" appearance.

For the funeral scene the bonnets were removed and the shawls worn over the head and held under the chin. The large shawls fell down over the body covering the form and creating a solemn, downcast mood.

A variety of silhouettes in the courtroom scene was achieved by the girls wearing various combinations such as a shawl but no bonnet, a bonnet without a shawl, neither bonnet nor shawl, and both shawl and bonnet. One had her bonnet tied but off her head, hanging in back. One carried her bonnet and one wore her shawl over her head like an old person. The director and I achieved such a variety of silhouettes that the characters seemed unrelated to those in church. They appeared to be all ages and sizes because of the different forms.

In the final scene when everything had ended well and there was a general feeling of relief and happiness all the girls wore their shawls tied around the shoulders and no bonnets. Their arms were free to be spread and raised for the dancing and singing number, achieving a carefree mood.

In each of these scenes the mood would have been apparent even if only back lighting had been used and the actors had actually appeared in silhouette. People in the back row may not be able to see the lines of a costume clearly but they will see the silhouette which is often the main element by which members of the audience identify characters. A unique shape will make a principal character stand out from the others.

Men do not like women to wear loose-fitting, full clothes which hide the natural form. They prefer clothes that show the figure, but they are "turned off" by too-tight, blatantly sexual clothes which show too much. This attitude can be used effectively in characterization through changes of form or silhouette. If you first analyze how you *want* the audience to feel about your women characters you can then use this knowledge to achieve it. The degree to which a silhouette hides or reveals the female form is as important to characterization as line, color, and historical period. (The rules are much the same concerning the male form.)

For comic characters think in exaggerated terms. Shoulders can be padded to any degree from slight to clown-like. The bosom and hips can be padded. One of the most famous examples of burlesque form is the Barnum-Bailey clown who wears balloons for breasts and

derrière under a huge dress. The comic dowager with narrow hips and enormous bosom has been used throughout the history of the theatre. Form, shape, or silhouette, then, can be achieved by design, fit, and manner of wearing.

Tone is light and dark values. If you make a chart of blocks going from a white square to a black one, there will be many shades of gray in the squares between the two. Any color has a wide tonal range as well. Red, for instance, can be anything from the palest pink to the deepest maroon.

It is possible to set the mood of the play by the predominant tone used. For instance, in *Oliver* the colors should be somber and grayed as opposed to the clear happy colors of *Hello, Dolly. Man of La Mancha* is usually seen in somber colors. Within a somber mood you can still have a range of color and tone taken from the medium-to-dark tones.

In a play of mixed tones one character or group of characters might wear clothes in somber or dark tones while other characters wear bright or light colors. Comics or the "fallen woman" characters can wear raw, bright colors with the "heavy" wearing "heavy" or dark tones. An innocent will need light, clear, "clean" colors. An unstable character might wear several tones of mismatched clothing as might an absent-minded type.

Color brings to mind the most symbols of all of the design elements. Color has the greatest emotional impact on the audience and is more directly felt than line, shape, or texture.

Today color plays an important part in advertising, packaging, and corporate identity. Personal things like cosmetics, food, and toiletries as well as clothes are carefully market-tested for reactions to color. Humans react emotionally to it but there are few real rules concerning color because it is so easily affected by its surroundings. A color might provoke one reaction in combination with one color and a very different reaction when combined with another.

Characters of like attitudes might be dressed in harmonious colors and contrasted with those of opposing groups. Some traditional examples are groups at war with each other such as the Union and Confederate sympathizers or feuding families. The "good guys" can contrast with the "other guys." Famous feuding groups in American history were the mountain families such as the Martins and the Coys, the farmers versus the ranchers, the cattle men versus the sheep ranchers, the ranchers versus the railroads, and the laborers versus the industrialists. The show *Oklahoma!* has a production number built around the "farmer and the cowboy."

Fabrics are available in such a range of colors today that costumes can be sweet, sharp, fleshy, dainty, old-fashioned, rebellious, heavy, light, masculine, feminine or anything that a designer chooses.

174

the bodice

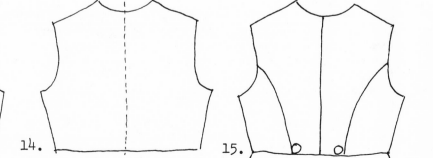

1. 2. 3. 4.

6. 7. 8.

10. 11. 12.

14. 15.

Artists of ancient and medieval times had to make all the characters in their paintings recognizable to the viewers. Until very recent times, few people could read so all works of art used symbols to a greater degree. Religious art was so full of visual symbolism that members of the church actually "read" the paintings. Each character was recognizable by his clothes, the objects he held in his hand, and by his placement within the composition. Colors became associated with certain humans or beings and have come to be associated with particular characteristics.

In more recent times advertising groups and industrial designers have done considerable research on color in order to increase product sales. Whether or not a theatre audience will react in the same way to a certain color as the customer in a store is a matter for further study. The information might be used to advantage in theatre design in many ways. For instance, if it is a fact that children react negatively to purple, then it might be skillfully used in children's productions for any character who is supposed to provoke negative feelings. If, as the advertisers suggest, young children like yellow, then it might be used to confirm positive feelings about certain characters.

The following discussions of color include both the traditional symbolism and the results of recent studies. My purpose is only to stimulate you to experiment and to become aware of the potential.

Red is considered the most appealing color by advertising experts. It is warm, even fiery. It stimulates and is a favorite color for restaurants and night clubs because it increases appetite. In the past it has been used to symbolize courage as in the military and in national flags. Red appears to advance or move closer to the viewer. In the women's clothing industry pink is considered sexy.

Blue is the color most often chosen by people in stores or in tests of color preference. It does not stimulate the appetite. It is preferred by older people. It has traditionally symbolized immortality and was always the color of the Virgin Mary's robe in Christian art. Blue suggests excellence in the ladies' clothing industry and might be considered by anyone entering a performing competition where you are judged by the impression you make (but what will happen if all the girls who enter an audition or contest show up in blue?). Navy is considered good taste and upper-class. Men who wear navy blue suits give the appearance of being powerful decision-makers. Navy makes one appear "in charge" of things. Blue appears to recede or move away from the viewer on a flat surface.

Green is soothing and refreshing and as a result is used for interiors of hospitals, schools, and other institutions. It has been referred to by maintenance supervisors as the "institution color." Green is the color of nature and suggests growth and vegetation. It also has symbolized birth. Men are believed to look upon a woman wearing green as a friend instead of a lover.

Yellow is energizing, encourages vitality and a sense of well-being. It can stimulate the appetite. Advertisers use yellow in ads directed at children because the young ones are known to like it. It is sometimes associated with a sunny disposition but in the past has been called the "color of treason." It causes mixed reactions among adults. Women who wear yellow are said to be considered intelligent by men.

Orange is a hot color. In today's clothing industry red-orange symbolizes anger. In advertising peach, orange, and beige are used to stimulate the appetite.

Purple is dramatic. It has been called the reconciling color since it is made of both stimulating red and soothing blue. It is sometimes associated with sweet tastes. Adults have no adverse feelings about purple as a rule but advertisers' surveys have shown that children often react negatively to it. In the past it has symbolized royalty and today is used a great deal by churches.

Black is considered heavy. Black or dark colors are sometimes used to give passengers a feeling of security in airplanes or other vehicles. Advertisers find that buyers are so convinced of the "weight" of black and dark colors that they often choose them in order to get more for their money! This is why black is often used for the "heavy" in theatre. It has been used in the past as a symbol of fear and the unknown.

White suggests innocence and lack of weight. In Christian art it was always used for the Christ child.

Brown is considered rural or middle-class in the men's clothing industry while in women's clothing it suggests confidence. Men are said to consider women in beige as independent according to reports of color engineers. In clothing beige is considered an upper-class power-wielding color for women. (Beige in advertising stimulates the appetite.)

Gray is considered noncommittal and produces little or no emotional response. In the clothing industry dark gray is considered the color of the power-wielding decision-makers.

The Carol Burnett—Rock Hudson production of *I Do, I Do* was one of the best examples of the skillful use of color I have seen. The young bride wore white, of course, then the following scenes through the years showed her in shades of pink and then red. In the "hot" number in which she proclaimed her anger and then her independence she wore hot orange! As she continued to age she was dressed in deeper tones until she wore a somber rose in her old age.

It has been observed that people in sunny regions like bright colors. When designing for a play which has a southern or tropical setting, you might use brighter, clearer hues. I personally experienced this on a tour of South America. I was asked so many times why I wore beige, black, and cream that I eventually began to feel drab. People there wear vibrant, glowing colors which

175

would seem garish in more northern climates but are perfectly at home, even subdued, among the incredible flowers that grow there the year round. What is tasteful in one region might not be so in another. When designing *Cat on A Hot Tin Roof* or some other play based on southern families this could be taken into consideration. Colors of green vegetation, bright flowers, and sunshine might be your inspiration.

In *Oklahoma!* you might, for instance, think of the wide-open spaces with blue skies. The colors of corn and wheat might be used in combination with the blue sky to suggest the physical characteristics of the state.

Remember that too much harmony will result in monotony while too much contrast will result in discord. Variety, overdone, can cause confusion. All these facts can, however, be used deliberately if that is the result you are seeking.

Texture as related to costume design means the degree of smoothness, roughness, or shine of a fabric. It can be soft or hard or sheer. Texture must often be exaggerated to be effective on stage.

Wool is considered businesslike, sophisticated, and the least sexy of the natural fiber fabrics. Linen is thought of as clean, fun, and wholesome with white linen symbolizing purity. White lace stands for aloofness, femininity, and elegance while black lace suggests sexiness. Silk is considered the most sensuous of all cloth in advertising but on stage it, or a good imitation of it, represents upper-class elegance. *Peau de soie* (or its synthetic imitations) and taffeta give a soft, elegant, expensive-looking sheen. Satin is hard with a showy or cheap-looking result (unless a fine quality synthetic or silk satin is used). Cotton is the most versatile of all cloth being available in a variety of blends, textures, patterns, weights, and colors.

We can cut cloth, tear it, wear it out, drape it, shrink it, weight it, wet it, stiffen it, iron it, or dye it. But that's not all, for we can paint it, puncture it, stretch it, wrinkle it, stain it, soil it, wash it, crease it, twist it, and sculpture it. You may very well think of still other things to do to cloth which will alter it.

There are not only many things that we can do *to* cloth but things that cloth *can do on its own as well*, either because we want it to or in spite of what we want! It will wrinkle, stretch, fray, tear, shine, move, reflect or absorb light, and it can reflect the body movement of the person wearing it. It can scratch, warm, or heat one's body.

First of all, when you purchase cloth try to anticipate what it is probably going to do under certain circumstances. Then think of the many ways in which you can alter it. If you aren't sure how it will act you might buy an extra half yard to experiment with.

In ancient Greece and then again in the early 19th century, garments were put on while still damp and then pressed, rubbed, stretched, and pulled to make them

conform to the body and fall in artistic folds and drapes. I have found that a sleeve that puffs up too much can be made to droop by dampening it and then manipulating it with my hands. A lace ruffle that is too crisp can be made to fall gracefully by dampening it; the same is true for skirt folds and bodice gathers.

Weights have been used throughout history to make clothes hang in the desired manner. Many of today's synthetic fabrics successfully imitate older natural fabrics in appearance but will not act in the same way because they are so light. I have used imitation suede for buckskin coats and weighted the coattails heavily so that the coat acted like real leather as well as looked like it.

Large sleeves like those of Figures 27, 42, 92, 179, 239, and 275 and draped skirts like those of Figures 106, 109, 139, 172, 264 can be made to fall beautifully with the addition of a few weights. Stoles and shawls will stay in place when worn over the arm, as in Figure 43, if weights are sewn into the points. The apron of Figure 177 or the caftan of Figure 207 might be enhanced by the use of weights if your fabrics do not have enough weight of their own as will the cape of Figure 262. So much depends on how a garment is cut, the weight and quality of the cloth, and the posture of the actor that draping and hanging are unpredictable. I have learned through the years to use weights, from light to very heavy, wherever and whenever they will enhance a costume. I arrived at this solution after examining antique garments and realizing that many of them were weighted for the very same reason!

An interesting exercise in design is to illustrate several versions of one costume in different fabrics. For instance, the girl's dress of Figure 246 might be made up in fine linen, taffeta, or silk with lace trim. The girl might wear white slippers with satin ribbons and a satin ribbon in her neatly arranged hair.

Next, it might be made of brown or gray cotton or wool, either checked or plain. With the plain dress she might wear dark stockings and high-button shoes like those of Figure 220 and her hair could be in braids or worn straight.

For the third version the dress might be muslin, cheap calico, or even feed-sack printed muslin. Her shoes might be well worn with her black stockings showing runs or she could even be barefoot. Her hair might be uneven and uncared for.

Your choice of fabrics and your treatment of them will depend on the lifestyle of the character you wish to portray.

Sound can be utilized as an element of costume design even though the costume designer is primarily concerned with visual media. Sometimes a character trait can be emphasized or exaggerated to any degree through the use of a squeaking shoe, rustling skirts, a swishing girdle, rattling shackles, jingling spurs, bangling jewelry, or a

fluttering fan. Ripping, tearing, or dragging sounds can be used as well.

Certain costume sounds bring to mind some traditional examples such as the court jester with bells on the points of his collar and hat. In more recent times in America the jingling spurs of a cavalryman or cowboy are a good example. Rustling petticoats were a part of the character of women's dresses in the 1880s.

Director-Designer Relations can be maintained on a pleasant and professional level with your creative ideas respected if you remember one bit of advice: the best way to get a director to see that an actor wears a costume the way you plan is to illustrate it that way on your costume plate. If you want a costume worn in different ways during different scenes in the play, then make extra sketches showing each manner in which it is to be worn. When I first presented my *Tom Sawyer* designs to the director (see "Form") I had a color plate showing the basic costume for the girls in the chorus. I had another plate of quick pencil sketches showing the different ways the outfit was to be worn in each scene, *clearly labelled* (as to scene) so that he knew exactly what I wanted. There was no problem; he was pleased with the way I had achieved so many moods so simply. Had I merely presented the one color plate and then later, during dress rehearsal, begun to tell him how his actors should wear their costumes during each scene he might understandably have felt that I was interfering with his direction. The result could have been not only hard feelings but, even worse, a less effective use of my designs.

It's only human nature that both the director and the actor will be more cooperative if *you know precisely what you want and make it perfectly clear to them*. That way it is part of the original design and not interference in someone else's job. Your ideas are always taken more seriously when they are on paper than when you talk about them. A hectic dress rehearsal is no time to suggest the creative use of your costume designs—do it when you present your designs.

CONSTRUCTING THE COSTUMES
Men's Bodice

Most of the costumes you will make from your basic man's bodice will open down the front. They can usually be constructed without darts although some men with small waists or extremely large chests might require them. The bodice should not fit too snugly.

1. To acquire your basic bodice pattern for men, begin with a large size woman's bodice, a man's vest pattern, or your own drafted on a live model or tailor's form. For double-breasted coats, first establish the center front and mark it with chalk or pencil as in Step 1.

2. Next, look at the shape and angle of the overlap on

the coat you are re-creatir 35.

3. This overlap or lape to each half of a bodice p

4. The completed dou

5. The lapels were som shown here, instead of c graphs show the lapels bu show the crease indicatir worn back. The crease is ill

6. The lapels were som 69, 75, and 234, instead of

7. Figure 58, left, has th as diagrammed.

8. A single-breasted co ranged in a design whicl double-breast similar to th

9. When drafting patte fold-down collars similar t and 90, establish your bodic the bodice with lapels is b around the neck, pin it in pl shape.

10. The double-breasted l in place.

11. In order to make cut- Figure 187 it is necessary to line while subtracting from t trated overlaps at the chest waist.

12. The cut-away coat bo

13. Boleros and short jac corners can be drafted from

14. A bodice back can be tr the front for drafting many

15. The curved back seam many years and continues coats. Many military coats o curved side back seam.

Trousers

The proper shape of trou thenticity of a costume. They spected piece of clothing in all is so easy to just allow an actor wardrobe. To the untrained ey pair of trousers, but to a good subtle diffferences in each dec

The belt and belt loop often cal costumes representing peric they were worn. Belts have be but they weren't worn as a par century. If your costume budg trousers, you can use old trou

loops, then add straps or fancy braces. Belts were some-times worn over trousers (without loops) which were higher waisted in the 19th century than they are now.

When constructing new trousers it will save time to just make a plain seam in front instead of a fly. I have found that volunteer seamstresses often recoil at the thought of sewing a complicated fly front, yet are not hesitant about making plain pants for women. Both directors and actors like the plain front (or fake fly) because there is no danger of one making an entrance with an unfastened fly.

1. Use a standard commercial trousers pattern with-out pleats or flares.

2. Place the outseams together, as shown, making one piece of the front and back sections.

3. For Indian leggings cut away as shown, leaving a strap up to the waistline. When the strap is folded over at the waist it makes a casing for the belt which holds the leggings or breeches in place. Those of Figures 5 and 89 are snug-fitting with fringe at the outside.

4. This is a variation of the leggings or breeches worn by the Indian and adopted by westerners. The flare is achieved by spreading the legs apart at the hem, and adding a small flare at the inseam as in Steps 4a and 4b. These full breeches are shown in Figure 95. The influence of the Indian clothing on the cowboy and western clothes is obvious here.

5. Women's biking bloomers (Fig. 213), divided skirts (Fig. 214), and riding outfit patterns are made by pulling the front and back sections apart at the hem and adding fullness at the outseam and inseam. The riding outfit of Figure 243 opens down the front of each leg.

6. Early cowboy chaps like those of Figure 125 were just Indian leggings used to protect the legs. The main difference was in the strap which went over the belt. The cowboys preferred wider straps. Remember to keep the strap to the *front* of the chaps. In the '70s chaps were snug-fitting, and they grew wider and looser into the '80s as demonstrated by Figures 126 and 162.

7. The famous cowboy batwing chaps shown in Fig-ure 162 are made by placing the inseams together (instead of the outseams) as in Step 7a. They are cut away at the hips and crotch as in step 7b. Fullness cut in scallops is added at the outseams to form the wings.

8. Riding breeches or jodphur patterns are made by adding a curved flare at the thighs and cutting away fullness at the ankles and calves on the outseam. The inseam is left straight. The earliest jodphurs were full length as in Figure 227 but they grew somewhat shorter by World War I when boots, puttees, gaiters or socks were worn over them.

9. Men's trousers of the '50s, '60s, and '70s were nar-row, sometimes quite snug. The hem was curved up over the instep in front and down to the floor in the back as shown in Figures 22, 23, 24, 35, 36, 81, 118, and 112.

10. The highwaisted pantaloons of Figures 28, 86, 87, and 159 are made by extending the top of the trousers.

They must be curved slightly to fit the torso. They were worn ankle-length early in the century and later with the cuffs turned up when they evolved into overalls.

Shirts

Originally shirts were constructed of a rectangle with sleeves gathered in very full. The gathers were often actually tiny pleats or rolls beautifully made by hand. A band was sewn over the fullness at the wrist leaving a ruffle to fall down over the hand. The shirt constructed of rectangles had to be made loose in order to fit properly; the drop shoulder line was the result.

It is interesting to know that the work and sport shirt is designed to be at ease or in its natural position when the arms are out. When a shirt is smoothed out flat the arms will be out almost straight. In contrast, a dress coat will have the sleeves down and close to the body when in its natural position. The arms can be raised and stretched in a denim jacket, exercise suit, or work shirt without dam-age. A woman's dress blouse and a man's designer suit will be strained, wrinkled, or even ripped when one's arms are outstretched or raised vigorously.

The double-breasted shirts of the 19th century were European inspired but eventually came to be American folk clothing. A plain shirt can be used with just braid and buttons or a panel added for a simple version. To draft a real double-breasted pattern, the method is much the same as described in the directions for a man's bodice.

1. The straight shirt with full sleeve (only half of shirt shown). When on the body this shirt naturally has a drop shoulder line like those of Figures 4, 6, 7 and 28 through 31. Those of Figures 86 through 88 are examples also.

2. A shaped shoulder and armhole with a shaped sleeve. The shaded area shows the relationship to the old straight shoulder.

3. A shirt with the sleeves smoothed out flat making them almost straight out in their natural position.

4. For a double-breasted shirt like those of Figures 37 and 161 draw a line down the center of the shirt front pattern.

5. Draw on the shape of the double panel.

6. When the shape of the panel is added to half the shirt pattern you have a pattern for a double-breasted shirt.

7. The shirt front with panel is shown in Step 7a, the finished shirt in Step 7b.

Sleeves

The sleeve is important to the silhouette and can in itself establish a period. It is possible to use a simple basic bodice and long full skirt for any period as long as you use the correct sleeve for each decade. It is also possible to back-date or up-date a costume by using a sleeve from an earlier or later period.

179

trousers

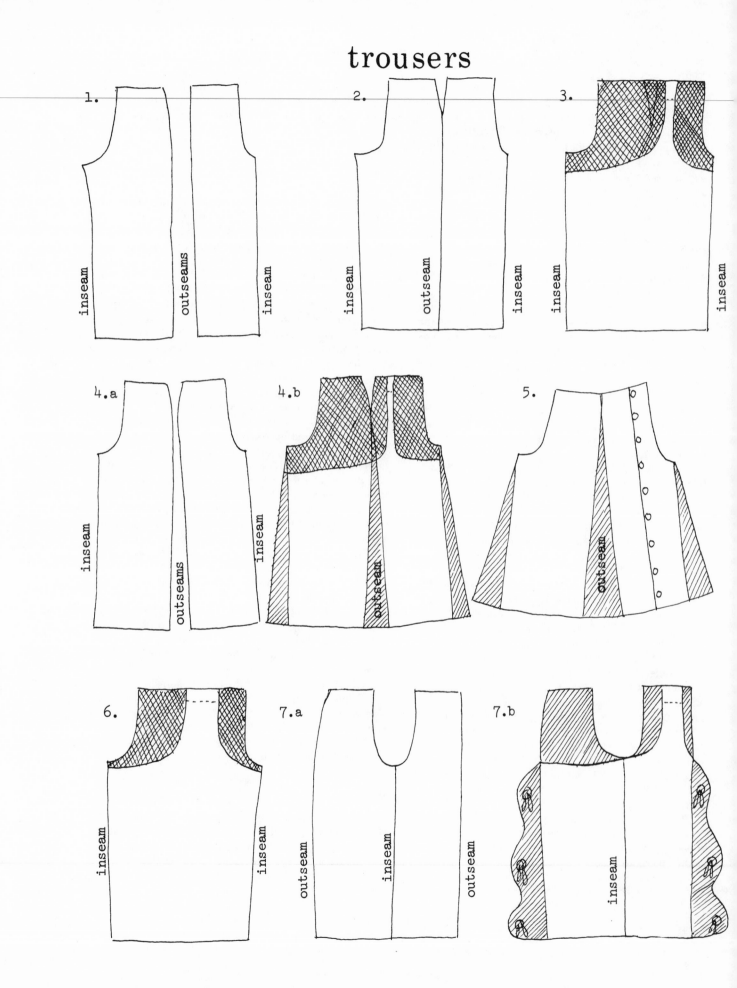

shirts

sleeves

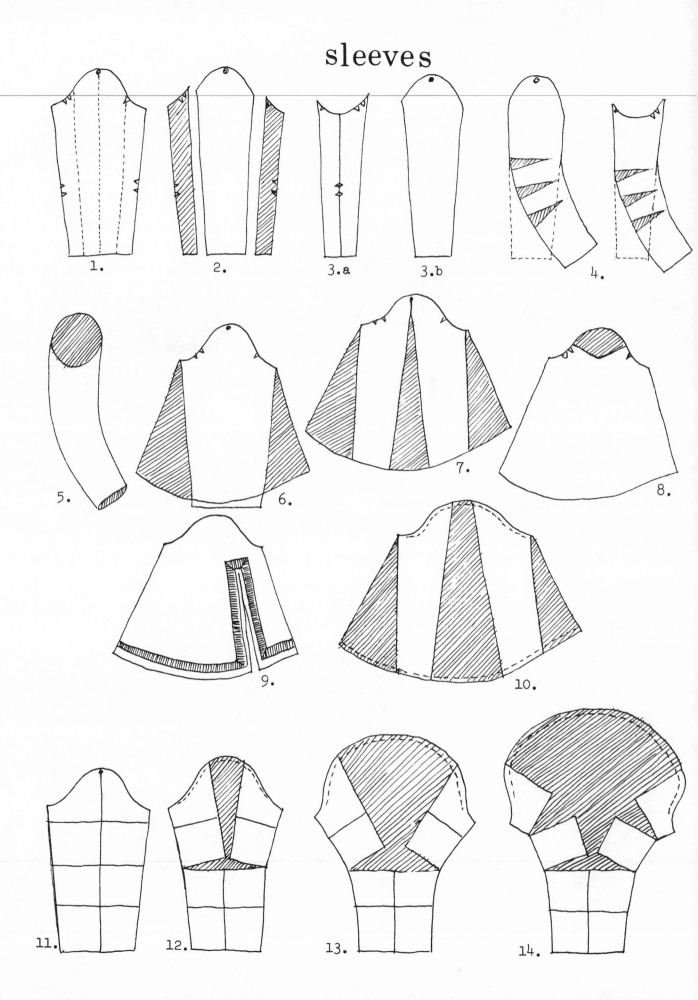

1. A period two-seam sleeve pattern can be drafted from a standard commercial pattern for a long fitted sleeve. There should be no gathers at the shoulder or wrist.

First, divide the sleeve in half vertically by drawing a line from the center top at the shoulder seam to the center at the wrist. Divide each of the two sections in half making four sections in all as shown.

2. Cut the pattern on the two side lines as shown.

3. Join the two side sections at the original underarm seam to make one inner sleeve piece as in Step 3a. Step 3b shows the outer sleeve. The pattern now has two seams.

4. The outer and inner sleeve sections now are ready to be curved as period sleeves were. (Men's suit jacket sleeves of today still have two seams and a slight curve.) Cut into the section with three cuts and spread apart as shown to form the basic pattern.

5. The completed curved, two-seam sleeve as in Figure 41. Figure 103 has the front seam left open in the manner of 17th century sleeves.

6. For the flared sleeves of Figures 17 and 108, extra fullness can be added as shown.

7. For very full sleeves gathered at the wrists like those of Figures 101 and 102, extra fullness needs to be added at the center as well as each side. Draw a center line and pull apart several inches.

8. Cut away the top of the sleeve to fit the extended shoulder styles like that of Figure 15. It is a good idea to baste the muslin sleeve to the bodice on a person or dressmaker's form before cutting the sleeve. Let the sleeve fit up under the shoulder, pin it in place, and mark with chalk or pencil.

9. The split in the sleeve of Figure 42 should be toward the front between the center line and the underarm seam as illustrated.

10. For full sleeves tathered in at the shoulder, as in Figures 111, 177, 209, and 244, the entire sleeve must be expanded along the center line, more at the wrist than at the shoulder. Add fullness at the underarm seam also as shown in the diagram.

11. For sleeves with full upper arms and slender lower arms divide the basic sleeve in half vertically and into four parts horizontally as shown.

12. For sleeves of the last half of the '80s such as those of Figures 172, 173, and 175, cut the pattern in the center both horizontally and vertically as illustrated. Spread the upper part as shown.

13. For a sleeve with more fullness as in Figure 207, spread the sections a bit more. The underarm seam edge must remain unbroken.

14. For the large leg-o-mutton sleeves of the 1890s like those of Figures 210, 211, 213, and 214, spread the two sections still more. In addition, cut the upper section horizontally and spread as illustrated keeping the underarm seam unbroken.

Women's Bodice

One of the best ways to achieve an authentic look in any period style is by the use of feather boning. It has to be sewn into the seams by hand and requires some extra care to make sure the ends don't poke the actress, but no dress is going to really look 19th century without it. A loose, wrinkled bodice just looks too casual and too modern.

Some professional theatres with large enough budgets sometimes construct period corsets to go under their period dresses, but there are plenty of all-in-one body foundations, long-line bras, and waist-cinchers available today so that a proper corseted look can be easily achieved. With proper undergarments and boning in the bodice seams it is possible to make very beautiful gowns.

1. One goal of every good costume designer should be to have a file of basic bodice patterns in a large range of sizes. You can begin by checking the commercial pattern books. If you make your own, pin or baste right on a live model or a dressmaker's form. Mark the center front and back and the bust and waist darts as shown.

2. Stitch the darts.

3. For the curved side-front seam, like Figures 44 or 110, draw a line with chalk or pencil from the waist dart in a curve up to the armhole. The point at the armhole will vary with different costumes so examine closely the one you intend to re-create. The line should go across the breast and follow the seam line of the waist dart as shown.

4. The separate front and side-front pattern pieces are ready for seam allowances. The side-front piece should press flat so that the bust dart can be disregarded when making your pattern. The curved shape of the newly drafted pieces will give the proper shape without darts. A waistline point is added here.

5. For the extended-shoulder bodice like those of Figures 14 and 15, add to the armhole as shown. The bodice is lengthened here for the longer style like Figure 15. It must curve out for the hips as illustrated.

6. Skirts can be added to the bodice pattern for the jackets and coats of Figures 41, 46, 139, and 140. There should be no waistline seam.

7. A narrower front like those of Figures 13 and 16 can be drafted in the same manner as the wider one of Step 3. For the bodices of Figures 14 and 16 the tucks can be sewn before the bodice pattern is cut. Tucked or shirred bodices should be made over a basic bodice lining.

8. Small shoulder extensions and a waistline point as in Figures 42 and 45 can be made as shown here.

9. For a basic princess-style bodice the line should run from the waist dart up to the center of the shoulder as in Step 9a, rather than to the armhole. Add flared extensions below the waist as in Step 9b for the classic princess-style coat or dress such as those of Figures 100 and 103.

10. For a bolero pattern sew the bust darts but not

those of the waist. Draw the shape of the bolero like that of Figure 102 on the bodice.

11. Here the bodice center is extended for the full front styles of the 1890s and 1900s.

12. For best results with the canezou blouses and bodices of Figures 102 and 107 or the tucked bodice of Figure 109, use a plain basic bodice for a lining and form the shirring and tucks over it.

Necklines

Any neckline shape can be drafted by beginning with a basic high-necked bodice and placing it on a live model or dress form. Sketch the shape you want with chalk or pencil.

1. For necklines which are off the shoulder such as Figure 13 cut across the bodice as illustrated.

2. High, wide necks like those of Figures 16 and 44 should be cut wide at the shoulder seam but kept high in the center.

3. Wide, low necks like Figure 208 should be cut all the way to the top of the armhole at the shoulder.

4. Deep V-neck openings for Figures 136 and 137 are cut wider than for Figures 172 and 237.

5. Formal necklines like Figure 99 are cut low and wide with extensions added across the shoulder as illustrated. A waistline point is added also.

6. Figures 40 and 135 have necklines similar to those of Step 5 cut into a point in center front.

7. and 8. Square or rounded-square necklines such as those of Figures 101, 235, or 267 can be cut in very low, wide, or high styles.

Skirts

One important rule to remember in making period skirts is that the petticoat should be made the same way. The proper petticoat will do a great deal to ensure that the skirt retains the proper shape.

After drafting the pattern, you can first construct a muslin petticoat. Any adjustments and refinements can be made in your pattern at that time so that the skirt will be exactly as you want it. You can then use the experimental muslin skirt for a petticoat.

In the '50s skirts were rounded at the hips because hoops had several wires all the way up to the waist. They later were cone-shaped as the wires were only placed at the hem.

The hoop could not be worn for mill work and some other activities as it could be dangerous. Judging from the many paintings showing the absence of a hoop it would seem that the huge hoop skirts were a luxury reserved for special occasions and for very fashion-conscious ladies. In the '60s waistlines were tiny and skirts over hoops were enormous.

The bustle began simply as extra fullness at the skirt back in the late '60s. Soon bows, ruffles, and extra fabric were added. When the padded bustle came in style in the early '70s it was high enough to force the dresses to be somewhat high-waisted as in Figures 135 through 139. It gradually moved down to the lower back (Figure 140) and finally to the hips (Figure 142).

The '80s saw bustles stay at the hips and even the thighs for a few years then rise back up to the lower back at the end of the decade. This last form of the bustle was larger than ever but short-lived.

By the '90s the bustle disappeared but the back remained full. Women had become so accustomed to the bustle that the full back remained until the turn of the century and even into the early 1900s on some clothes.

Since some form of back fullness was part of women's clothes from the Civil War on into the 20th century, it is important to learn the subtle differences during the "rise and fall" of the bustle.

1. Using a standard, four-gore, fitted skirt pattern (1a and 1b) patterns can be drafted for most skirt styles.

2. For making a full, four-gore skirt first divide the front in half making two fronts and two side fronts as shown in Steps 2a and 2b. The back is done the same way.

3. Add fullness to each of the four front pieces as shown. Do the same to the back pieces.

4. When the expanded gores are joined the skirt becomes full. It can be expanded to any degree. This skirt can be fitted at the waist or expanded, as shown, to be gathered. This flared design can have gathered fullness without bulk at the waist and as a result is more slenderizing to the figure than a straight gathered skirt.

5. The skirts of the 1860s were so full that they sometimes measured as much as ten yards around the hem. The gores must be flared (Step 5a) because ten yards gathered into the waist is out of the question except in sheer fabrics. The back of the skirt was growing fuller and longer during the '60s as it evolved toward the bustle of the '70s.

Step 5b shows the skirt lengthening at the side seam and curving down in back toward the center back seam to form a train as in Figures 41 and 101 through 106.

6. The front grew narrower and the back longer in the '70s as in Figures 135, 139, 140, and 142. Here the skirt back is only slightly fuller at the side seam. The back center is very full and long. It is worn over a bustle pad.

7. Skirts of the '80s had shorter trains and straight fronts. Although skirts were often pleated at this time they were straight in front, not flared.

8. During the '90s skirts still had full backs but they were flared in both front and back as in Figures 208 through 211. The flare, slight in front, increased at the sides and ended in full pleats at the back.

9. Several gores were used in early 20th century skirts. Six-gore styles were popular, seen in Figures 237 and 238.

First, divide the front and back into three gores each as in Step 9a. Separate the three gores and add a flare at the

the bodice

1.

2.

3.

side center front

4.

5.

6.

7.

8.

9.a

9.b side front

10.

11.

12.

lower part of each one as in Step 9b. This skirt should fit snugly at the hips, have only the slightest flare at the thighs, and then flare out quickly at the knees or calves. Flared or ruffled flounces were often added at the bottom.

Petticoats

In every period of history, including today, women's undergarments have been designed especially for the current fashion. The petticoat is the shape underneath that fills out the dress to the proper shape. A petticoat of the wrong style can make a dress hang improperly.

Crinolines appeared in the mid-'50s. Cages or metal hoops appeared about 1858. They were of tempered watch-spring steel which was very flexible. These first hoopskirts were quite round in shape.

In 1862 the front began to flatten and by 1865 the front was almost flat while the back had grown into a train. By the late '60s the metal was used only at the hemline with two or three rows of steel.

The bustle was a natural outgrowth of this back interest. The bustle of the '70s was called a tournure. By 1876 drawstrings were used to draw in the back as the bustle moved down.

By the 1880s petticoats, like dress skirts, were very slender and form fitting in front with stiff crinoline ruffles and boning in the back.

Late in the '80s the steel hoop returned in the form of a huge bustle. It was flat in front with steel hoops holding out the back. A flounce was snapped onto the bottom of the tournure and could be removed for laundering.

The exaggerated bustle of 1888 and 1889 was short-lived and disappeared in the '90s. The full back, though, would remain popular into the 20th century.

Combinations and Drawers

In the 1840s and 1850s pantalets were ankle-length. Drawers gradually grew shorter. By the '90s the corset cover and drawers were combined to become the one-piece "combinations." The knees were gathered in at first then grew wider. Eventually drawers became quite wide legged as in Figure 216.

Corsets

During the 1840s and 1850s corsets were long and flared out over the full petticoats. They laced in back and had a little ruffle across the arm. Elastic gussets were used at the breasts.

By the '60s front clips were used for front openings and the corset became quite short. It became lower at the top as well and remained much the same during the '70s.

Corsets of the '80s were long again as dress bodies grew longer. Some no longer had elastic inserts.

Jersey webbing was used for corsets in the early '90s. The elastic inserts were gone and steel stays were mostly vertical instead of diagonal as the side ones had been earlier. Straps were added at this time. (See also Figure 216)

TRIMMINGS

In each decade there were many dresses of similar line which differed only in the decorations and materials. These embellishments were sometimes the dominant feature of the costume. Each dress shown in the historical chapters can be interpreted in several different versions by simply changing the color and trim.

Braids, lace, ribbon, floral or patterned ribbon, and fringes can be quite expensive, especially when several yards are used. Nineteenth century costumes often require rather large amounts of trim so through the years I have experimented by making my own. We have found at Nashville Academy Theatre that custom-made trims actually are better anyway because the expensive commercially made trims are often rather boring in their lack of variety. For instance, even if you live in a large city where floral ribbons are available and you have the budget to afford them, you will find that there are few to choose from.

On the other hand, when you shop for floral striped fabrics you will find many more choices at lower cost. If you learn to spot them in each store, purchase a few yards when they are available, and store them away you can, in a short time, acquire a wide choice.

Some of the trims such as the bias tube, braided and crocheted yarn ropes, and tassels cost very little. They are so inexpensive that you can afford to use them extravagantly.

I usually have volunteer seamstresses who range from professional to novice. Some jobs like braiding, crocheting chains, taping fringe, drawing or cutting felt designs, and sewing on buttons can be done by children as well as the grown-up novice. The jobs, though simple, are very important and give a person a feeling of accomplishment.

You will eventually begin inventing your own trimmings and collecting materials.

Fur Cloth

There is a wide choice of fur cloth colors and pile lengths which can be used for coats, stoles, muffs, hats, Indian wraps, and trim on clothing. The main thing to remember is to always cut from the back side, cutting only the backing, as in Step 1, not the pile.

For ermine tails in white fur use black yarn tufts and pull them to the back side over a few threads and back out to the front as shown in Step 2. Small pieces of long-pile fur cloth can be sewn into the white fur. Part the pile, stitch a small circle of fur cloth in place and then brush with a hair brush.

necklines

1.   2.   3.   4.

5.   6.   7.   8.

skirts

center back   center front

1.a   1.b

center front

2.a   2.b

side seam   side seam

3.   4.

skirts

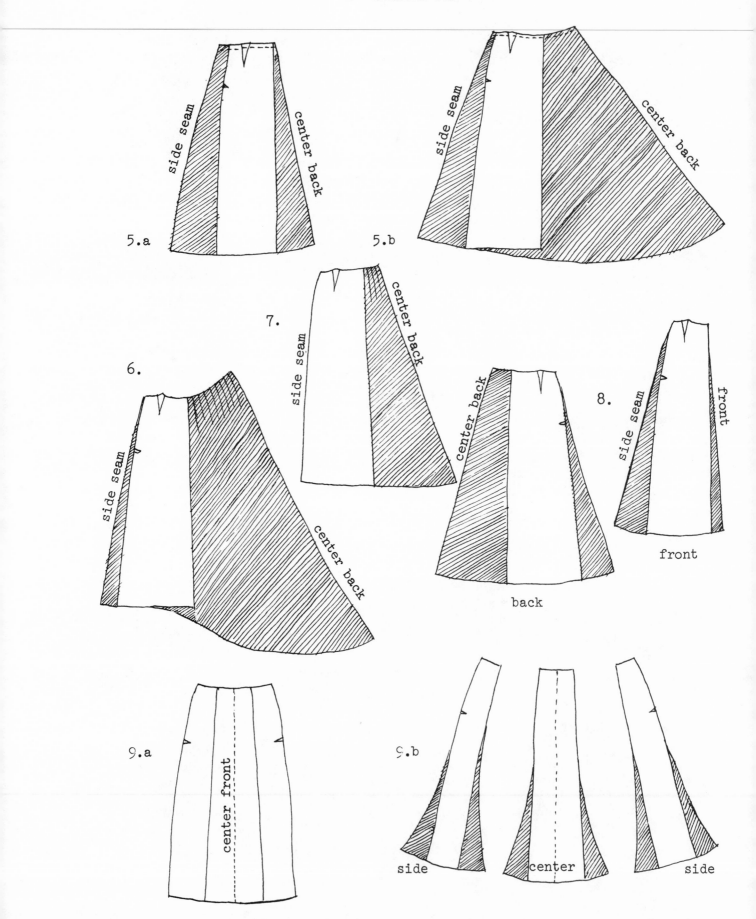

5.a

5.b   side seam   center back

6.   side seam   center back

7.   side seam   center back

8.   side seam   front

front

back   center back

9.a   center front

9.b   side   center   side

petticoats

1858

1860

1870s

1870s

1865

1876

1872

petticoats

1881

1882

1881

1888

1889

1898

1892

1897

1880s
&
1890s

combinations

drawers

corsets

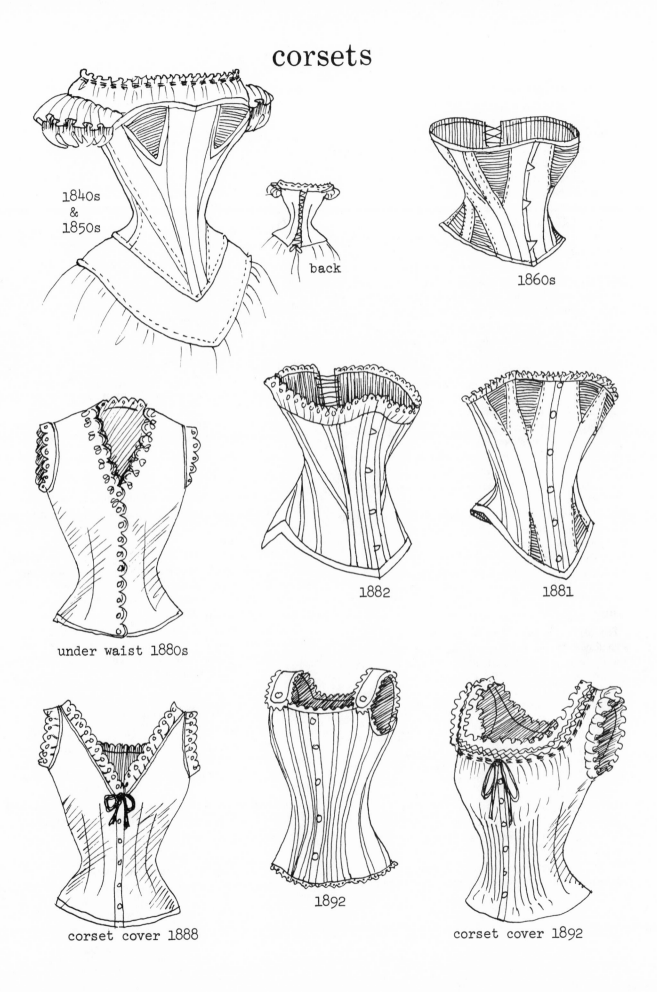

1840s & 1850s

back

1860s

under waist 1880s

1882

1881

corset cover 1888

1892

corset cover 1892

Trims From Fabrics

I once found a striped fabric which looked like rows of Indian bead or quillwork design. I used it for Indian costumes in *Indian Captive*. I have found classical designs, authentic 18th and 19th century motifs, and Tyrolean and Pennsylvania Dutch design stripes.

The secret of building a store of fabrics for trim is to buy a couple of yards of a good one when you run across it. Train yourself to buy on impulse because it won't be there when you go back later.

Some fabrics have one stripe design repeated over and over while others have two, three, or four different ones alternating. Sometimes I find one that is so beautiful I build a costume around it while other times I plan the dress and then look through my collection of fabrics and find one that coordinates.

1. Cut along the stripe with scissors, do not tear. The edges can either be basted in a hem or turned under and ironed.

2. By mitering the corners as illustrated the floral bands can be used in the same manner as ribbons and braids.

3. Lace cloth often comes in a striped design which can be cut into strips. It is available in delicate or heavy lace patterns. Sometimes it even has flowers embroidered in color or ribbons woven in. In the spring it can be found in a small range of colors as well as black, white, or cream.

4. An all-over lace cloth can be used as a source for lace flowers and designs to be sewn onto costumes.

5. Flowers or other design elements can be used on skirts, bodices, and sleeves for endless variety. Lace flowers combined with ribbon bands are especially feminine. The flowers or designs from two different pieces of lace cloth can be combined into a fancy lace appliqué.

Fringe

Fringes vary in price. Cotton ones are usually inexpensive. Rayon fringes move and shine beautifully. Drapery and upholstery departments or shops often have a good assortment.

1. Victorian fringes were often complicated designs with beads and fancy braids. They sometimes were scalloped or pointed.

To cut fringe in designs hold it so that the fringe hangs in a straight line allowing gravity to keep everything straight. Press it gently against a strip of wide masking tape (1a). Use a cardboard template for tracing the design on the back side of the tape and cut on the lines. The masking tape can be cut in half-yard or yard long lengths to facilitate sticking it to the long strip of fringe (1b).

2. Designs can be points, scallops, or combinations of the two.

3. Fringe can be rolled and sewn into tassels which will coordinate with the scalloped fringe for a very elegant costume. Since fringe is available in several widths you can make tassels from tiny to very large.

Cotton Ball Fringe

Ball fringe can usually be found in variety or department stores and mail-order catalogs. It is usually less expensive than that in drapery shops. Experiment with a few yards and design your own trims.

1. The plain, inexpensive cotton ball fringe.

2. Using two strips with the balls arranged as illustrated.

3. The tape can be looped or tucked in various designs drawing the balls closer together.

4. One tape can be sewn directly on top of the other so that the balls are at the same level as shown.

5. Several rows can be used for more complicated designs.

6. Any of the designs can be used with two or more colors to coordinate with the color of the costume.

7. When using two tapes as in Step 4, the balls on the tape underneath can be wrapped around to the front (or back) and sewn above as shown.

8. Two rows of balls can be twisted around each other and sewn in place as illustrated for an open, lacy design.

Cut Fringe

1. For best results use felt or imitation suede fabrics for buckskins and Indian tunics. Decide on the length you want the fringe to be and draw a line as a guide *on the back side* of the garment.

2. At regular intervals draw perpendicular lines to be used as guidelines for cutting. If you have trouble cutting the fringe in straight lines first cut in the center of each section, and then keep dividing each remaining portion in half until a section is done.

3. For cutting fringe on curved edges measure the length as in Step 1. The cutting guide lines should fan out in relation to the flare of the garment. Start with a straight line in the center as indicated.

Trimmings From Cotton Rug Yarns

There is a great deal of room for creative impulses to be expressed with the inexpensive, colorful rug yarns. They can be made into beautiful, authentic, and expensive-looking trims. When using black braid, so popular during the last half of the 19th century, small single black sequins can be occasionally stitched into the design. It will give a subtle glint now and then which will look like jet heads.

1. Inexpensive cotton rug yarn can be *crocheted* into a long chain in a very short time for braids of different widths, depending on the size of the yarn.

2. The chains can be used as plain braid in rows.

trimmings

fur cloth

1.

2.

from fabrics

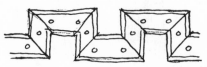

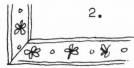

2.

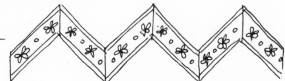

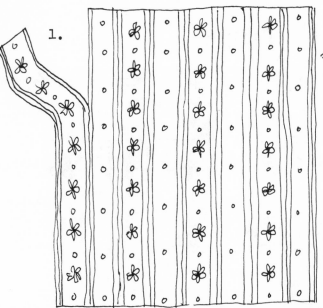

1.

cloth

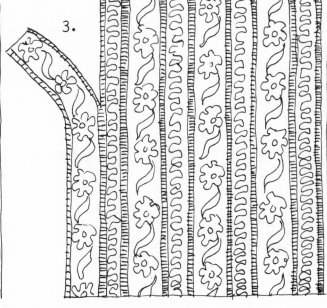

3.

lace

4.

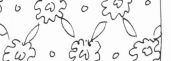

lace

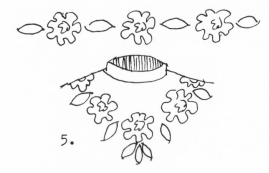

5.

fringe

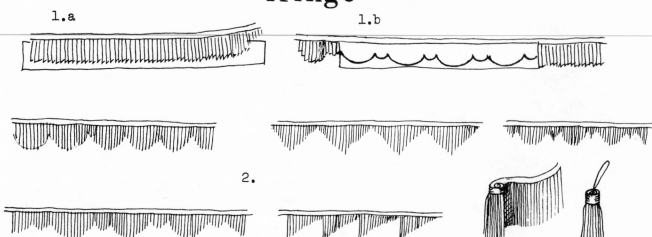

1.a

1.b

2.

3.

cotton ball fringe

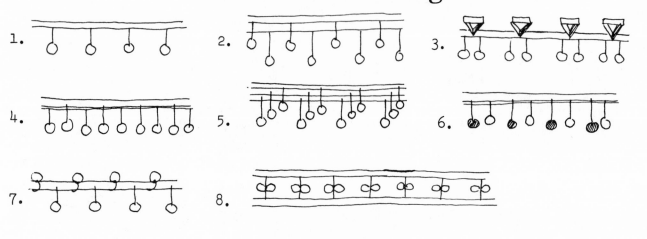

1.

2.

3.

4.

5.

6.

7.

8.

cut fringe

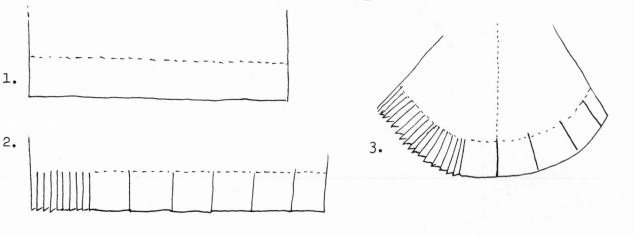

1.

2.

3.

3. A chain can be crocheted with loops or other decorative stitches by someone with experience. If not, the long chain can be sewn onto the garment in decorative loops and designs.

4. Medallions can be made by simply coiling the chain. Matching tassels can be made for a coordinated look.

5. Instead of crocheted chains, another inexpensive trim is the *plaited* or *braided* chain. Even a very young person can help with this project and turn out yards of braid. Use inexpensive cotton rug yarn.

6. Flatten the braid and apply as you would any other braid.

7. Both this and the crocheted chain can be used for military braid on uniforms. It isn't necessary to have metallic braid because the deep yellow or gold yellow is surprisingly attractive.

8. Yarn tassels can be made in any size to coordinate with the crocheted or plaited braids. Rug yarn comes in a wide range of colors.

9. Tassels can be used extravagantly on costumes when they can be made for so little money. All these tassel trims were taken from museum costumes and are authentic. Step 9a was the sleeve and the skirt of a dress. Step 9b shows wide ribbon applied in a zig-zag design with a tassel on each fold-down top point. Step 9c shows tassels suspended from buttons.

10. *Knotting* is another method of creating inexpensive trims for costumes. Shown here are strands of yarn punched through the hemmed edge of a shawl, coat, ribbon, or strip of cloth. Several or single strands can be punched. Use a crochet hook.

11. Knot each strand or group of strands at the edge of the fabric then divide the yarn at each knot and join it with half that of the next knot as illustrated in Steps 11a and 11b.

12. Repeat the process for as many rows as you want. This makes an elegant fringe which has a lacy look.

13. The tuffs can be as close together as you want to place them. The rows of knots can be up as close together or far apart as you like.

14. This design shows three knots on the second row instead of one on each row as in Steps 12 and 13.

The Bias Tube

1. Cut bias strips ¾-inch wide and join with diagonal ends to make a strip several yards long. Fold over and machine sew with a large stitch.

2. Turn the tube by sewing one end to a "bone" needle or ribbon threader and working through as shown.

3. The finished tube. Iron it flat with the seam in the center back.

4. Make a cardboard template of the design you want and draw around it with chalk or pencil. Baste the tube to the garment in any design you choose. When the basted

design pleases you, stitch it on with the machine or by hand.

The tube can be stretched and manipulated to curve in any direction. It can be mitered at sharp corners.

Bias tape can be used in this manner but since it has two folded edges it is more difficult to work with than the simple tube.

Reverse Facings

1. Contrasting facings of light-weight felt turned to the outside are simple to make and eliminate hemming. If other fabrics are used the edges should be turned under or covered with braid.

2. Stitch as shown, clip off the corners, and then turn and press.

3. Add buttons for accents as in Step 3a. Step 3b shows the edges cut into points while Step 3c illustrates scallops. Step 3d has edges covered with braid.

4. Braid loops or cut-out lace designs can be added to the edges as in Step 4a. Step 4b shows fringe added to the facing. Heavy lace embellishes the edge of the facing in Step 4c, fabric or lace cut-outs are used in Step 4d. The designs can be cut of felt also.

Ruffles and Ruchings

1. Cut strips of soft fabric on the true bias as shown.

2. Join with diagonal ends as in Step 2a. Step 2b shows the joined pieces.

3. Bias-cut ruffles and ruchings were not always hemmed. Many museum examples of 18th and 19th century dresses show ruffles simply pinked on the edges. The bias-cut strip can't ravel because the threads *all* go diagonally across the strip. The stitching further anchors them in place. Even if a loose-weave fabric does ravel, it only fringes on the edges; the threads do not come out as on a straight-cut strip.

4. Stitch both sides of the strip for ruchings. The rows of stitching can be close to the edges or near the center depending on how much heading is wanted on each side.

5. The stitching line on ruffles can be curved or zig-zaged for interesting effects.

6. Ruffles can be pleated or gathered. The pleats can be left to puff out or ironed flat for a tailored trim.

7. Scallops with pinked edges can be gathered or pleated. Step 7b shows how to pleat the scallops to make them cup.

8. Swags should be measured carefully and pulled up at regular intervals on a straight strip.

9. Stitching at regular intervals drawn up tightly makes rounded poufs. If lined with nylon net they will stay crisp and rounded. For formal gowns this is particularly attractive with small flowers, bows, or beads at the places where the stitching is pulled in.

10. A different pouf can be made by stitching laterally

trimmings from cotton rug yarns

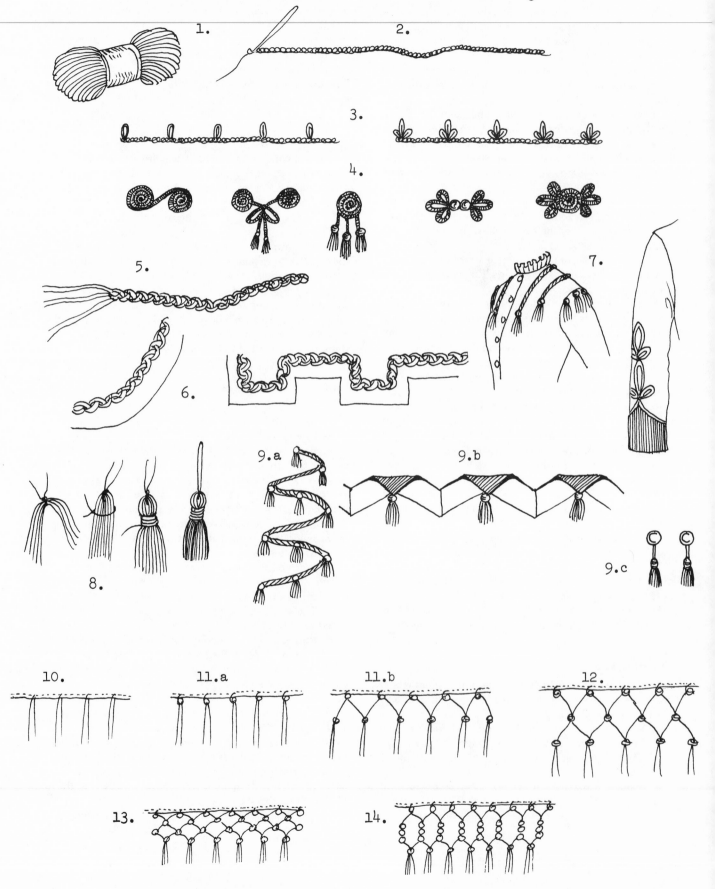

1.

2.

3.

4.

5.

6.

7.

8.

9.a

9.b

9.c

10.

11.a

11.b

12.

13.

14.

bias tubes

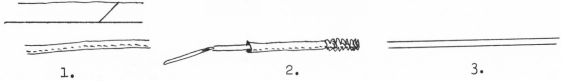

reverse facings

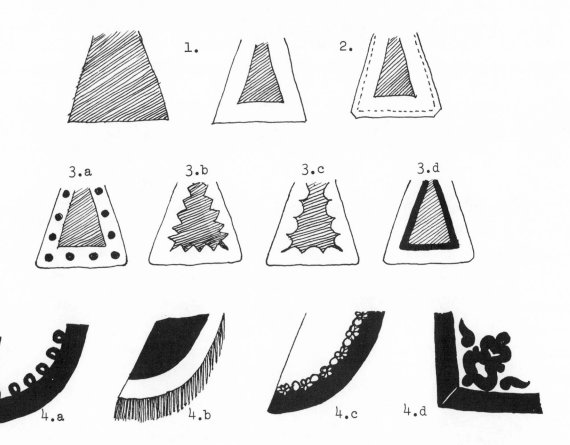

ruffles & ruchings

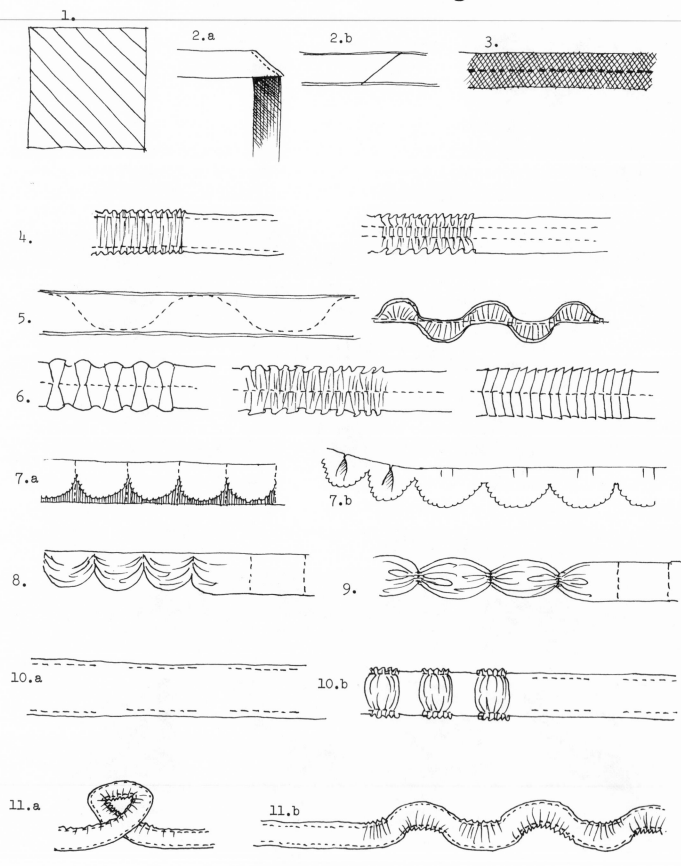

1.

2.a

2.b

3.

4.

5.

6.

7.a

7.b

8.

9.

10.a

10.b

11.a

11.b

ribbons & fabric bands

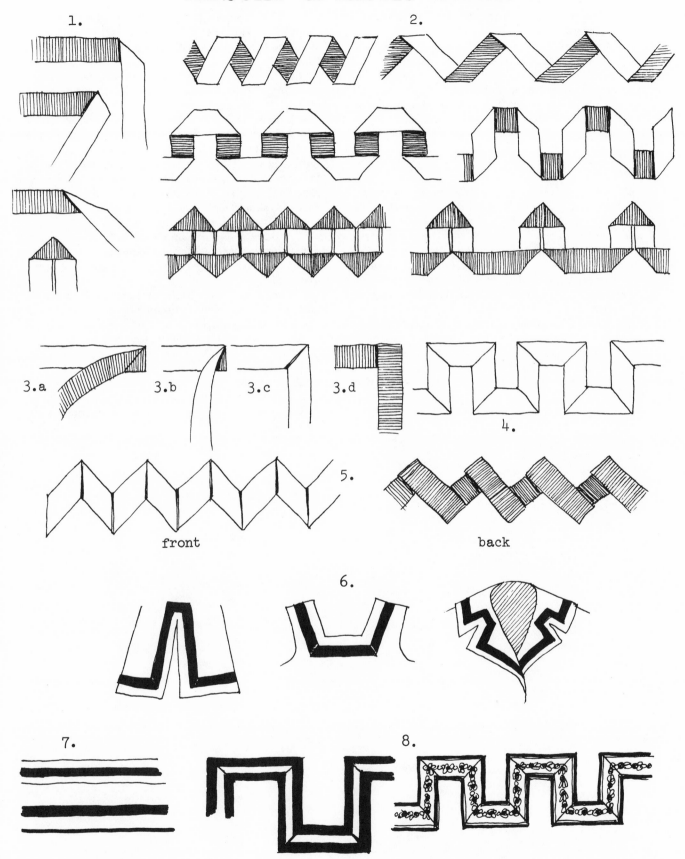

1.

2.

3.a 3.b 3.c 3.d 4.

5.

front back

6.

7. 8.

at intervals as illustrated in Step 10a. Step 10b shows the completed poufs.

11. Ruchings can be applied in loops and curves if the gathers are arranged to force them into shapes. Step 11a shows a loop design caused by gathering one side. The gathers are pushed or spread out as needed. Step 11b shows how the curves can go in both ways if the gathers are pushed into bunches on alternating sides.

Ribbons and Fabric Bands

Grosgrain, velvet, and satin ribbons are especially beautiful on Victorian costumes. Satin and velvet, being different on their two sides, are particularly interesting when applied in spirals.

Bands of any fabric can be used on costumes: taffeta, satin, velvet, cotton, and synthetics. The edges can be turned under and basted but the easiest method is to sew a long tube on the straight of the fabric and then turn it like a belt.

The spiraling and mitering methods of application can be used for ribbons, braids, fabric bands, and lace in plain, striped, floral, and other patterned designs.

1. Fold the ribbon or band in a diagonal fold revealing *both the front and back side* as illustrated. It can be folded at any angle.

2. The back side of the ribbon is shaded to show the direction of the folds more clearly. There are many fold patterns which accent the dull and shiny sides of velvet or satin ribbon. These designs are also attractive when both sides are the same as with grosgrain ribbon or fabric bands.

When using fabric bands, you can sew two different colors together (or two shades of one color) for a dramatic effect.

3. Mitering the corners involves folding the ribbon so that *just one side shows*. First, fold the ribbon back against itself as in Step 3a and make a diagonal fold. Next, bring the face of the ribbon back to a position perpendicular to the original direction as in Step 3b. Step 3c shows the completed mitered corner fold. Step 3d shows how the back side should look.

4. A design with mitered corners.

5. Another design showing both front and back of the ribbon. Remember that the miter joint keeps the *same side of the band on top throughout the design, never revealing the reverse side.*

6. Some ways of applying fabric bands or ribbons with miter joints. This method of application is particularly good for following the edges of coattails, sleeves, necklines, and collars as well as for geometric designs.

7. One ribbon can be sewn on top of a wider one or several colors can be sewn together for interesting designs.

8. Striped cottons or taffetas are easy to use and make striking designs. Floral striped fabric or floral ribbons are particularly beautiful.

Index

References to drawings are printed in boldface type.

Alabama Light Infantry uniform, 45
Alamo, Battle of, 18, 19
apron overall, **127**
apron, 39, 40, **93, 113,** 150
　allover, **150, 152**
　baby, 172
　girls, **24,** 78, **79, 117, 152**
　mens, **31, 85, 145**
　tea, **112**
　tennis, **114**
Arapahoe Indian, 70, 105
Army cap, 16, 34, 35
Army officers, **34, 35, 129**
　Confederate, **53**
　1916, **157**
　Union, **57**
Army of the Potomac uniform, **50**
artillery, **35, 58,** 159
ascot, 82
asymmetric dress, **109**
athletes, **102,** 143
automobile coat. See duster coat
automobile helmet, **123**
aviator, 158, **160, 161**
　cap, 123

babies, **42, 80, 98, 137, 153, 172**
　Indian, 36, 69
ball gown, 71
bandanna, 24, 65, 86
bandit, 33
banker, 82

bartender, 82, 127
baseball player, **83, 102, 142**
baseball uniform, boys, **168**
bathing
　cap, 148
　cape, **75, 113**
suit, mens, **101, 143**
suit, womans, **75,** 113, **149, 167**
bathrobe. See dressing gown
batwing chaps, 105
　construction, 179
batwing sleeves, 113
bedrolls, 54
bedroom slippers, 144
bell-bottom trousers, **56, 159**
belt loops, 83, 86, 122, 129, 170
belt
　ladies, 111, 131, 132, 146
　mens, 32, 45, 54, 55, 158
bertha collar, 24, 162
bib overalls, **127,** 144
bicycling outfit
　ladies, **110, 111, 133**
　mens, **30, 100, 101, 121, 123**
Black Bart, 82
Blackfoot Indian, 36
blacksmith, 31
blakeys (shoe taps), 115
blankets, **21, 36, 70**
bleached hair, 162
Bloomer, Amelia, 15, 23, 75
bloomers, **23, 133**
　construction, 179
blouse, 23, 72, 75, 76, 109, 111, 131,

132, 164, 165, 166. See also canezou,
guipe
"blue collar uniform," **127**
boa, 162
boating reefer, **171**
bodice, 109, 146
　boned, 22, 38, 90
　calico dress, 40
　construction
　　ladies, 183–84
　　mens, 177
　corsage, **72**
　formal, **108**
　front opened, 23, 39
　little girls, 24, 41
　tucked, 22, 24, 33
　V-shaped, 91, **108**
body language, 13–14
boleros, 37, **72,** 112
　boys, 79
boned bodice, 22, 28, 90
bonnets, **23, 24,** 38, 71, 73, 74, 76. See
also hats, sunbonnets
　girls, 25, 98
boots, 32, 57, 64, 65, 104
　boys, 41, 78, 96
　cowboys, 85, 87, 104
　firemens, 84
　girls, 97
　Indian, 106
　riding, 32, 157
　Wellington, 31, 32, **34,** 35, 54, 57, 65
Boston National Lancers uniform, **47**
border ruffian, 35

Index

bowler hat, **29**, 82, 100, 121
bow tie, 78
boys, 18, **25, 26, 41, 42,** 78, **96, 97, 98, 115, 116, 135, 152, 171**
  caps, 25, 135, 136, 152
  dresses, **25, 42, 79, 98**
  in the Navy, 56
  play clothes, **25, 153, 168, 170.** *See also* brownie suit, rompers
box coat, 16, **29**
boxer, **102,** 143
breechcloth, 69, 70, 90, 107
breeches, boys, 79. *See also* railroad breeches
brogans, 145, 169
Brooklyn Thirteenth Militia uniform, 46
brownie suit, **136, 153**
buckskin hunting clothes, **33, 66, 87**
bustle, 74, 90, 92, 94, 108, 109, 110, 115, 184
butcher, 127
butternut soldiers, 8, **54**

caftan, **130**
calico dress, **40**
California vigilante, **34**
Camel Corps uniform, **35**
campaign hat, 158, 159
canezou blouse, 72, **75,** 77
canvas, 32
caps. *See also* hats
  baseball, 102
  bathing, 148
  boys, 25, 135, 136, 152
  driving, 123
  engineers, 127
  farmer, 65
  forage, 78
  immigrant, 19
  miner, 19
  overseas, 159, 160
  policeman, 34
  sailors, 68
  shako, 34, 35, 41, 44
  sport, 30, **122,** 156
  touring, 156, 170
  "Turkish" or "house," **30,** 63
  Union Navy, 55
  U.S. Army, 19, 34, 35
  womens, 23, 93, 153
capes
  bathing, 75, **113**
  combing, 95, **113**
  Confederate soldier, **55**
  cyclists, 123
  girls, **98**
  ladies, 108, **111, 132, 147**
  lounging, **113**
  morning dress, 92
  nurses, **161**
  oiled, **126**
  rain, **126**
  soldiers, **59**
carpenters, 103, 144, 145
cavalry uniforms, **19, 57, 88, 158**

Confederate, **54**
chaps, **33, 85, 86, 87, 105**
  construction, 179
  ladies, **112**
Chaplain, Navy, 128, 158
checked trouses, 16, 65, 82
cheek whiskers, 82, 83
chemise, **164**
Cherokee Indian, **20**
Chesterfield coat, **121**
Cheyenne Indian, 36, 70, 105
Chickasaw Indian, 20
Chinese immigrants, **67**
Choctaw Indian, 20
christening dress, **80**
Cincinnati Red Stockings, 8, **83**
civilian scout, **89**
city gent, **16**
clerical collars, 67
Clinch Rifles, Augusta, Georgia, uniform, 44
cloak, **73**
cloche hat, 163, 165
club meeting dress, **147**
coal miner, 156
coats,
  boys, **116**
  girls, 77, **80, 116, 137, 153, 170, 171.** *See also* reefer
  ladies, **73,** 92, **95, 147, 165, 166**
    duster, **148**
    fur trimmed, **163**
  mens
    Army officer, 34
    bicycling, **30**
    Confederate Army, **53,** 55
    cutaway, **17**
    firemans, **17**
    morning, **28, 120,** 156
    raglan sleeved, **29**
    utilitarian, 85
    Union Army, **57, 58, 59**
    Union Navy, 55
    vigilante, **34**
coat suit, 156
collars
  bertha, 24, 162
  calico dress, 40
  clerical, 67
  detachable, 29, 31, 124
  ladies, white, 38, 39
  mens shirt, 16, 124
  shawl, 16, 28, 124
  smoking jacket, 63
colors, use of for effect, 174–76
combing cape or sacque, 95, **113,** 134
Confederate Army officers, 53
Confederate sailors, 52
Confederate soldiers, 8, **54, 55**
Confederate Floating Battery uniform, 49
Connecticut Tenth Militia, 50
construction worker, 127
cooks, 127
"coppers," 8, **68**
Cordeliere cloak, **73**
corsage bodice, 72
corsets, **134,** 155, 186

cowboy boots, 85, 87, 104
cowboy kerchief, 85, 86
cowboys, **33, 85, 86, 87, 104, 105, 126,** 127
crash suit, **122**
cravat, 16, 28
Creek Indian, 20
crocheted gaiter, **98**
cuffs
  detachable, 29, 124
  dress, 22, 23
  girls dress, 41
  smoking jacket, 63
  trousers, 156
culottes, 133, **150,** 163
curling iron, 149
cutaway coat, **17,** 30
cyclists cape, 123

Dakota Indian, **69**
daytime dress, **147**
deerskin hunting shirt, 49
deerskin tunic, **18, 36.** *See also* buckskin hunting clothes
  womans tunic, 20, 21, 36, **69**
denim, 31, 86, 144
derby hat, 29, 82, 100, 121
design principles, 173–77
detachable collars, 29, 31, 124
detachable cuffs, 29, 124
diaper cover, rubber, 136, 137
diapers, 42
dickey, 91
director-designer relations, 177
"ditto" suit, 28
divided skirt, **112, 133, 150**
  construction, 179
doctors, 82
"dog collar" necklace, 146
double breasted coat, **116**
double breasted dress, **170**
double breasted shirt, **32,** 35, **54, 104**
  construction, 179
Douglas, Stephen A., 28
dragoons, 19, 34, 35, **45, 88**
draped skirt, **162,** 163
drawers, 134, 135, 186
dresses, **23, 39,** 76, **94, 130, 146, 170**
  asymmetric, **109**
  baby, **137**
  bloomer, **23**
  boys, **25, 42, 79, 98**
  calico, **40**
  daytime, **147**
  deerskin, **20, 36, 69**
  double breasted, **170**
  formal, 37, **71, 130, 146, 162**
  girls, 24, **25, 41, 42, 75,** 77, 78, 79, 97, 98, 114, 115, 136, 137, 151, 153, 170
  Indian, **20,** 21, **36, 69,** 107
  jacket, 37, **40,** 110
  knit, **165**
  meeting, **147**
  middy, **152**
  morning, **92**

Norfolk style two-piece, 165, **169**
office, **91**
party, **22**
princess style, **71**
rural womans, **39, 40**
shirred, **22**
skating, **96,** 114
sport, **110**
two-piece, **77, 169**
walking, **91**
working, **39**
dressing gown, **30, 84,** 125
  ladies, 92, 95, **113, 134, 149**
driving cap, 123
drummer boy, 59
Duncan, Isadora, 162
dungarees, 144
  sailors, 158, 159
dust ruffle, 94
duster coat, **123**
  ladies, **148**

Ellsworth's Zouaves, **50**
embroidered waistcoat, 16
engineers, 127
English walking suit, **120**
explorer, 18

fabric, used for effect, 176
factory workers, **65, 127,** 156
  children, **151**
  woman, 39, 77
farmers, **18, 31, 65, 144,** 156
  smock, **17**
Federal Army of the Cumberland
  uniform, 44
fedora hat, **140**
Fire Zouaves, 50
fireman, **17,** 84
  hats, 17, 65, 84
flounce, 22, 23, 38
flying helmet, 160, 161
flying suit, **161**
footed drawers, boys, 135
football outfits, 123, **142**
forage cap, 78
form, use of, 173–74
formal bodice, **108**
formal gown, **37, 71, 130, 146,** 162
formal suit, mens, **156**
Fort Sumter, uniform worn at, **44**
fringe, 18, 21, 36, 66, 192
frock coat, **16, 28,** 55, 62, **120,** 128, 140,
  158
front open bodice, 23, 29
frontiersman, **33, 66**
  hat, 39
fur coat, mens, **141**
fur hat, 18
fur scarf, **147,** 148, 162
fut trimmed coat, **163,** 171

gaiters, 30, 47, 62, 96, 97, 101, 111,

129, 133, 164. *See also* puttees
  boys, 171
  crocheted, 98
gamblers, 82
garters, sleeve, 145
gauntlets, 45, 57
  ladies, 150
gentlemen, **16, 28, 82, 120**
Georgia Clinch Rifles, uniform, 46
Georgia Heavy Infantry uniform, 45
Georgia Sumter Light Guards,
  uniform, **46**
Ghost Dancer, **105**
girls
  aprons, **117**
  bodice, 24, 41
  boots, 97
  cape, 98
  coat, **77, 80, 116, 137, 153, 170, 171**
  dresses, **24, 25, 41, 42, 75, 77, 78, 79,**
    97, 98, 114, 115, 136, 137, 151, 153,
    170
  play clothes, **25, 152**
  skating dress, **96**
gloves, 86, 123, 133. *See also* gauntlets
gored skirt, **147**
grain elevator operator, 144
Great Basin Indians, **105**
grocer, 144, 145
guimpe (blouse), 97, 151

hair, bleached, 162
hairpants, **86**
hairstyles, 14, 22, 23, 37, 39, 71, 72, 90,
  91, 108, 109, 130, 131, 134, 146, 149,
  162, 164, 165, 166, 167, 169
  boys, 25, 42, 78, 79, 171
  girls, 24, 41, 42, 79, 97, 114, 170
  Indian, 20, 21, 36, 89, 90, 106, 107
  mens, 16, 28, 124, 143, 156
half-breed, 13
hard-knock shoes, 127
hard times, ways of expressing, 13
harvester, 144
hats
  Alabama infantry, 45
  army officer, 47, 53
  automobile, 148
  baby, 172
  boys, 26, 79, 96, 97, 115, 116, 135
  cavalry, 57, 158
  Cherokee Indian, 20
  Confederate soldier, 54
  cowboy, 85, 86, 87, 105
  fireman, 17, 65, 84
  frontiersman, 39
  fur, 18
  mens, 16, 52, 62, 64, 65, 82, 100,
    121, 127, 144
  Mexican, 33
  opera, 156
  plug, 28
  policeman, 145
  prospector, 32
  stetson, 104
  straw, 16, 18, 31, 121

  ladies, 24
  stovepipe, 28
  summer helmet, 100
  top hat, 28, 62, 65, 66, 120, 123
  Union Army, 58
  womens, 37, 38, 39, 73, 92, 93, 94,
    95, 108, 109, 110, 111, 131, 132,
    146, 147, 148, 150, 163, 164, 165
headdress, Indian, 36
Heavy Infantry, Georgia, 45
helmet, dragoon, **45**
helmet, flying, 160, 161
"high-lows," 26
hobble skirt, **163**
homburg, 120
hoop skirt, **37, 38, 39, 40, 72, 90**
Hopi Indian, **106**
hour glass figure, 130
house cap, 30, 63
house dress, 146
Huck, Finn, 12
hunter, 18
hunting clothes
  buckskin, **33, 66,** 87
  shirt, **33,** 48, 49
  smock, **18,** 87

Illinois Miltia, Nineteenth, 44
immigrants, 17, **18, 32,** 64, 88, 101, 104
  Chinese, **67**
  Irish, **66**
  Mexican, **33**
Indian, **20, 21, 36, 69, 70, 105, 106,**
  107. *See also specific tribes*
  baby, **36, 69**
  boots, 106
  dresses, 20, 21, 36, 89, 90, 106, 107
  headdress, 36
  leggings, 18, 20, 21, 32, 33, 66, 69,
    89, 105
  construction, 179
Indiana Militia, Eleventh, **50**
infantry uniform, 19, 45, **159,** 160
  Confederate, 54
Injun Joe, 13
Irish immigrant, **66**

jabot, 109
jackets
  boys, **97**
  cavalry, 88
  cowboy, 86
  dress, 37, **40,** 110
  girls, sailor, **136**
  infantry uniform, 159
  ladies, 92, 133, 169
  Norfolk, 157, 161, 169
  pea, **56,** 68
  poke, **24**
  sport, **100**
  work, **127**
jeans, 104, 144
"jellybags," **84**
jewelry, 22, 36, 37, 90, 108

Index

jodhpurs, **142, 157, 158, 159, 160**
  construction, 179
jumper, 151

Kansas Free State Battery uniform, 35
Kentucky Rifle Brigade uniform, 49
kepis (cap), 34, 35, 44, 45, 46, 47, 48,
  50, 54, 58, 88
kerchief, 40, 52, 56, 66, **76,** 88, 106,
  158, 159
kilt, boys, **98**
kimonos, **149,** 163, **168**
knee breeches, boys, 115, 135
  boxers, 102
knickers, **83,** 97, **100, 102,** 115, **121,**
  123, 135, 156, 157
  ladies, 166, **169**
knit dress, **165**

laborer, 103
lace, 37
ladies suits, **110,** 132, **147, 164, 166,** 169
lawyers, 82
Lee, Robert E., 53
leggings, 171
  bicycling, 133
  Indian, 18, 20, 21, 32, 33, 66, 69, 89,
    105
Lincoln, Abraham, 28, 65
line, 173
linen coat, 15
"London style" suits, **169**
Louisiana Tigers uniform, 50
lounging cape, **113**
lounging robe. *See also* dressing gown
love scenes, 13–14
lumberman, 144
Lyon's Federal Troops in Missouri
  uniform, **47**

machinist, 145
Mackintosh, **100**
mail agent, 144
Mandan Indian, 36
marines, 47
marshall, 82, 87
Mary Jane shoes, 171
Maryland, First Militia uniform, **46**
Massachusetts Militia
  Eighth, 45
  Seventh, 50
  Sixth, **44, 46,** 52
  Twenty-fifth, 50
  Twenty-first, 50
  Twenty-third, 50
maternity smock, 77
meeting dress, **147**
mens
  hats, 16, 52, 62, 64, 65, 82, 100, 121,
    127, 141
  shirt collars, 16, 124
  suits, 28, 30, **83, 122, 140, 156, 157**
merchant seamen, 68

merchants, 82
Metternich sack coat, **73**
Mexican miner or railroad worker, 33
Michigan First Militia uniform, **44**
middy
  boys, **135, 136**
  Confederate sailor, **52**
  dress, **152**
  Spanish-American War sailor, **128**
  Union sailor, **56**
  World War I sailor, **159**
militia uniforms, 43–59
military escort, officer, **34**
mill owner, 82
mine owner, 82
miner, 18, 10, 32, 65, 144
  cap, 19
  coal, 156
  Mexican, 33
minister, **67**
minstrels, 40, **64**
Mississippi Rifle Militia uniform, **49**
monobosom, 130
monocle, 28, 29, 38
Mormon pioneer, 18, **24**
morning cap, 93
morning coat, **28, 120,** 156
morning dress, **92**
Moscow coat, 16
mountain men, 19
muff, 146, 147, 163
mustaches, 30, 82, 101

Navajo Indian, **106**
navy chaplain, 128, 158
navy enlisted mens uniform, **159**
navy officer, **55, 157, 158**
navy officer, Spanish-American War,
  128
necklines, 184
New Jersey Militia uniforms, **44,** 50
New York Militia uniform
  Fifth German Rifles, 44
  Fifty-Fifth, 50
  Fifty-First, 50
  Fourteenth, 44
  Ninth, 50
  Seventh, **44**
  Seventy-First, 46
  Twelth, 50
  Wide Awakes, **44**
newsboy, 135
Nez Percé Indian, **90, 107**
nightcap, 84
night dress, 95, **134**
night shirt, **125,** 143
Norfolk jacket, **157,** 161, 169
Norfolk suit,
  boys, 115, **170**
  mens, **122**
  womans, **164**
Norfolk style dress, 165, **169**
North Carolina Mounted Rifles,
  uniform, 55
nurses, **161**

office dress, 91
officers, cavalry, **34**
officers, navy, **55,** 157, 158
  Spanish-American War, **128**
Ohio Militia uniforms, 44, 46
oiled (rain) cape, **126**
older lady, 23
opera hat, 156
outing suit, **122**
overall suit, aviators, **161**
overalls, 31, **64, 103, 127,** 144
  apron, 127
  bib, 127, 144
  boys, **153**
overcoat, 29
  uniform, 44, 59
overdress, **94,** 164
overseas cap, 159, 160
overskirt, **74, 90, 91, 92,** 108, 110, **162**
Oxford shoe, 169

painters, 103, 127, 144
paisley shawl, 38, 74
Paiute Indian, **105**
pajamas, **103,** 125, **144**
pajamas, ladies, **167**
paletôt coat, **73**
Panama Canal workers, 127, 144
pantalets, 24, 41, 42, **75,** 78, 98
  boys, 42
pantaloons, **18, 103**
  boys, 25, 41, 78, 97
  farmers, **31,** 65
  immigrants, 19
  miner, 19
  minstrel, 64
paper hanger, 127, 144
papoose board, **36, 69**
party dress, 22
  girls, **79**
pea jacket, **56,** 68
peg top skirt, **162**
Pennsylvania Militia uniforms, 44, 47,
  48, 50
petticoat, 76, 134
  construction of, 184, 186
petty officer, navy, 128, **158**
pillbox hat, 109
pince-nez, 29, 38
pioneers, Mormon, 18, **24**
pistols, 33, 63, 83, 88, 89, 158
Plains Indians, **21, 36, 69, 70,** 89
Plateau Indians, **107**
play clothes, **25, 78, 152, 153,** 170, **171**
play overalls, **136**
pleated skirt, 169
plug hat, 28
points, collar, 16, 28
Poiret, Paul, 163
poke jacket, **24**
policeman, 8, **68, 145**
policemans cap, 34
polanaise, **94**
poncho, 33, 54, 87
Pony Express rider, 65
pouch, belt, 32, 34

Pouch, shoulder, 29, 30, 33, 57, 58, 65, 100
poverty, use of costume to show, 13
preacher, **67**
Prince Albert coat, **120, 125**
princess style dress, **71**
prospector, **32**
Pueblo Indian, 106
purse, 24, 162, 163
puttees, **158, 159, 160**
    ladies, **164, 166**

quillwork, 21, 36, 69

Raglan, Lord Henry, 29
raglan sleeved coat, **29**
railroad breeches, **41, 64, 66,** 84
railroad workers, 33, 144
rain cape, **126**
raincoat, 121, 141
    ladies, **166**
    policemans, **145**
rainy day suit, 147
redingote, 163. *See also* frock coat
reefer (coat), 131, **136, 152, 171**
repairman, 103
retail clerk, 145
retainer, skirt, 132
reticule purse, 24
Rhode Island Militia uniform
    Artillery, 48
    First, **48**
    Fourth, 50
riding
    boots, 32, 157
    outfits, 75, **93,** 110, **112,** 166
        construction, 179
    skirt, **150**
rifles, 18, 32, 33, 34, 54, 66, 70, 89, 129, 158
riverboat man, 18, 31
romper play suit, **153, 171**
Roosevelt, Theodore, 102, 144
rubber diaper cover, 136, 137
ruching, 91
rural lady, **39, 40,** 76
Rush's Lancers uniform, 47

sack coat, 58, 62, **82, 121, 140, 142,** 156
    boys, 135
    Metternich, **73**
sacque, combing, 134
saddle coat, **126**
sailing suit, mens, **83**
sailor
    dress, **152**
    jacket, girls, **136**
    middy. *See* middy
    suit, boys, **115, 135, 136**
sailors
    Confederate, **52**
    merchant, **68**

Spanish-American War, **128**
    World War I, **160**
Sam Browne Belt, 158
scarf
    aviator, 161
    boys, 25
    cavalry, 88
    soldier, 55
schapka headdress, 47
schoolmarm, **108**
Scottish outfit, boys, **98**
scout, civilian, **89**
scuff, womans, 40
seaman, **68,** 159. *See also* sailors
seaside coat, **121**
Seminole Indian, 20
serape, 33
settler, 18
shako cap, 34, 35, 41, 44
shawl collar, 16, 28, 62, 124
shawls, **74,** 95
    mens, 55, **62,** 64
    paisley or lace, 38, 74
shipbuilder, 52
shirred bodice, 42
shirred dress, **22**
shirring, 22
shirt, **18,** 28, **64, 65,** 89, **104,** 143, 145
    baseball, **102**
    boys, **41, 78**
    collarless, **124**
    construction, 179
    cowboys, 86
    double breasted, **32, 35, 54, 104**
    farmers, **31**
    firemans, 17
    hunting, 17, **18, 33, 47, 49**
    immigrants, **19,** 32
    miners, 19
    soldiers, **35, 47, 48,** 54, **58,** 158
    work, **31**
shoes, 100, 124
    boys, 25, 26, 41, 42, 96, 98, 115, 135, 151, 152, 170
    girls, 41, 42, 75, 77, 78, 151, 152, 169, 170
    ladies, 22, 23, 39, 40, 76

    mens, 16, 24, 30, 31, 32, 100, 101, 121, 122, 125, 127, 140
    sport, 30, 83, 101, 102, 121, 122, 123, 142
    work, **18,** 145
shorts, 143
Shoshone Indian, 107
sideburns, 16, 28, 29, 30
silhouette in design, 173
Sioux Indian, 70, 105
skating dress, 75, **96, 114**
skirt flounce, 22, 23, 38
skirt retainer, 132
skirts, 39, 76, 111, **131,** 132, 146
    construction, 184
    divided, **112, 133, 150**
    draped, **162,** 163
    gored, **147**
    hobble, **163**

hoop, 37, 38, **39, 40,** 72, **90**
peg top, **162**
pleated, **169**
slaves, 18, 30, 31
sleep dress, **95**
sleeping suits, **103**
sleeve garters, 145
sleeve protectors, 131, 145, **150**
sleeves
    batwing, 113
    construction, 179, 182–83
    dress, 38, 109, 130, 131, 146, 147, 162
    false blouse, 23, 39, 91
    girls, 24
    ladies, coat, 95
    mens dressing gown, 30
    partial, 23
    party dress, 22
    shirred, 22
slicker, **87,** 126
slippers, 144
slops, 56, **68**
smock
    baby, 172
    boys, **25, 41, 78**
    double breasted, **32, 35, 54, 104**
    farmers, **17, 18, 47,** 48
    firemans, 17
    hunting, **87**
    maternity, 77
smoking jacket, 30, **63,** 84, 124, 143
socks, 171, 172
    sport, 122
soldier
    artillery, **35, 49, 58**
    British, 159
    Camel Corps, 35
    cavalry, **88,** 158
    Confederate, **54,** 55
    dragoons, 88
    infantry, **160**
    militia, **44–59**
    1916, **157**
    Spanish-American War, **129**
    War with Mexico, **19**
    Union, **57, 58, 59**
    World War I, **160**
sound, use of, 176–77
South Carolina militia uniform, **44**
South Carolina Light Infantry, 49
South Carolina Palmetto State
    Artillery, **49**
southern farmer, **65**
southern sympathizer, 52
Spanish-American War uniforms, **128, 129**
Spanish jacket. *See* boleros
spats, 100, 120, 156
sporran, 98
sport caps, 30, 122, 156
sporting dresses, **110, 111**
sports jacket, **100**
sports suits, **157**
    ladies, **166**
sportswear, 27, 29, 30, **62, 100,** 101, 121, **122**
Stanton, Elizabeth Cody, 15, 23
steamboat rider, **28**

Index

steelworker, 31
Stetson, John B., 86
stetson hat, 104
stockings, boys, 79, 96, 115, 135
stockjobbers, 82
stole, **74**, 95
stovepipe hat, 28
straw hat, 16, 18, 31, 121
  ladies, 24, 112
Stuart, J.E.B., 44
suit
  boys, 115
  ditto, 28
  flying, **161**
  formal, **156**
  ladies, 132, **147**, **164**, **166**, 169
  London style, **169**
  mens, **140**
  Norfolk, 122
  overall, **161**
  sailing, mens, **83**
  sailor, boys, **115**, **135**, **136**
  sleeping, 103
  walking, **120**
    ladies, **92**, **132**, **148**
    girls, **98**
summer helmet, 100
sunbonnets, **40**, 78
suspenders, **18**, 19, **30**, 32, 58, 64, 124, 129, 135
sweater coat, **143**, 153
sweater dress, **165**
sweater
  bike, **123**
  boys, **135**
  coat, **143**, 153
  dress, **165**
swords, 53

tam
  boys, 41, 97, 98, 171
  Confederate sailors, 52
  girls, 136
  Union sailor, 56
tango dancing, 156, 163
taps, shoe, 115
tea apron, **112**
teddy bear, 172
telephone operator, 113
Tennessee Sharpshooters uniform, 46
Tennessee Twenty-sixth Militia
  uniform, 46
tennis
  apron, **114**

coat, **121**
dress, **110**
  shoes, 83, 101, 167
  texture, use of, 176
tone as design principle, 174
topcoats, 29
top hat, 28, 62, 65, 66, 120, 123
touring cap, 156, 170
train (dress) 91, **94**, 108, 146
trapper, 18
trench coat, **165**
trimming, 186
trouser cuffs, 156
trousers, 28, 29, 62, 121, 122, 156
  bell bottom, 56, 159
  boys, 41, 56
  checked or plaid, 16, 65, 82
  Confederate sailor, 52
  construction, 177–79
  immigrant, 19
  Indian, 90
  khaki, 129
  ladies, **23**
  miner, 19
  sailor, 56
Truman, Harry S., 159
tucked bodice, 22, 33, 124
tunic, Indian, 21, **36**, 69
Turkish or house cap, 30, 63
Turkish trousers, **133**
turtleneck sweater, **123**, 129, 135, 143, 157
tuxedo, 140, 156
two-piece dress, **77**, 165, **169**

Ulster coat, **108**
  mens, **141**
Uncle Sam suit, 64
undershirt, **108**, **110**
underwear, mens, 143
Union Army
  cape, 59
  hat, 58
  officer, **57**, **58**, 59
Union Navy, **55**
unionsuit, 19, 58, 85, 88, 103, 145
U.S. Marines, 47
utilitarian coat, **85**

V-shaped bodice, 91, **108**
velvet dress, **130**

velvet suit, boys, 41, 79
vests, 16, 28, 65, 86, 120, 122, 156
vigilante, **34**
Virginia Calvary, **45**, **46**, **47**
volunteer fireman, **17**, **84**
volunteer infantry, 47

wagon maker, 31
wagon train escort, officer, **34**
waist, boys, **97**
waistcoat, 16, 156
waiter, 127
walking dress, **74**, **91**
walking stick, 28, 29, 82, 120, 121, 140
walking suit, **120**
  ladies, **92**, **132**, **148**
  girls, **98**
Wallaces Zouaves, **50**
warbonňet, **69**
Washington Artillery, New Orleans, uniform, 46
watches, 38, 82, 101
watch fob, 16
Waud, Alfred R., 40
wealth, showing levels of, 12–13
Wellington boots, 31, 32, **34**, 35, 54, 57, 65
western settler, 18, **63**. *See also* Mormon pioneer
windshield, **166**
Wisconsin Eighth Militia uniform, 45, 48
womans caps, 23, 93, 133
womans club meeting dress, **147**
womans hats, 37, 38, 39, 73, 92, 93, 94, 95, 108, 109, 110, 111, 131, 132, 146, 148, 150, 163, 164, 165
work dress, **39**
work jacket, 127
workers
  children, 151
  lady, 39, 77, 131
  men, **31**, **52**, 65, **85**, **103**, **127**, 156
Worth, Charles Frederick, 37, 61
wrapper cloak, baby **153**

zouave,
  boys suit, **79**
  drummer boy, 59
  uniform, **50**, **59**
Zuni Indian, 106

A popular writer and lecturer on Americana, ESTELLE ANSLEY WORRELL is a well-known authority on early American clothing styles, and designer and maker of cloth dolls, dollhouses, puppets, miniatures, and costumes.

After earning a degree in art education from Peabody College, she write *The Dollhouse Book,* a how-to volume on miniature furniture designs in authentic American period styles. Her appearance on NBC's Today Show to discuss this book drew more letters than any previous guest. *The Doll Book* followed with detailed instructions for miniature period clothing. The English Speaking Union of the United States chose her *Americana in Miniature* to be sent around the world to teach American culture as an Ambassador Book. Mrs. Worrell is also author of *Be a Puppeteer!* and *Dolls, Puppedolls & Teddy Bears. Early American Costume,* published by Stackpole in the bicentennial year, was endorsed by the Early American Society.

In between books, Mrs. Worrell has found time to design the costumes for one play each year for the Nashville Children's Theater (of which she is a former board member), appear frequently on the lecture circuit, write music, and exhibit her miniature historical settings.